IMPLEMENTING MICROSOFT AZURE INFRASTRUCTURE SOLUTIONS

PRACTICAL GUIDE FOR ULTIMATE BEGINNERS

Contents

About this Book

This book has been written for the candidates who want to learn and use the Microsoft Azure cloud platform, candidates who have just started his career with Cloud services, who is already working with Azure cloud services. This is also dedicated to those who are preparing themselves for one of the most popular cloud certifications **Implementing Microsoft Azure Infrastructure Solutions** Exam.

This is mainly focused on the hands-on lab exercises and real-world best practices rather than deep theoretical and conceptual lectures. However, we have covered enough concept and theory part of each of the mentioned topics. There are hundreds of theoretical documentations are available on the Microsoft Azure official documentation site and a few other sites on the Internet community. But, there are very few articles on the step by step how to guide to implement, use, and configure Azure Cloud services.

This guide will help you to become handy and expert on most of the Microsoft Azure Cloud services that will help you start your career with Cloud technologies. However, this guide also contains various real world, enterprise-level, best practices to implement and use for the production services.

These step by step lab exercises will help you to design a highly-secure, scalable, and well-architecture enterprise-level Cloud solutions and designs.

We assume that you know at least the basic terminology of knowledge about the Windows and Linux Operating Systems, Networking concepts and virtualization platforms.

About the Author

This book is written by an Author who has over 9+ years of experience in various IT domains such as Microsoft, Red Hat, Cisco, AWS, OpenStack, and CompTIA. He has worked with many reputed organizations as various profiles such as Content Designer, Subject Matter Expert, Technical Expert, and Solution Architect. He currently holds 15 + IT Global certifications. Some of the major Global certifications held by him includes Microsoft Azure, MCP, MCTP, MCITP, MCSA, MS Hyper-V, CCNA, RHCSA, OpenStack, and AWS Certified Solutions Architect – Associate.

Other Helpful IT Books for You

You may also be interested in the following eBooks:

1. AWS Solutions Architect Associate - Exam Practice Questions
2. Step By Step Windows Server 2016 Lab Manual/Practical Guide
3. Step By Step AWS Cloud Lab Manual/Practical Guide for Ultimate Beginners
4. Step By Step CCNA Lab Manual/Practical Guide for Ultimate Beginners
5. Step By Step Windows Server 2012 R2 Lab Manual/Practical Guide
6. Step By Step VMware Workstation Player Lab Manual/Practical Guide
7. Docker Container: Concepts and Hands-on Exercises for Ultimate Beginners

Disclaimer

While writing the content of this book, author (publisher) has tried his best to keep the content as up-to-date and accurate as possible. However, being a human, there might be some typo or grammatical errors. It might also be possible that due to the rapid changes of IT technologies and services, some of the features, limitations, and terms might get change or updated by the respective IT vendors. Author or publisher does not provide any guarantee for such changes. The lab exercises mentioned in this book should be performed in the testing environment, not on the production servers or environment. Author or publisher will not be liable for any loss of data, service interruptions caused by candidates either intentionally or unintentionally.

Copyright

Note: Since few of the information (such as account number, email ID, public IP address, instance ID, etc.) in the mentioned screenshots are private and confidential, so those might be blurred. However, and obviously, this will not impact your learning experience at anyhow.

Cloud Computing Introduction

Cloud compute technologies are the fastest growing technology in the current era. Many of the major and startup organizations have already moved their infrastructure to Cloud platform or in the process of moving on-premise data centers to the Cloud platforms. You must upgrade your skills from the traditional IT support skills to Cloud and DevOps skills, otherwise you will not be able to grow in your career, or even may not be able to survive yourself in the IT sector.

Some of the quick facts about the Cloud computing technology are:

- Cloud computing provides a modern alternative to the traditional on-premises data center.
- Allows you to lease access to hardware and software resources that would be too expensive to purchase.
- Cloud environments typically provide an online portal experience, making it easy for users to manage compute, storage, network, and application resources.

Cloud Service Providers

There are various cloud service providers in the IT industry. However, AWS and Azure are the market leaders in this field. Few of the major cloud service providers are:

1. Amazon Web Services (AWS)
2. Microsoft Azure Cloud
3. Google Cloud
4. Alibaba Cloud
5. Digital Ocean

Types of Cloud

Depending on the types of network, services, and resource control you have in a Cloud platform, there are majorly three types of cloud platforms:

1. **Public**: In a Public cloud, a cloud service provider is completely responsible for hardware purchase and maintenance and typically provides a wide variety of platform services that you can use.
2. **Private**: In a Private cloud, you create a cloud environment in your own datacenter and provide self-service access to compute resources to users in your organization.
3. **Hybrid**: A Hybrid cloud integrates both public and private clouds, allowing you to host workloads in the most appropriate location.

Cloud Offering Classes

There are basically three types of Cloud based on the control and responsibility of Cloud provider and customers. These are:

1. **SaaS: Software as a Service**
   SaaS is software that is centrally hosted and managed for the end customer. It usually is based on a multitenant architecture.
   Examples: Microsoft One Drive, Dropbox, WordPress, and Amazon Kindle.
2. **PaaS: Platform as a Service**
   With PaaS, you deploy your application into an application-hosting environment provided by the cloud service vendor.
   You (developer) provide the application to be hosted, and the PaaS vendor provides the ability to deploy and run it.
   Examples: Azure Websites and Azure Cloud Services (web and worker roles).
3. **IaaS: Infrastructure as a Service**

An IaaS cloud, the vendor runs and manages server farms running virtualization software, enabling you to create VMs that run on the vendor's infrastructure.

In IaaS, you can create a VM running Windows or Linux and install anything you want on it.

Example: Azure VM.

Microsoft Azure Introduction

1. Azure is Microsoft's cloud computing platform which provides you a wide variety of cloud services.
2. Azure has the second largest cloud platform after the AWS Cloud. But, the year-by-year growth of Azure Cloud is faster than AWS Cloud.
3. You can use the Azure cloud services without purchasing and provisioning your own hardware.
4. Azure enables the rapid development of solutions and provides the resources to accomplish tasks that may not be feasible in an on-premises environment.
5. Azure allows you to start with very low cost and scale rapidly as you gain customers.

Lab 01: Getting Started with Free Azure Subscription

You can use the Azure Portal to create virtual networks, use cloud services, create VMs, configure storage
accounts and so on.

There are basically two versions of the portal. The **Azure Management Portal** and the new one called
Azure Portal. Azure Portal has advanced features, easy to use, better look and design.

Before you cloud login to Azure Portal, you must have an active Azure subscription. We assume that you
don't have yet. So, let's follow the below instruction and get a new free Azure subscription. You will also
get a $200 credit to use, explore, and learn the various Azure cloud services with the limited
functionalities for limited period. These $200 credits maximum could be used for 30 days.

Signing Up for Free Azure Subscription

As discussed earlier, Microsoft free Azure subscription gives you $200 credit that you can use to explore
Azure cloud services up to 30 days. If you consume $200 credit before 30 days, you will be asked to
upgrade your free trial subscription to paid account. However, many people don't create Azure free
subscription because they fear to submit their credit/debit card details and think Microsoft may charge
if they mistakenly go beyond the given free credit limit. But, Microsoft will not charge you until you
manually upgrade your subscription from free to paid account. Here, let's follow us to sign up for the
free Microsoft Azure account and let's get started with Azure Cloud services. The $200 credit is enough
to learn and explore most of the major Azure cloud services. So, let's get started.

1. Visit the following free sign up link to create a free azure subscription.
   - https://azure.microsoft.com/en-in/free

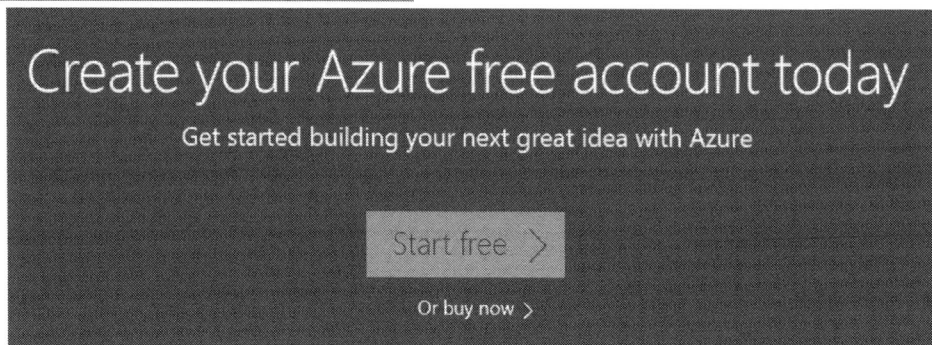

Create your Azure free account today

Get started building your next great idea with Azure

Start free >

Or buy now >

2. Click **Start free** button to proceed next. On the **Sign-Up** page, type the Microsoft's account
   associated Email ID you want to use, or create a new Microsoft account if you don't have already.

3. On the next page, you need to fill few information about you and the purpose of using Azure Cloud. Fill all the required information appropriately and proceed to the next page.

1 About you

Country/Region ℹ️

India	▾

First name

Microsoft Azure

Last name

Cloud

Email address ℹ️

████████████@outlook.com

Phone

████████

Organization

Own

4. On the next page, you need to verify your phone number.
5. On the next page, you need to verify your identity, setting up payment method, and billing address. You would not be charged until you exceed your free credit limit and or convert your free subscription to paid account manually.
6. Finally, accept the license agreement and finish the Sign-Up process.
7. After completing the Sign-Up process, you will get the Credit summary details similar like the following.

Microsoft Azure

HOME   PRICING   DOCUMENTATION   DOWNLOADS   COMMUNITY   SUPPORT   ACCOUNT

subscriptions   marketplace   profile   preview features

Portal →

Summary for Free Trial

OVERVIEW   BILLING HISTORY

ⓘ Your Free Trial expires in 30 day(s). Click here to automatically convert to Pay-As-You-Go and avoid service disruption.

₹ 13,300.00

₹ 0.00   ₹ 13,300.00

Your monthly credit expires on 1/31/2018   Pricing calculator

You have not used any services recently with this subscription.

SUBSCRIPTION STATUS

30
days left

₹ 13,300
credits remaining*

Upgrade now →

8. Once your sign-up process completes successfully and your free subscription is created, you can login to Azure Portal and start exploring Azure services.

Lab 02: Getting Familiarized with Azure Portal Options

The Azure Portal is GUI based console to manage Azure cloud services. In the later sections, we also discussed other Azure cloud management tools such as Azure PowerShell, Azure CLI, xplat-cli etc. But, Azure Portal remains the most popular and primary tool to manage Azure cloud services. The various panels, blades, options, sidebars, etc. are shown in the following figure. We recommend spending some time to get dirty hands-on about various portal options.

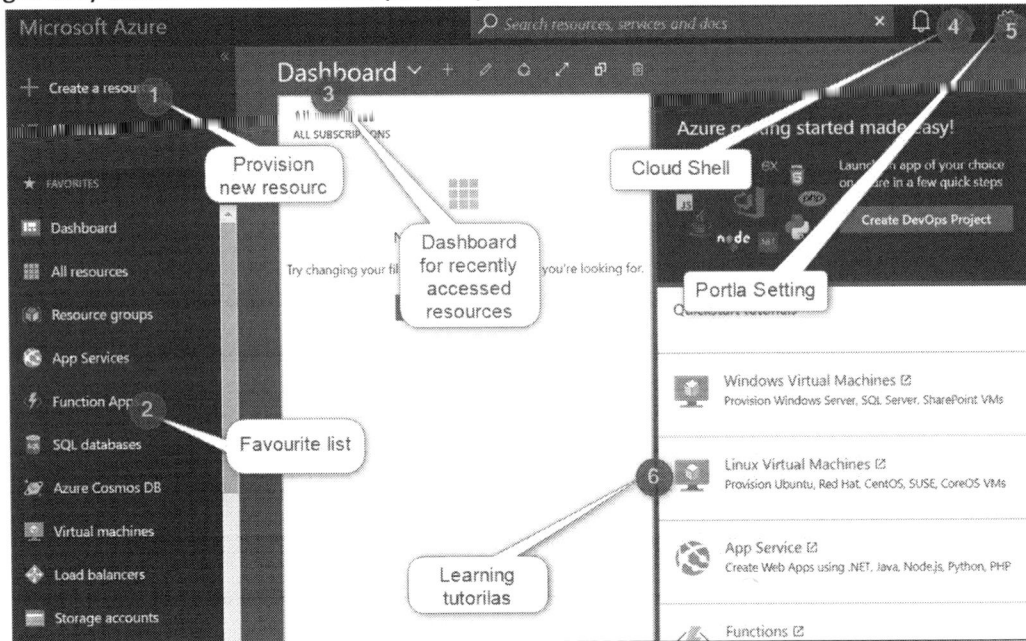

In Azure Portal, a new window opens with the configuration steps are called Blades. You can always close the currently opened blade to go back to previous blade. This whole chain of blade selections is called a journey. Let's have a look at the following figure about Blades and Journey.

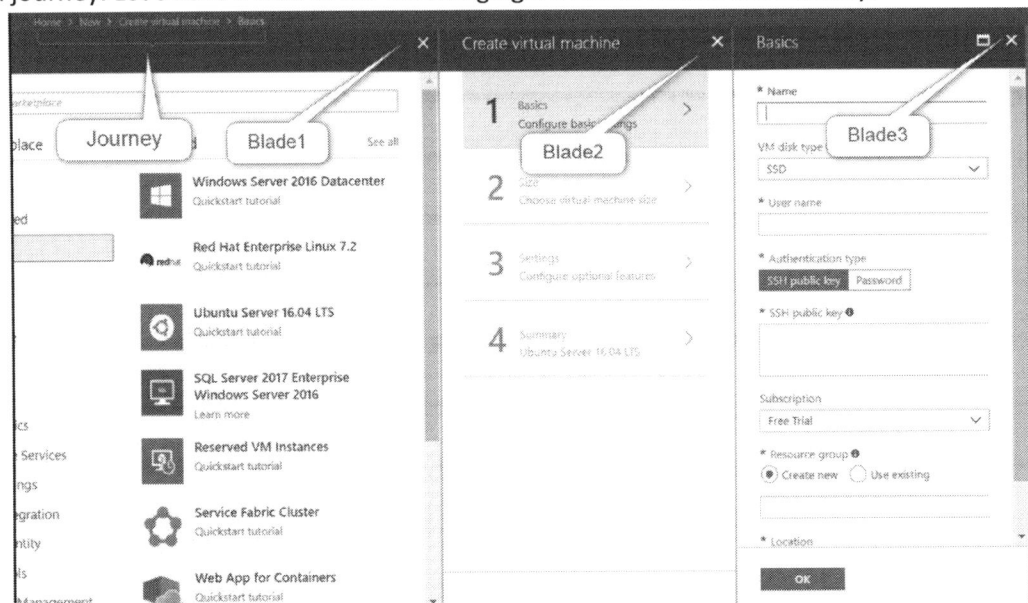

Sometimes we noticed that if you made some changes using the Azure Portal in Azure cloud services, you may need to refresh the browser to get reflected the changes. So, keep this in mind while working with the Azure Portal.

Lab 03: Getting Azure Subscription Details

The features and services allowed for you to deploy depends on the type of Subscription you are using. Apart from this, you can also add more and more subscriptions to this account in order to manage centralized billing of your multiple Azure subscriptions.

Here, we are going to explore few basic options to get familiarized with the Azure Subscriptions. Just perform the following steps:

1. In **Azure Portal**, click **All services** in the left pane and then search for the **Subscriptions** as shown in the following figure.

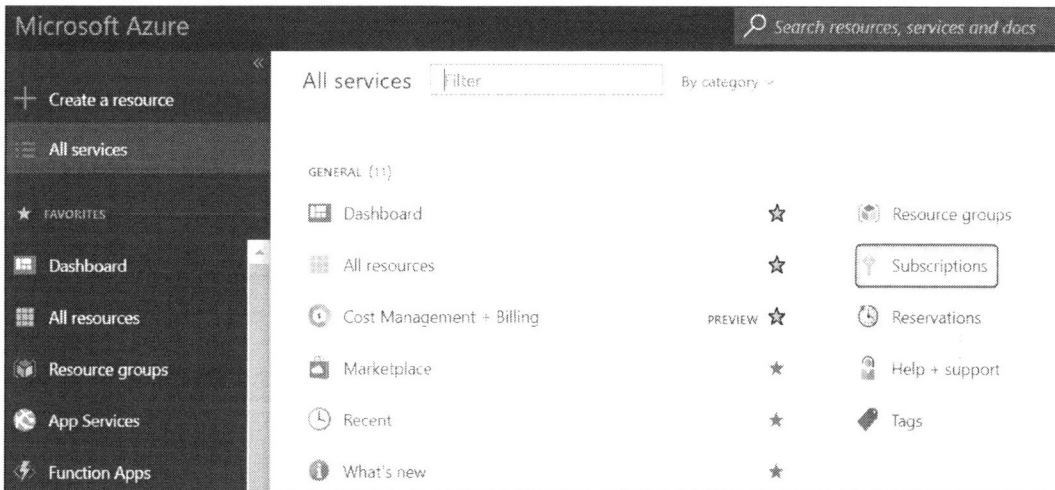

2. In the **Subscriptions** blade, you will see your subscription type and ID as well the roles added to your user account as shown in the following figure.

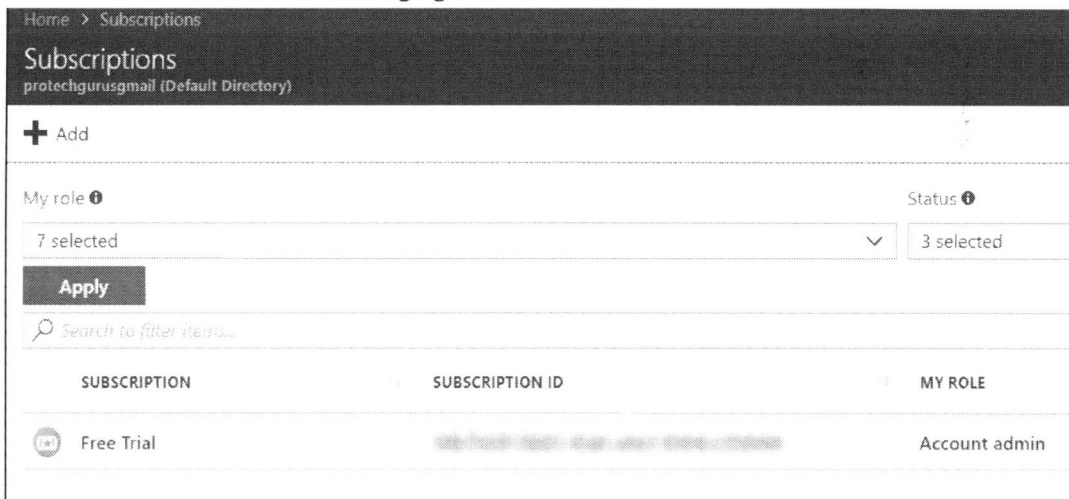

3. To view more details about your subscription, open the subscriptions details blac the various options as shown in the following figure.

4.   We recommend you spend some time each of the options to just get familiar with them.

Lab 04: Creating Administrative Users for Azure Cloud Management

The account you used for Sign Up has all the administrative rights to manage Azure services. However, this account should only be used for the centralized billing and manage other users. It is not recommended to use the default administrative account for a daily basis tasks. This is done by using Role Based Access Control (RBAC) that allows you to grant more granular permissions to account management than just full access to a subscription. To give someone access to modify the resources in a subscription in the Azure Portal, you need to add the OWNER role for the subscription to the user's account.

Here, we are going to show you how to create and manage Azure users and groups using the Azure Active Directory (Azure AD).

1. To create a new Azure user, select the **Azure Active Directory** in the left pane and then select **Users** as shown in the following figure.

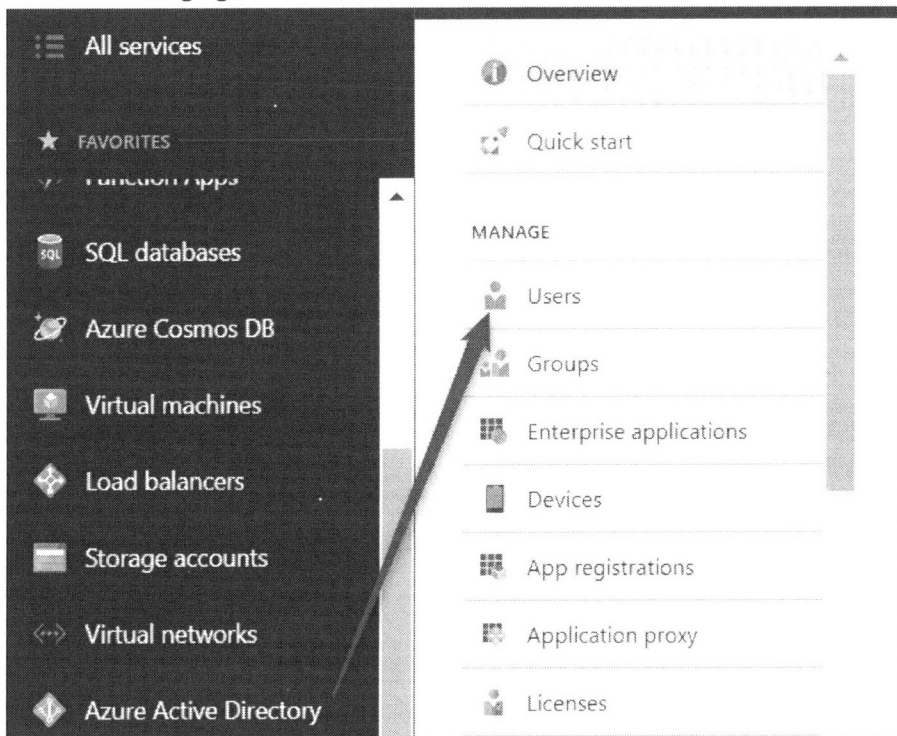

2. On the **Users** blade, click **New User** to add a new user account.
3. On the **User** blade, specify the user details as follow:
   - Name: **Admin**
   - User name: **<user>@<your-azure-ad-domain-name>.onmicrosoft.com**
   - Directory Role: **Global Administrator**
   - The following figure shows the User blade.

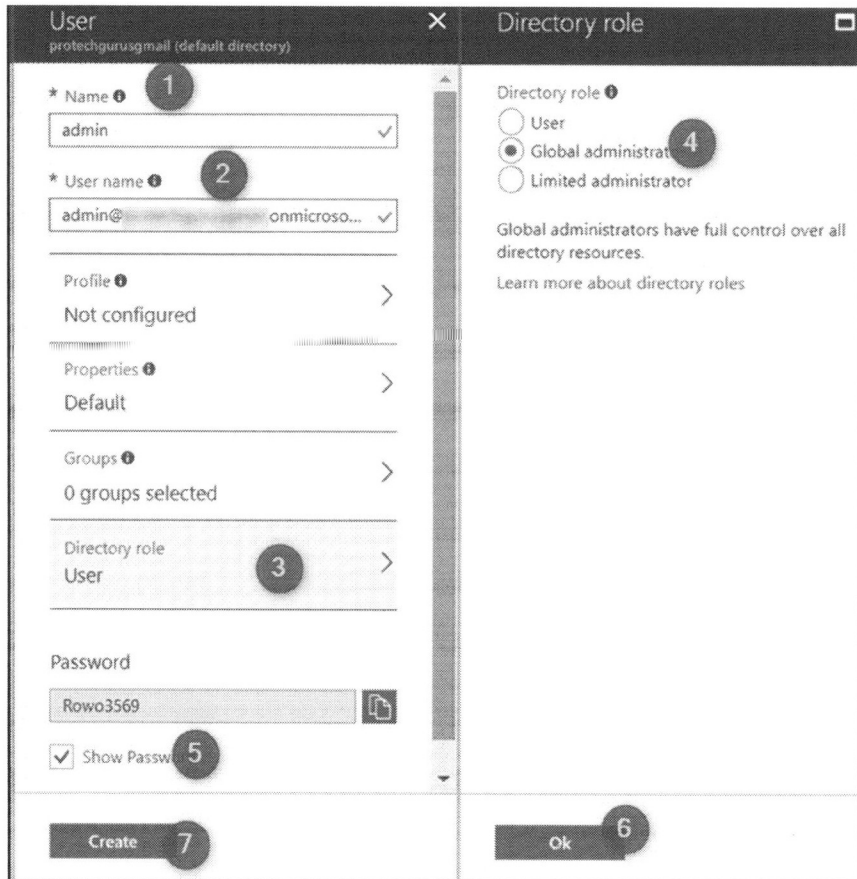

4. Once you defined the required values, click **OK** and then click **Create** to create Azure AD account. The Admin user will be created with Global administrative role and will be listed in your Azure AD users list.

Note: There are various types of roles for an Azure AD account. However, we do not cover detailed of them here. You are advised to visit the following link to know more about the Azure AD roles.

---

https://docs.microsoft.com/en-us/azure/active-directory/active-directory-assign-admin-roles-azure-portal

---

5. In the Azure AD user list, select the created user. You will see various user's related options such as reset password, delete user, **Multi-Factor Authentication** etc. as shown in the following figure.

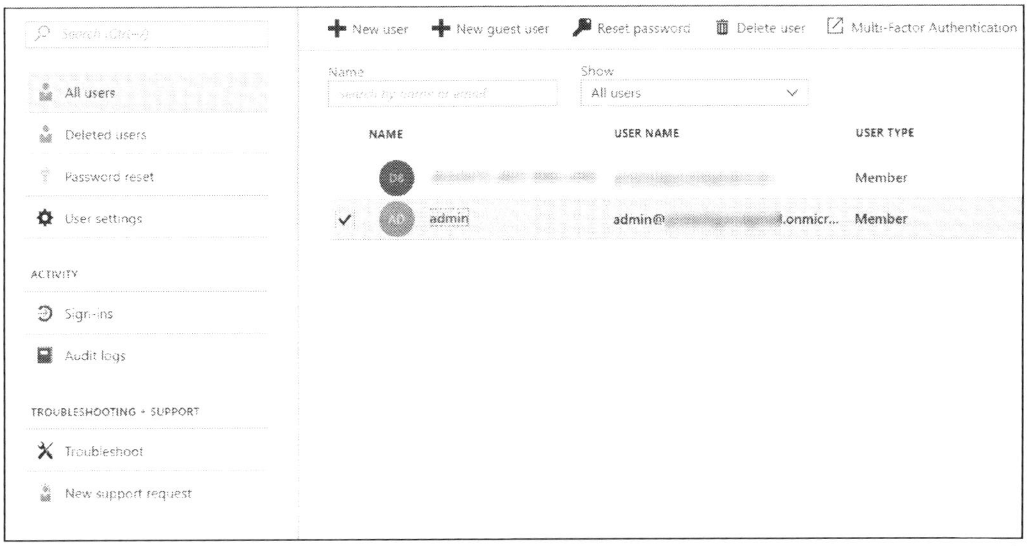

+ New user   + New guest user   🔑 Reset password   🗑 Delete user   ☐ Multi-Factor Authentication

🔍 search (Ctrl+/)

🧑 All users

🧑 Deleted users

🔑 Password reset

⚙ User settings

ACTIVITY

🕘 Sign-ins

📊 Audit logs

TROUBLESHOOTING + SUPPORT

🔧 Troubleshoot

🧑 New support request

Name
search by name or email

Show
All users

NAME	USER NAME	USER TYPE
DB		Member
admin	admin@................onmicr...	Member

6. Now sign out from your default azure admin user and login back with the user you created recently that is **admin**. You will be asked to reset your password for first time login. Once logged in, you can provision Azure resources with this Admin account.

Lab 05: Enable Multi-Factor Authentication for Azure Accounts

Multi-Factor Authentication is an additional security layer to protect your Azure account. When you enable MFA, users are required to provide two-factor authentication code along with their username and password.

To enable MFA for the Azure account, you need to perform the following steps:

1. Login to **Azure Portal** and navigate to the **Users** section of the **Azure Active Directory**.
2. Select the user for which you wish to enable MFA and then click **Multi-Factor Authentication** option as shown in the following figure.

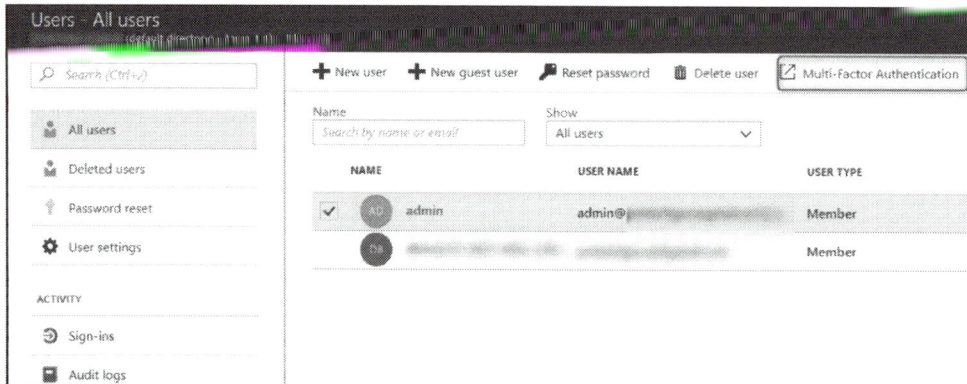

3. On the **multi-factor authentication** page, select the user and then click **Enable** to enable MFA as shown in the following figure.

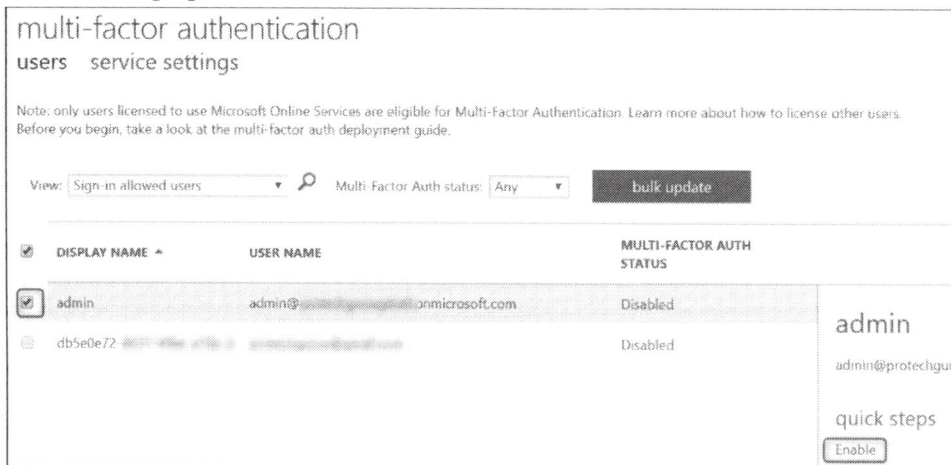

4. On the next page, click the **enable multi-factor auth** button to proceed as shown in the following figure.

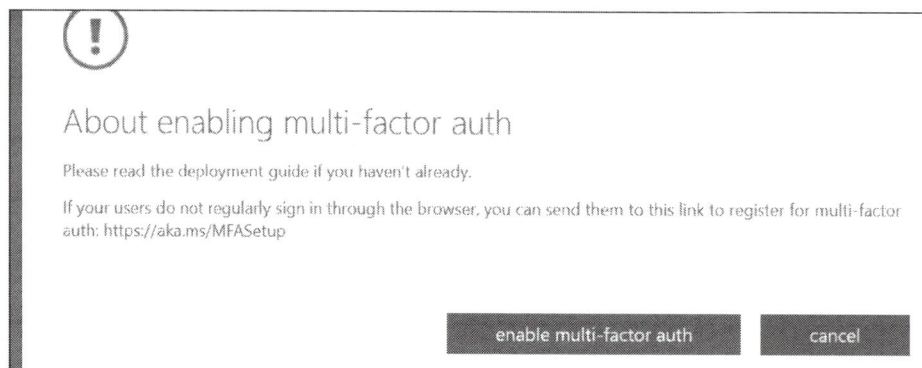

5. Users are required to setup a **two-steps authentication app** on their mobile. For this, you need to send the following link to users to register for MFA.
   - https://aka.ms/MFASetup
6. When a user will sign in using the above link, he will be asked to setup MFA option as shown in the following figure.

7. On the **Additional security verification** page, select the authentication method such as **Mobile app**, select the verification method such as **Use verification code** and then click the **Set up** button as shown in the following figure.

Additional security verification

Secure your account by adding phone verification to your password. View video to know ho[w]

Step 1: How should we contact you?

Mobile app ▼

How do you want to use the mobile app?

○ Receive notifications for verification

◉ Use verification code

To use these verification methods, you must set up the Microsoft Authenticator app.

Set up   Please configure the mobile app.

8. The **Configure mobile app** page will be displayed as shown in the following figure.

Configure mobile app

Complete the following steps to configure your mobile app.

1. Install the Microsoft authenticator app for Windows Phone, Android or iOS.

2. In the app, add an account and choose "Work or school account".

3. Scan the image below.

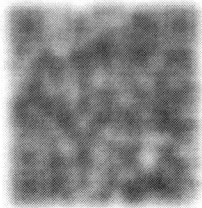

Configure app without notifications

If you are unable to scan the image, enter the following information in your app.

Code: (

Url: https:/

If the app displays a six-digit code, choose "Next".

9. We assume that you have the Microsoft authenticator app installed on your mobile. If you don't have already, please install it using the following appropriate link depending the mobile platform you are using.

- Microsoft Authenticator Windows
  https://www.microsoft.com/en-in/store/p/azure-authenticator/9nblgggzmcj6?rtc=1
- Microsoft Authenticator Android
  https://play.google.com/store/apps/details?id=com.azure.authenticator
- Microsoft Authenticator IOS
  https://itunes.apple.com/app/id983156458

10. On the **configure mobile app** page, open the **Microsoft Authenticator** app on your mobile.
11. Click **Add account** and select **Work or school account** as account type.
12. Scan the QR code displaying in the previous image and then click **Finish**.
13. On the next page, type a dynamic code shown in your mobile app and add your mobile number as an alternative method (recovery option) in case you lost your phone.
14. Finally, click **Done** to complete the process.
15. Your account will be added into **Microsoft Authenticator app**. Alternatively, you can also use your **Code** and **URI** values shown in the QR code page to add account instead of using the QR scan code.
16. Once your account is added, the successful configuration message will be displayed as shown in the following figure, click **Next** to finish the wizard.

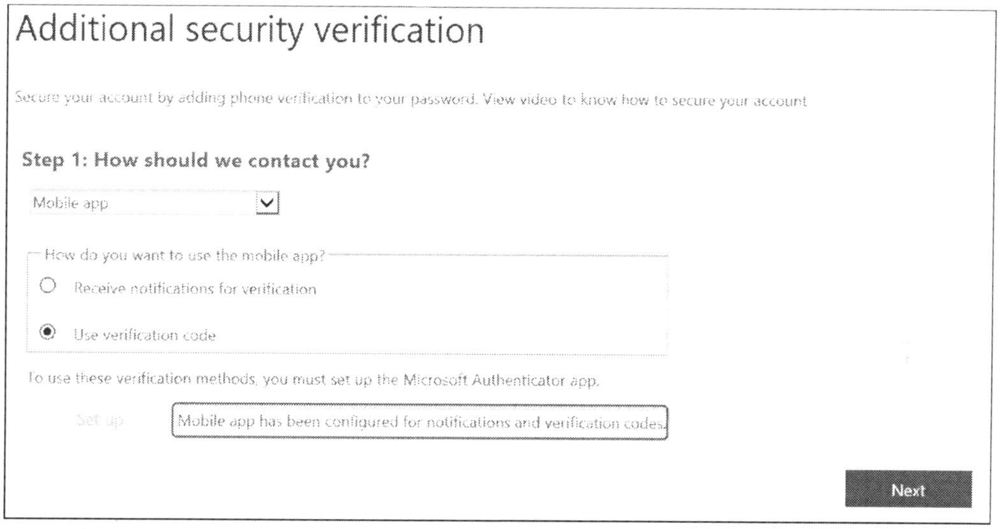

17. Now, your MFA has been enabled for the Azure account using the Microsoft Authentication app. If you are interested, you can also explore other options instead of using Mobile app to setup MFA for Azure account. Please visit the following link for more details about the Azure MFA.
    - Azure MFA Deployment Guide.

Lab 06: Azure Pricing Calculator

You might have heard from many people that Cloud is much less expensive than on premise hardware infrastructure and data center. But, this may not be always true, because you have to be so careful about using suitable cloud services. Otherwise, you may end up by paying a huge unnecessary cloud cost. For example, you created a VM with 2 vCPU and 4 GB RAM, but you didn't check the actual resource consumption by the running services on this VM. It may be possible that services running on this VM only require 1vCPU and 2 GB RAM. The other possibilities: keep running Development and testing VMs 24*7, but you should keep your dev/test VMs powered off during off-hours and weekends. Before to provisioning any cloud resource, you must be familiar with the pricing model and factors regarding that service. Here, we are going to explain you how to calculate the pricing of Azure cloud services before to go ahead.

1. To calculate Azure cloud service price, visit the following link. The Azure pricing calculator page will be displayed as shown in the following figure.

   - https://azure.microsoft.com/en-us/pricing/calculator

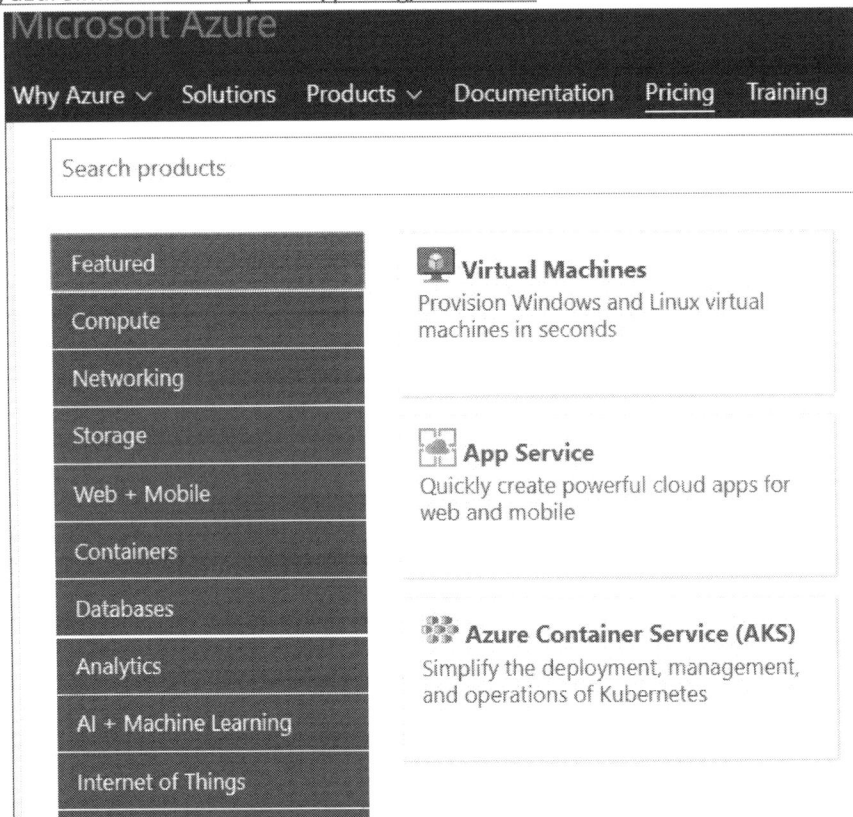

2. In the left pane, select the service for which you want to calculate pricing.
3. For example, let's calculate the price of a virtual machine with following configuration:
   - Region: **South India**
   - vCPU: **2vCPU**
   - RAM: **4 GB**
   - HDD: **64 GB**
   - OS: **Linux**
   - Platform: **Ubuntu 16.04**
   - Billing option: **Pay-as-you-go**
   - Running hours: **24*7**

4. For this, select **Compute** in the left pane and then select **Virtual Machines** in the right blade.

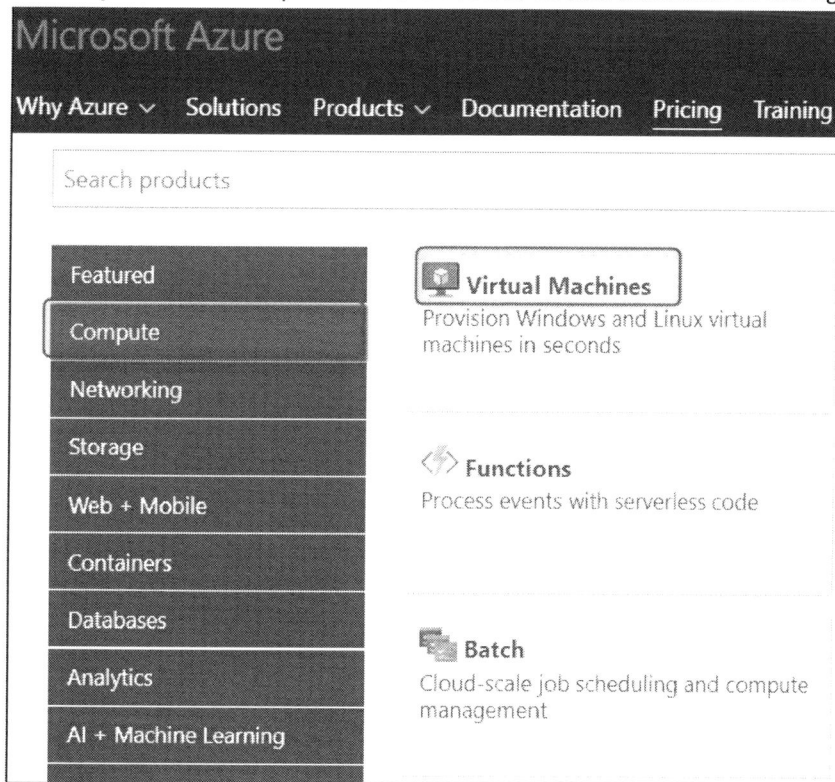

5. Scroll-down to the Virtual machine section and select the below-mentioned settings and refer the following figure.

- Region: **South India**
- Operating System: **Linux**
- Type: **Ubuntu**
- Tier: **Standard**
- Instance type: **A2 v2**
- Billing: **Pay-as-you-go**
- Running hours: **730**

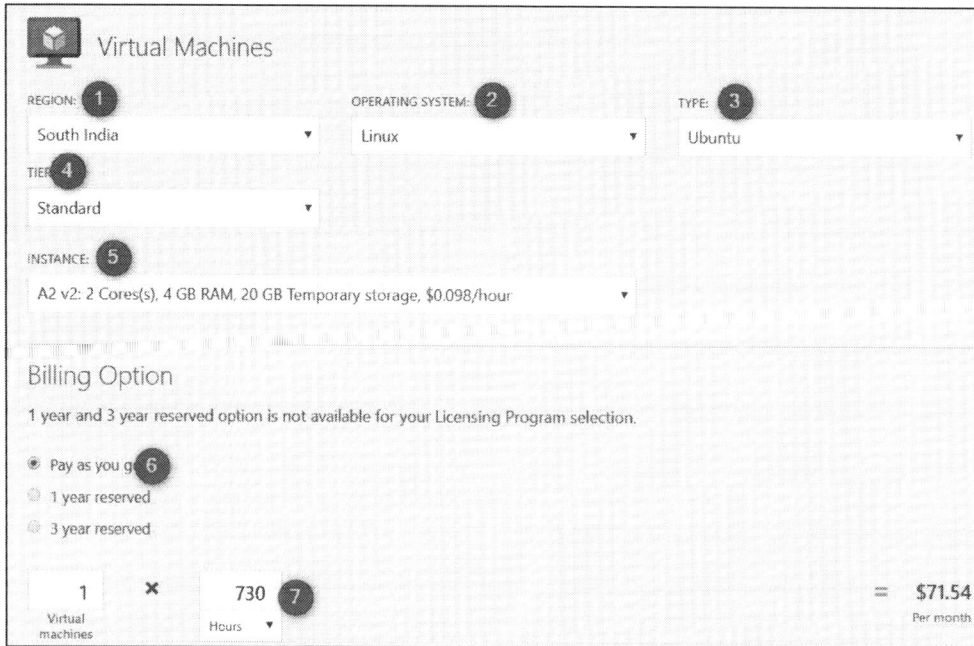

Virtual Machines

REGION: ① South India

OPERATING SYSTEM: ② Linux

TYPE: ③ Ubuntu

TIER ④ Standard

INSTANCE: ⑤ A2 v2: 2 Cores(s), 4 GB RAM, 20 GB Temporary storage, $0.098/hour

Billing Option

1 year and 3 year reserved option is not available for your Licensing Program selection.

- ⦿ Pay as you go ⑥
- ○ 1 year reserved
- ○ 3 year reserved

| 1 Virtual machines | × | 730 Hours ▾ ⑦ | = | $71.54 Per month |

6. Next, scroll-down to the Managed OS Disks page and select the following settings as shown in the following figure.
   - Tier: **Standard**
   - Disk Size: **64 GB** (without Snapshot)
   - No. of disks: **1**

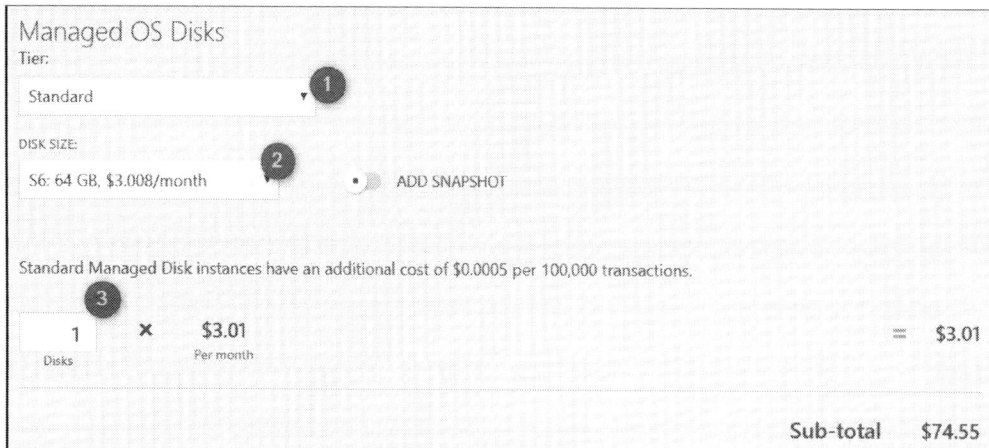

Managed OS Disks

Tier: ① Standard

DISK SIZE: ② S6: 64 GB, $3.008/month ⦿ ADD SNAPSHOT

Standard Managed Disk instances have an additional cost of $0.0005 per 100,000 transactions.

| ③ 1 Disks | × | $3.01 Per month | = | $3.01 |

Sub-total $74.55

7. In the above figure, you can see the total calculated price is around $74.55. Similarly, you can calculate the cost of other Azure cloud services appropriately.

Lab 07: Introduction Azure Virtual Network (vNet)

Similar to your on-premise network, you need to define the logical network components for your Cloud platform as well. Azure Virtual networks (vNets) are used in the Azure Cloud to provide a layer of security and isolation for your services. Each virtual network should have separate IP address ranges.

Let's have a quick look about the few facts about Azure Virtual Networks:

- VMs and other cloud services that are part of the same virtual network can access to each other.
- Azure services that communicate to each other with a virtual network do not travel through the Azure Load Balancer.
- You can add a Virtual Network Gateway to a virtual network that allows you to connect your on-premises network to Azure.
- When you set up an Azure virtual network, you define the topology of the virtual network, which includes the available address spaces and subnets.
- If the virtual network needs to be connected to other virtual networks, you should select IP address ranges that are not overlapping.
- The IP address ranges are private and cannot be accessed from the public Internet. You should always use non-routable IP addresses. These are specified in CIDR notation, such as 10.0.0.0/8, 172.16.0.0/12, or 192.168.0.0/16.
- CIDR notation uses xxx.xxx.xxx.xxx/n format, where **n** is the number of leftmost '1' bits in the subnet mask. For example, 192.168.10.0/22 applies the network mask 255.255.248.0 to the 192.168 network, starting at 192.168.10.0.
- After specifying your virtual network address space(s), you can create additional subnets for your virtual network. You can do this by breaking your network into more manageable logical sections. For example, you might assign 10.10.0.0 to front-end servers, 10.20.0.0 to back-end cloud services, and 10.30.0.0 to SQL Server VMs.
- Azure cloud reserves the first four IP addresses in each subnet for its own use. Hence, you cannot use these.
- By default, there is no security restriction between azure network subnets.

Lab 08: Creating an Azure Virtual Network

To create VMs into a virtual network, you first need to create the virtual network and then you select the virtual network and subnet where the VMs will belong. The network settings for VMs and cloud services are acquired during the VM deployment process. When you deploy multiple VMs into a virtual network or subnet, the IP addresses are assigned as the VMs boot up. A Direct IP (DIP) is the internal IP address associated with a VM.

If you created a VM and later decide to move this VM into a different virtual network, you cannot do it straightforward. In this case, you need to redeploy the VM into the desired virtual network.

Here is the process of creating an Azure virtual network with the following configuration settings:

- Virtual Network Name: **MyTestvNet**
- Region: **South India**
- vNet range: **10.10.0.0/16**
- Private Subnet name: **MyPrivateSubnet1**
- Private Subnet range: **10.10.1.0/24**
- Public Subnet Name: **MyPublicSubnet1**
- Public Subnet range: **10.10.2.0/24**

To create and configure Azure virtual network and subnet as per the above configuration, you need to perform the following steps:

1. In the **Azure Portal**, select **Create a resource**, select **Networking**, and then select **Virtual network** as shown in the following figure.

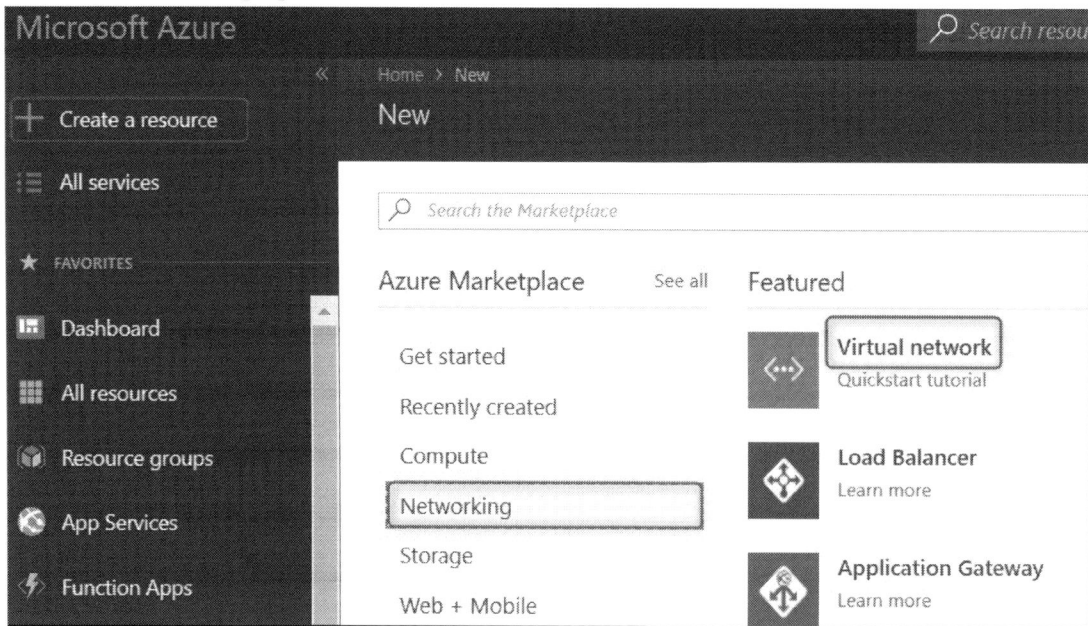

2. On the **Create virtual network** blade, specify the following configuration values:
   - Name: **MyTestvNet**
   - Address space: **10.10.0.0/16**
   - Subscription: **Free Trial**
   - Resource group: Create new and name it as **MyTestRG**
   - Location: **South India**
   - Subnet name: **MyPrivateSubnet1**
   - Address range: **10.10.1.0/24**

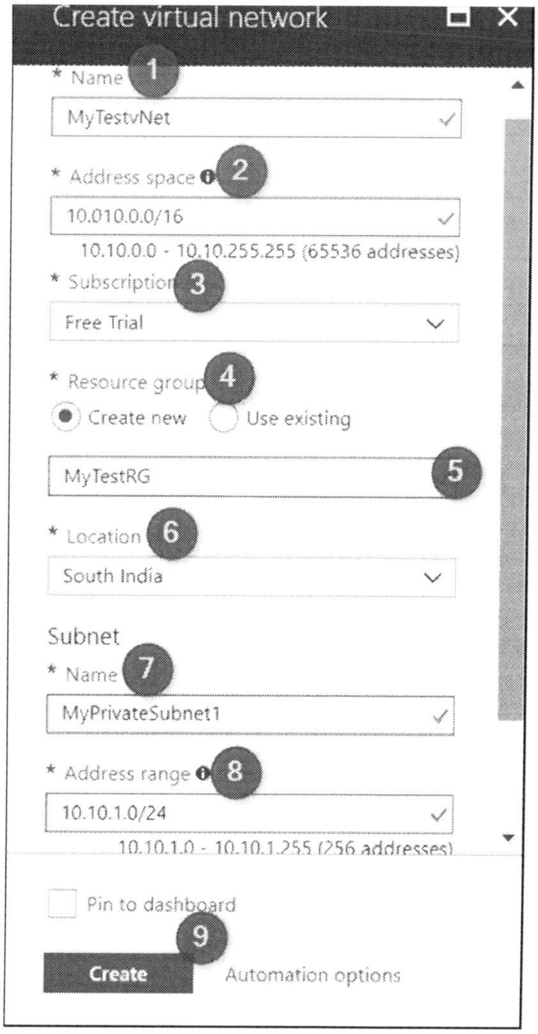

Create virtual network

* Name ①

| MyTestvNet | ✓ |

* Address space ❶ ②

| 10.010.0.0/16 | ✓ |

10.10.0.0 - 10.10.255.255 (65536 addresses)

* Subscription ③

| Free Trial | ⌄ |

* Resource group ④

⦿ Create new   ◯ Use existing

| MyTestRG | ⑤ |

* Location ⑥

| South India | ⌄ |

Subnet

* Name ⑦

| MyPrivateSubnet1 | ✓ |

* Address range ❶ ⑧

| 10.10.1.0/24 | ✓ |

10.10.1.0 - 10.10.1.255 (256 addresses)

☐ Pin to dashboard

⑨

Create   Automation options

3. Finally, click **Create** to create a new **virtual network** along with a private subnet. Once created, verify your virtual network by navigating the Virtual networks section.

Creating Additional Subnets

Now let's create another subnet named as MyPublicSubnet1 with the following configuration values:

- Name: **MyPublicSubnet1**
- Range: **10.10.2.0/24**
- Location: **South India**
- Resource Group: **MyTestRG**

To add more subnets in your virtual network, you need to perform the following steps:

1. Navigate to the **Virtual networks** section, select the earlier created virtual network "MyTestvNet".
2. On the **MyTestvNet – Subnets** blade, select **Subnets**.
3. In the right blade, click **+Subnet** to add a new subnet as shown in the following figure.

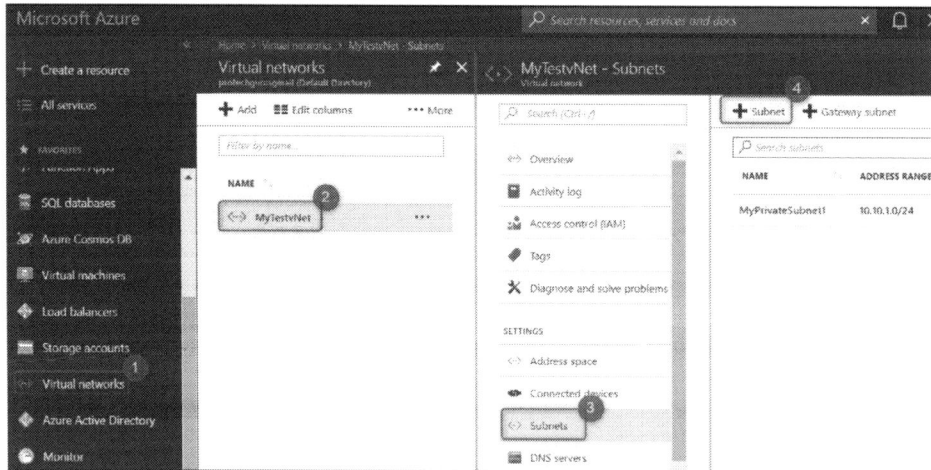

4. On the **Add subnet** blade, specify the subnet name, subnet range, and then click **Create** to create a new subnet as shown in the following figure.

Note: We have covered the rest of the options, such as Network Security Group and Route Table, in the upcoming sections.

5. Your public subnet will be created and listed in the **Subnets** list as shown in the following figure.

NAME	ADDRESS RANGE	AVAILABLE ADDRE...	SECURITY GROUP	
MyPrivateSubnet1	10.10.1.0/24	251	-	...
MyPublicSubnet1	10.10.2.0/24	251	-	...

Note: In the later section, we will also cover Gateway subnet along with App Gateway.

Using A Network Configuration File

Apart from the above-mentioned manual method, there is another method to configure Azure virtual networks. You can do it by uploading a network configuration file. You define all of your network configuration settings in a file and then upload this file as a base template for configuring virtual networks.

The network configuration file applies to the entire subscription. One scenario where you might be interested to use network configuration file is "you have an Azure subscription with preconfigured virtual networks in it and you want to clone one or more of them to another Azure subscription". However, we will not cover it here. If you are interested, please refer the following link for more detail about using Network Configuration File in Azure cloud.

*   https://docs.microsoft.com/en-us/azure/virtual-network/virtual-networks-create-vnet-classic-netcfg-ps

Lab 09: Introduction to Azure Resource Groups

One of the best features of Azure cloud we love most is **Resource Group**. A resource group is a container that contains the closely related resources of Azure cloud. A resource group can contain all the resources of your Azure subscription. However, you can include only those resources that you want to manage as a group.

Suppose you created a resource group named as DemoRG and you put all of your testing resources in this resource group. Once your testing is over, you can delete this resource group and all of the related resources belonging to DemoRG will be deleted in just a few clicks. Otherwise, you need to delete resources individually, which might be a tedious job. AWS Cloud is lacking in comparison of Azure Cloud Resource Group and AWS Resources Group.

Few important factors to consider when defining your resource group are as follows:

- All the resources in your group should share the same lifecycle.
- A resource in Azure cloud can only belong to one resource group.
- You can add or remove a resource to a resource group as per your choice.
- You can move a resource from one resource group to another group.
- A resource group can also contain resources that belong from different regions.
- A resource can interact with resources in other resource groups.

Lab 10: Managing Resource Groups

You can create and manage resource groups in Azure cloud using the Azure CLI, PowerShell, and Azure Portal. Here, we will focus only with Azure Portal.

To create a new resource group in Azure subscription, you need to perform the following steps:

1. Select the **Resource groups** in the left pane of Azure Portal.
2. Click **Add** to add a new resource group.
3. On the **Resource group** blade, specify the appropriate name, subscription, and location for the resource group as shown in the following figure.

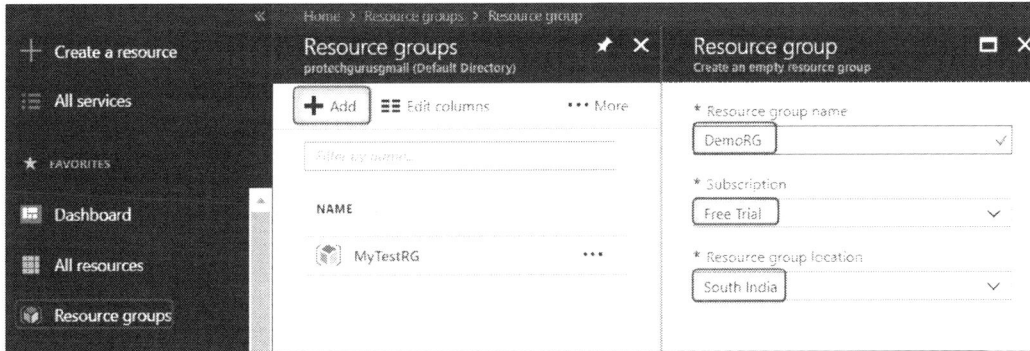

4. Finally, click **Create** to finish the wizard.
5. To delete a resource group, just click **Ellipsis (...)** button in front of the resource group that you want to delete.
6. Select **Delete** resource group as shown in the following figure.

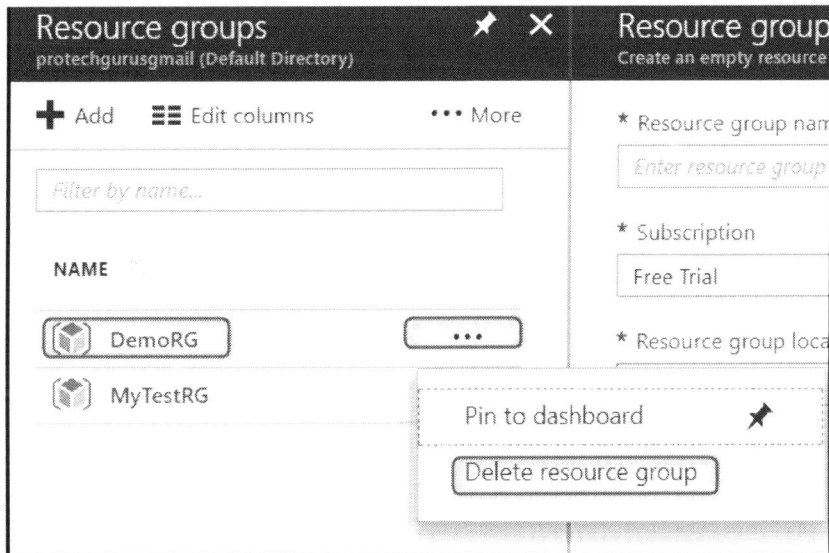

7. You will see the list of all the resources belonging to this resource group.
8. Type the exact name of your resource group, select all or few of the resources as per your choice and then click **Delete** to delete the selected resource group.

TYPE THE RESOURCE GROUP NAME:

Affected resources

There are 1 resources in this resource group that will be deleted.

NAME	LOCATION
MyTestvNet (Virtual network)	South India

9. The selected resources of the resource group will be deleted.

Lab 11: Introduction Azure Virtual Machines

Azure Virtual Machines are one of the central features of any Cloud platform. It's an Infrastructure as a Service (IaaS). In the Azure cloud, you can create Windows virtual machine as well Linux virtual machines. In the IaaS cloud model, you have total control over your deployed virtual machines. You are responsible for software installation, configuration, and maintenance, patching and updating VMs.

Azure VM Status

VMs in Azure cloud have three possible states. These are: Running, Stopped, and Stopped (Deallocated). Let's have a quick look about each of these:

- **Running**: The VM is powered on and running normally. The VM will be charged in this state.
- **Stopped**: The VM is stopped (powered off), but it is still consuming compute resources of Azure cloud. The VM will not be charged in this state.
- **Stopped (Deallocated)**: The VM is stopped (powered off), but it is not consuming compute resources of Azure cloud. The VM will be charged in this state.

By default, when you stop a VM using Azure Portal, the VM goes into the **Stopped (Deallocated)** state. In this state, few of the VM's settings, such as DIP, will be free to use by other VMs or other customers. If you want to stop the VM, but also want to keep it as allocated, use the following PowerShell cmdlet:

```
> Stop-AzureVM -Name "vm-name" -ServiceName "vm-name" -StayProvisioned
```

If you shut down the VM from inside the operating system of VM, the VM will be stopped, but it's attached resources will not be deallocated.and you will be charged it as running VM.

Lab 12: Understanding Azure VM Series Types

Virtual machines in Azure cloud have a variety of categories and types. Depending on the need of application, you can select the desired type of series and configuration for your VM. Before to deploy any virtual machine in any cloud platform, you must be well familiar with the VM categories and series provided by the cloud services provider. The following are the Azure virtual machine series. We recommend you have a quick look at each of the following VM series:

- **D Series**: Used by most applications, relational databases, and for in-memory caching and analytics purposes.
- **Dv2 Series**: Ideal for applications that require faster CPUs, better local disk performance, higher memories and offer a powerful combination of many enterprise-grade applications.
- **E Series**: Used as SAP HANA and other large in-memory business critical workloads.
- **F Series**: Used for batch processing, web servers, analytics and gaming.
- **G Series**: Used for large SQL and NoSQL databases, ERP, SAP and data warehousing solutions.
- **H Series**: Used for high performance computing, batch processing, and analytics.
- **L Series**: Used for NoSQL databases, data warehousing applications, and large transactional databases.
- **M Series**: Used for large in-memory business critical workloads which require massive parallel compute power.
- **N Series**: Used for graphics rendering, video editing, remote visualization, high performance computing and analytics.

Lab 13: Creating Azure Virtual Machine

Here we are going to show you how to create an Azure virtual machine using Azure Portal. Let's create a virtual machine as per the following configuration values:

- VM Name: **MyTestVM1**
- Resource Group: **MyTestRG**
- vNet: **MyTestvNet**
- Subnet: **MyPrivateSubnet1**
- OS: **Linux/Ubuntu**
- VM Type: **B1S (1vCPU/1GB)**

To do this, you need to perform the following steps:

1. In Azure Portal, select **Virtual machines**. On the **Virtual machines** blade, click **Add** to create a new virtual machine as shown in the following figure.

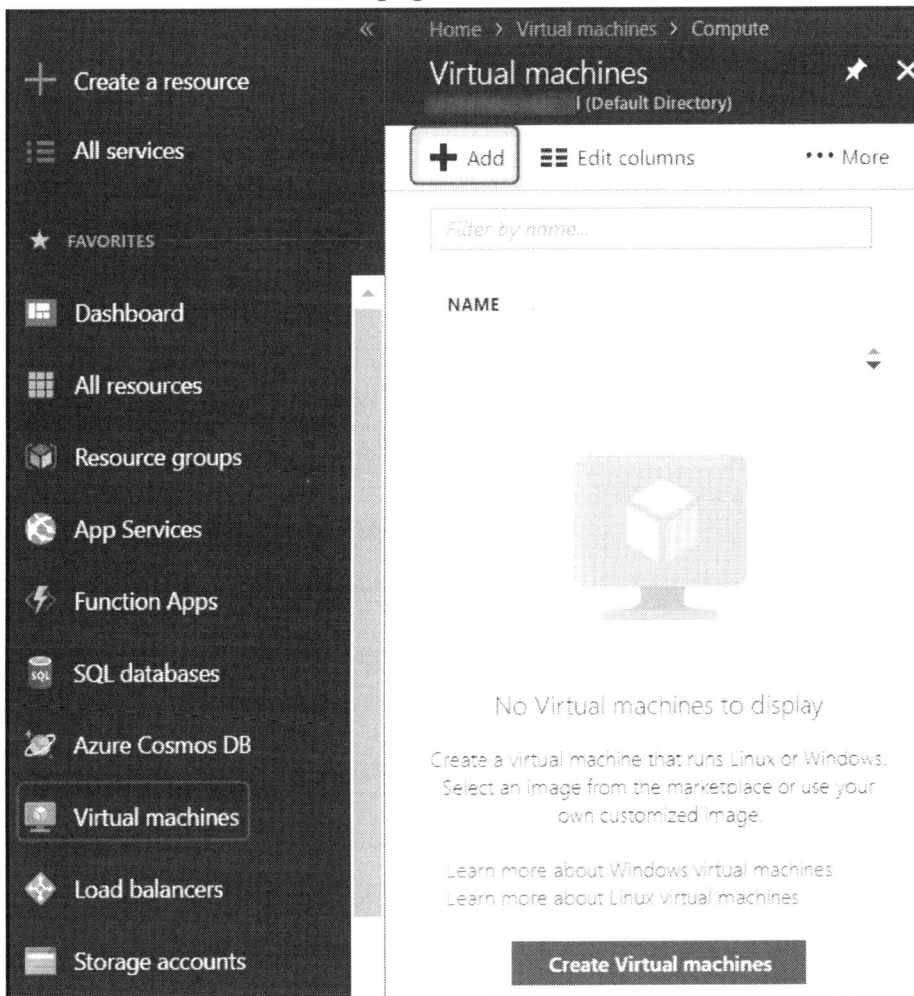

2. On the **Compute gallery** blade, type **ubuntu** in the search box, select **Ubuntu 16.04** provided by the **Canonical** publisher as shown in the following figure. However, you can select any other OS platform and publishers (such as RHEL or Windows) depending on your need and choice.

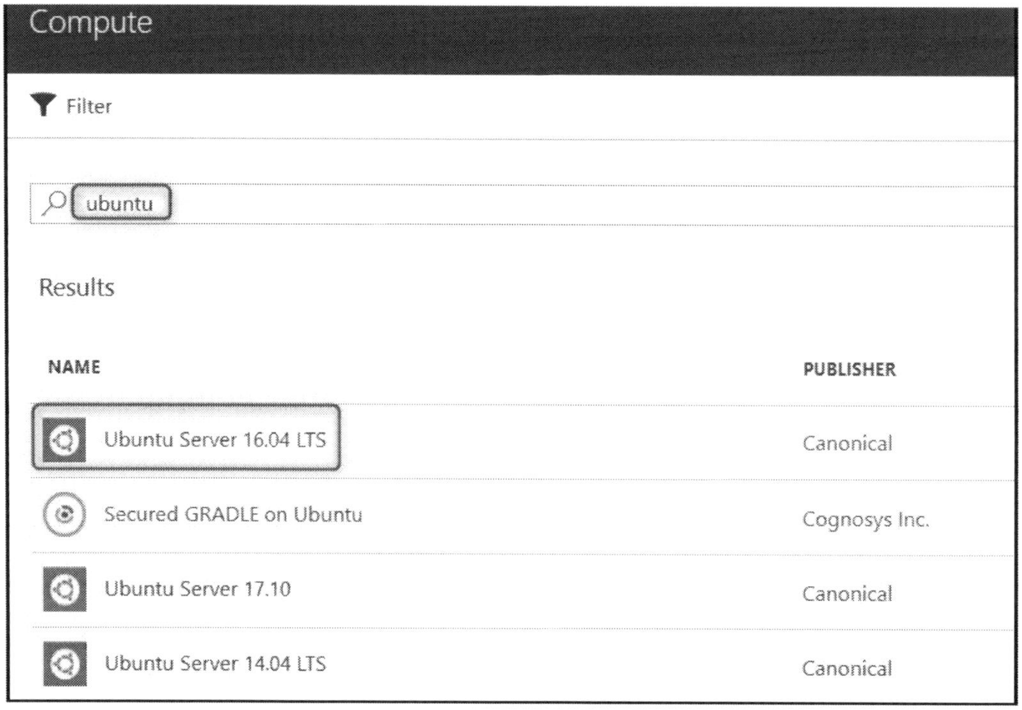

Compute

Filter

ubuntu

Results

NAME	PUBLISHER
Ubuntu Server 16.04 LTS	Canonical
Secured GRADLE on Ubuntu	Cognosys Inc.
Ubuntu Server 17.10	Canonical
Ubuntu Server 14.04 LTS	Canonical

3. On the **VM publisher intro** blade, make sure that **Resource Manager** is selected as the deployment model (old one is called classic) and then click **Create** as shown in the following figure to proceed.

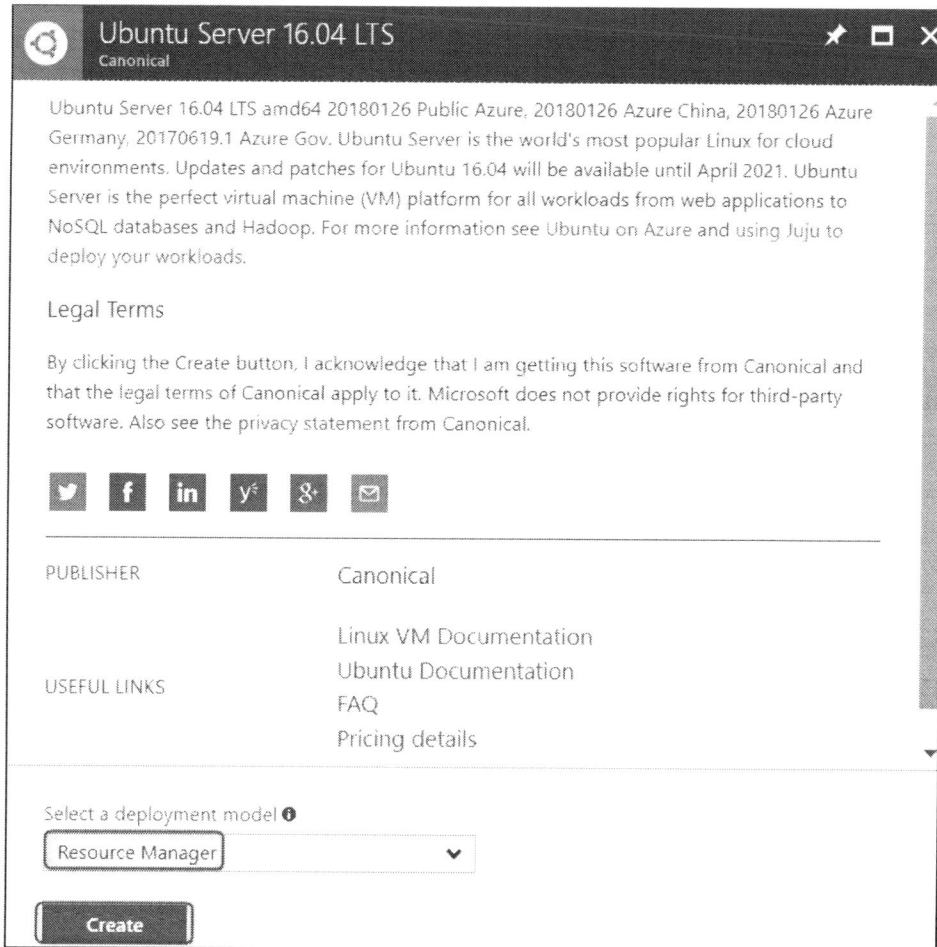

Ubuntu Server 16.04 LTS
Canonical

Ubuntu Server 16.04 LTS amd64 20180126 Public Azure, 20180126 Azure China, 20180126 Azure Germany, 20170619.1 Azure Gov. Ubuntu Server is the world's most popular Linux for cloud environments. Updates and patches for Ubuntu 16.04 will be available until April 2021. Ubuntu Server is the perfect virtual machine (VM) platform for all workloads from web applications to NoSQL databases and Hadoop. For more information see Ubuntu on Azure and using Juju to deploy your workloads.

Legal Terms

By clicking the Create button, I acknowledge that I am getting this software from Canonical and that the legal terms of Canonical apply to it. Microsoft does not provide rights for third-party software. Also see the privacy statement from Canonical.

PUBLISHER   Canonical

                   Linux VM Documentation
                   Ubuntu Documentation
USEFUL LINKS   FAQ
                   Pricing details

Select a deployment model

Resource Manager

Create

4. On the **Basics** blade, specify the following VM details:
   - Name: **MyTestVM1**
   - VM Disk type: **SSD** (HDD for lower performance and SSD for better performance)
   - User name: **Ubuntu**
   - Authentication type: **Password** (you can also upload SSH key if you have already generated).
   - Subscription: **Free Trial**
   - Resource group: **MyTestRG**
   - Location: **South India**
5. Refer the following figure for the sample configuration.

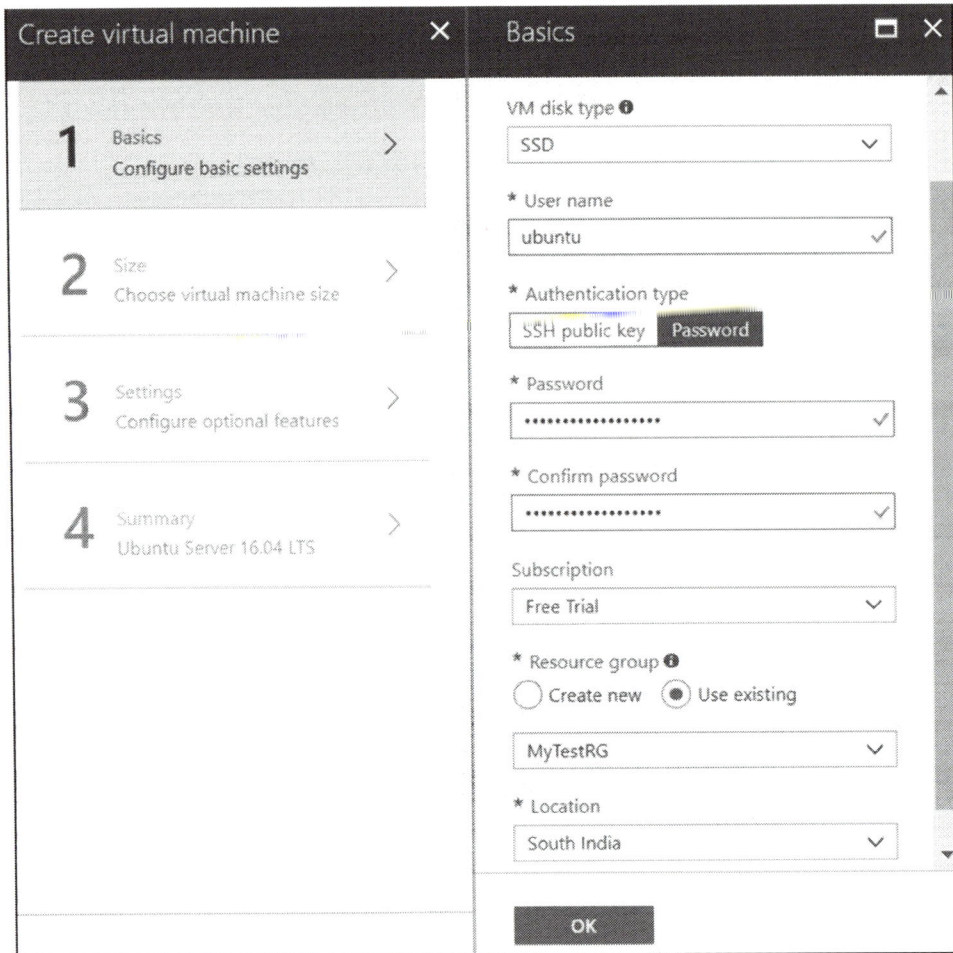

6. Click **OK** to proceed.
7. On the **Choose a size** blade, click **View All**, scroll-down and select **B1S Standard** VM size as shown in the following figure.

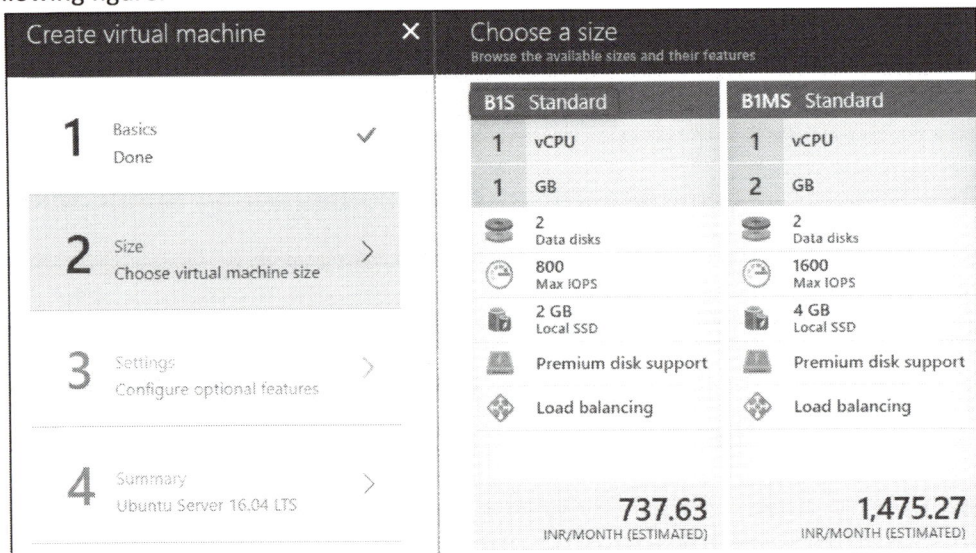

8. On the **Settings** blade, set the following settings:
   - Availability set: **None**

- Use managed disks: **Yes**
- OS Disk Size: **Default size (30 GB)**
- Virtual Network: **MyTestvNet**
- Subnet: **MyPublicSubnet1**
- Public IP Address: **Accept default selection**
- Network Security Group: **Accept default selection**
- Extensions: **No extensions**
- Auto Shutdown: **Off**
- Boot diagnostics: **Enabled**
- Guest OS Diagnostics: **Disabled**
- Diagnostic storage account: **Accept default selection**
- Backup: **Disabled**

9. Once your settings are set appropriately, click **OK** as shown in the following figure to proceed.

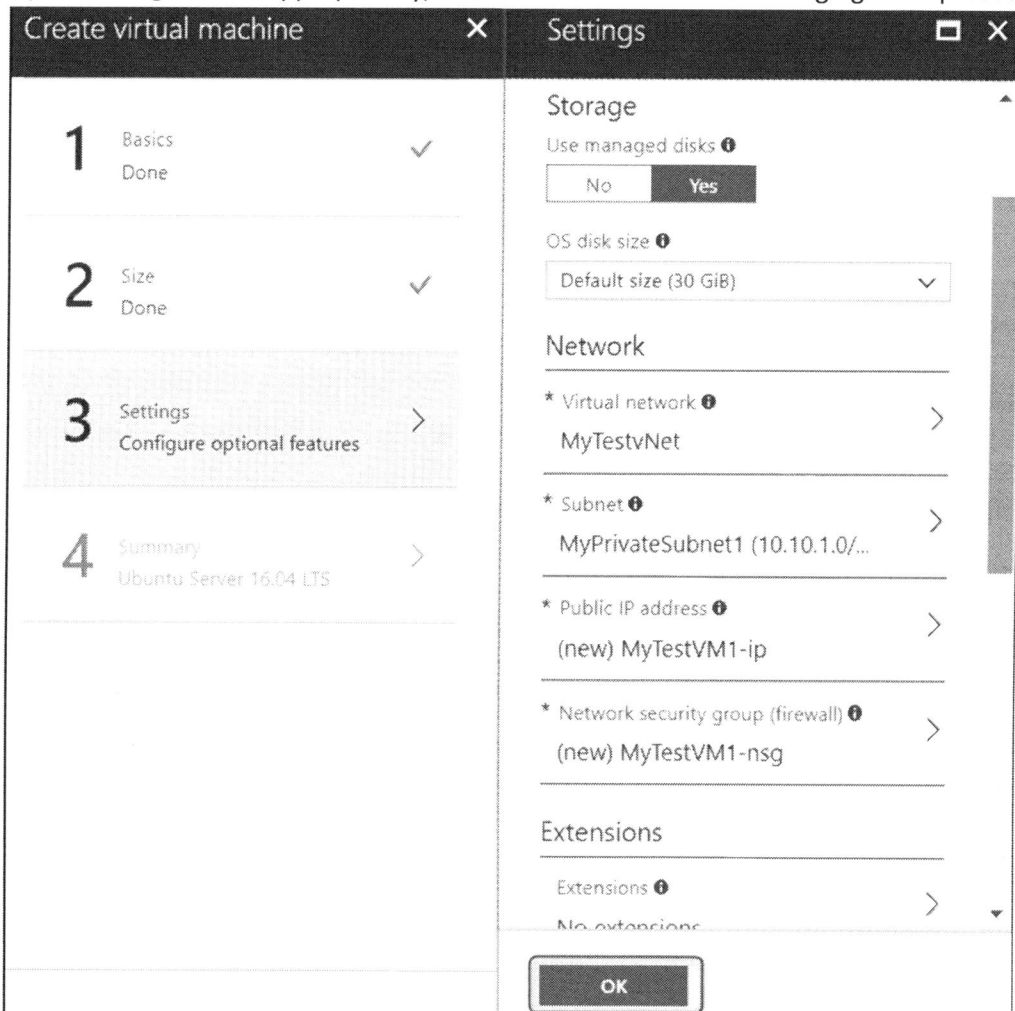

10. On the **Create** blade, check out the summary of your virtual machine and then click **Create** as shown in the following figure to proceed.

Offer details

Prices presented are estimates in your local currency that include only Azure infrastructure costs and any discounts for the subscription and location. The prices don't include any applicable software costs.

Ubuntu Server 16.04 LTS
by Canonical
Terms of use | privacy policy

Pricing details

Standard B1s
by Microsoft
Terms of use | privacy policy

0.9914 INR/hr
Pricing for other VM sizes

Terms of use

By clicking "Create", I (a) agree to the legal terms and privacy statement(s) associated with each Marketplace offering above, (b) authorize Microsoft to charge or bill my current payment method for the fees associated with my use of the offering(s), including applicable taxes, with the same billing frequency as my Azure subscription, until I discontinue use of the offering(s),

☐ I give Microsoft permission to use and share my contact information so that Microsoft or the Provider can contact me regarding this product and related products.

Create   Download template and parameters

11. The VM deployment process will be started. It may take a few minutes to complete the deployment process. The status will be shown in the notification bar.

Lab 14: Connecting Azure Virtual Machines

Once you create a virtual machine in Azure cloud, next you need to connect it. So, you can deploy application and other required configurations inside the virtual machine. The process of connecting azure virtual machine depends on the OS platform. If you create a Windows VM then you need to use RDP to connect VM. Otherwise, for Linux VM, you need to use SSH to connect VM. Since we have created a Linux virtual machine in the previous exercise, hence we need to use SSH method.

Depending on the platform of your local machine (Windows or Linux), you need to use an appropriate tool to connect azure VM using SSH. For Linux based machine, you need to use the SSH command on the terminal. If you are connecting Azure VM from Windows machine, you can do it using either PuTTY or GitBash. If you don't have these tools already, you can download from the following links.

- Download Gitbash for Windows
  https://git-scm.com/downloads
- Download PuTTY for Windows
  https://www.putty.org/

Connecting Azure Linux VM using Gitbash

1. To connect your Azure Linux VM using Gitbash, open the Gitbash terminal and execute the following command:
   ```
   ssh <username>@<vm-public-ip-address>
   ```
2. If you don't know the public IP address of your Azure VM, click **Virtual machines** in Azure Portal.
3. Select the virtual machine you want to connect, click **Overview** and then click **Connect** in the presented blade as shown in the following figure.

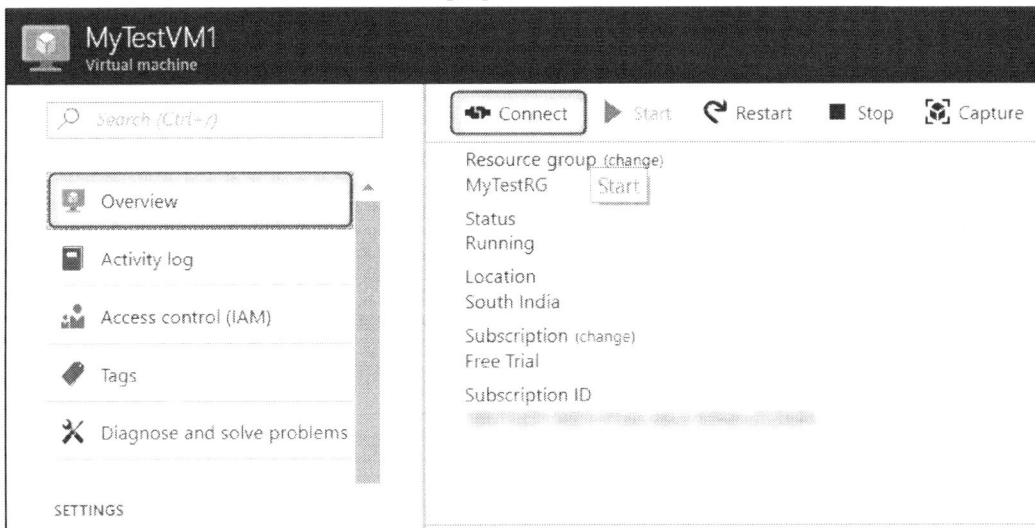

4. The SSH connection string will be displayed as shown in the following figure. Copy it and use it on Gitbash (or any other terminal) to connect this VM.

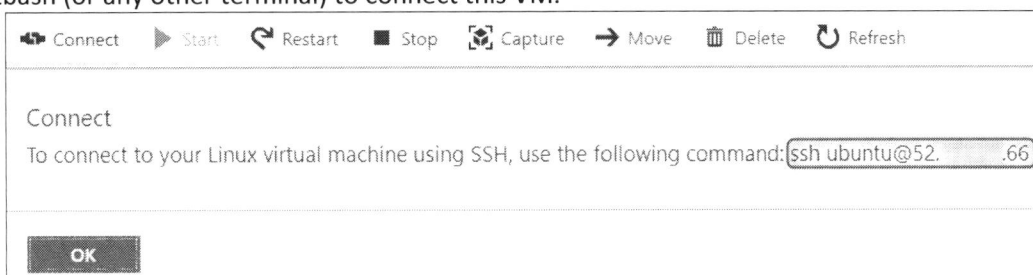

5. Use the username and password you set during the VM deployment. You will be connected to your Linux virtual machine as shown in the following figure.

Connect Azure Linux VM using PuTTY

1. If you are using PuTTY, then open PuTTY tool, and specify the public IP address of your Linux Azure VM. Click **Open** as shown in the following figure.

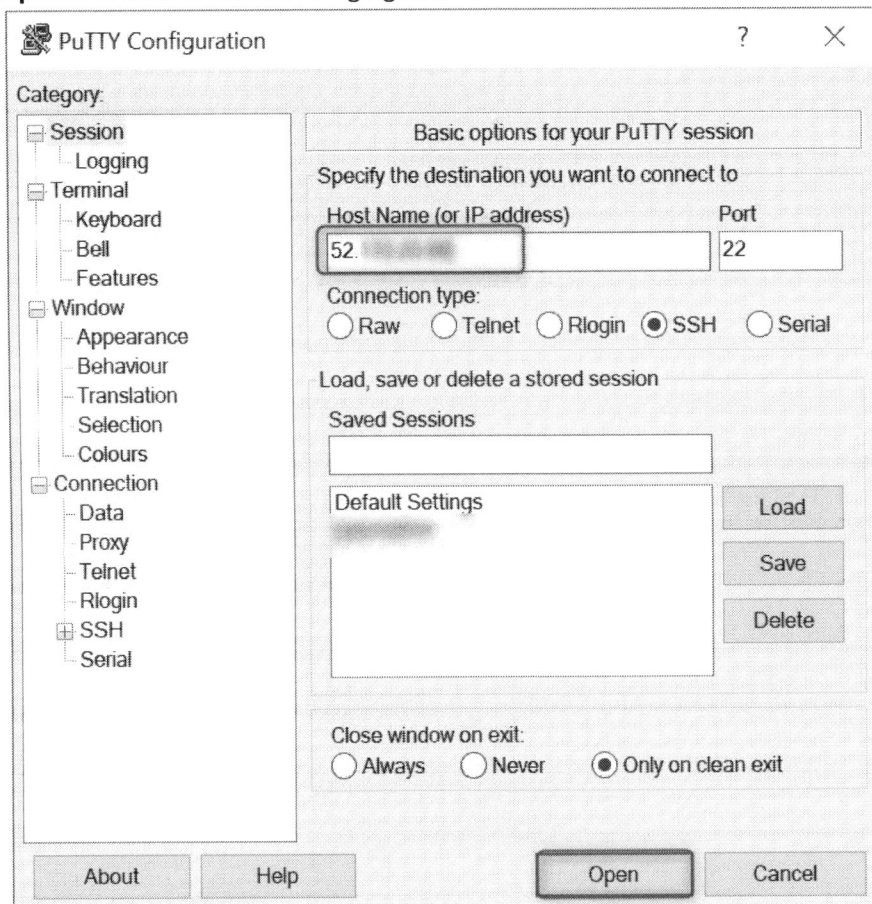

2. Type your username and password when asked and you will be connected to you Linux virtual machine prompt as shown in the following figure.

```
ubuntu@MyTestVM1: ~                                    —    □    ✕

login as: ubuntu
ubuntu@          s password:
Welcome to Ubuntu 16.04.3 LTS (GNU/Linux 4.13.0-1011-azure x86_64)

 * Documentation:  https://help.ubuntu.com
 * Management:     https://landscape.canonical.com
 * Support:        https://ubuntu.com/advantage

  Get cloud support with Ubuntu Advantage Cloud Guest:
    http://www.ubuntu.com/business/services/cloud

0 packages can be updated.
0 updates are security updates.


Last login: Fri Mar  2 14:53:25 2018 from
To run a command as administrator (user "root"), use "sudo <command>".
See "man sudo_root" for details.

ubuntu@MyTestVM1:~$
```

3. In a separate section, we will also cover how to connect your internal Windows and Linux VMs using private IP addresses (which would not have public IP addresses assigned). That's all you need to know to connect your Linux Azure VMs remotely. We have covered the Windows machine RDP connection in a separate section.

Lab 15: Detailed Explanation of Azure Virtual Machine Options

When you select a VM in Azure cloud, you see various options to manage the selected VM. It is very important that you become familiar with all the major and most useful VM properties options. Let's have a quick look of few most useful azure VM properties options:

1. **Overview:** It displays the basic information such as IP address, VM hostname, location, VM status etc. of your selected VM. It also allows you to **Connect**, **Start**, **Stop**, **Restart**, **Capture**, **Move**, and **Delete** virtual machine as shown in the following figure.

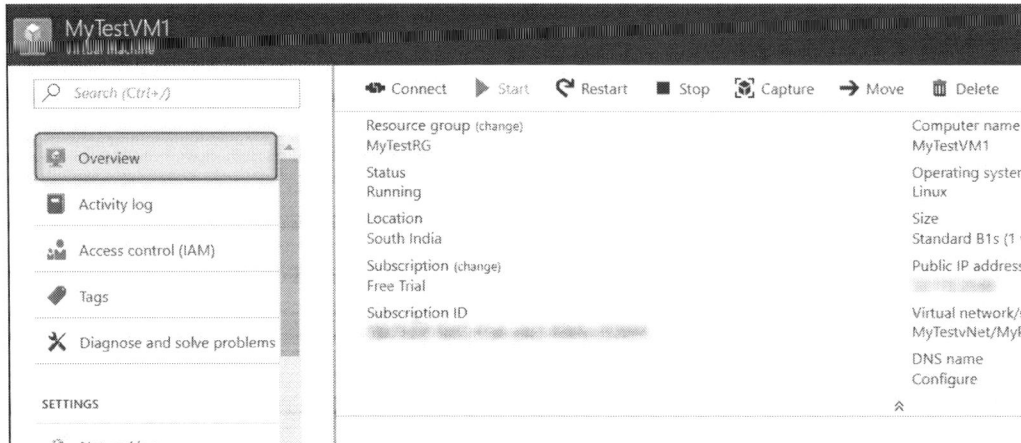

2. **Access control (IAM):** It allows you to show the current owner of VM and add additional users to manage this VM.

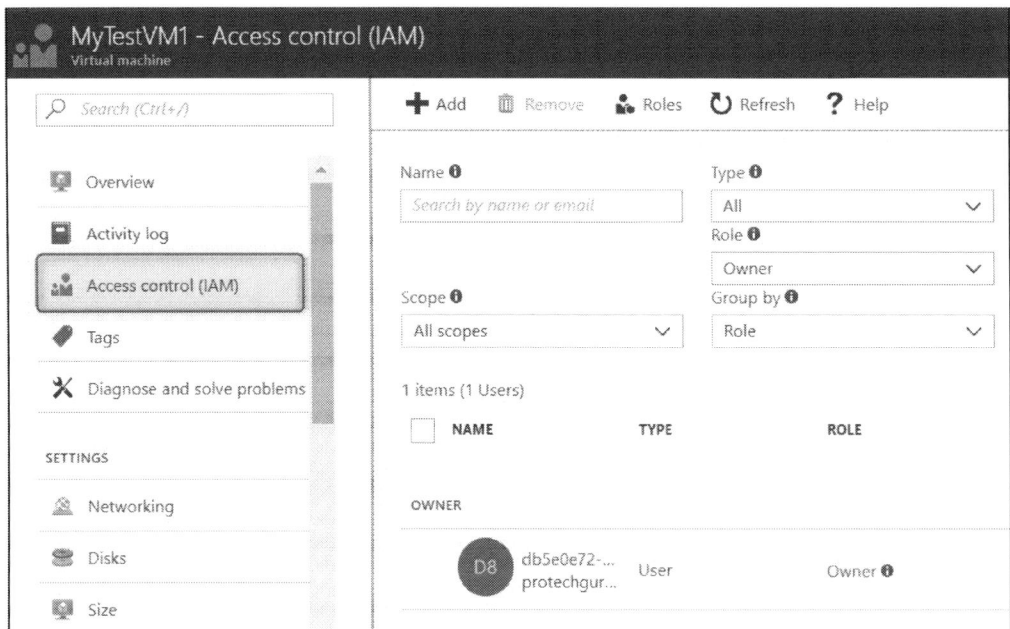

3. **Tags**: It allows you to categorize your virtual machine by specifying different tags. You can set various tags in **Key** and **Value** pair format. For example, set **Environment** as Key, and Value as **Testing** to categorize all testing VMs. Another example is - let's assume you have many VMs for different projects in a single Azure subscription, how will you differentiate their project-wise costs? Yes, you can set tags. For example, set Key as **CostCenter** and Value as **DemoProject** to categorize all demo VMs to keep its cost separate from other VMs.

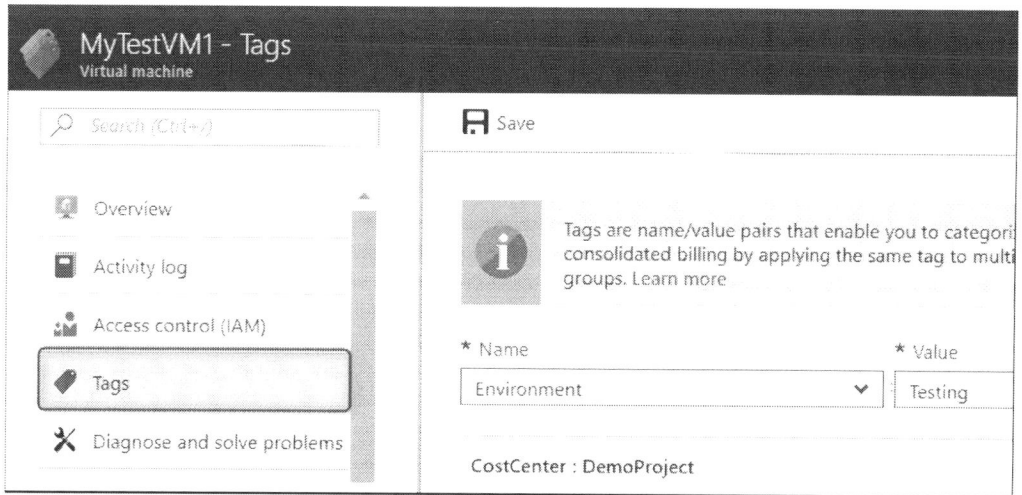

MyTestVM1 - Tags
Virtual machine

🔍 Search (Ctrl+/)

💾 Save

🖥 Overview

📋 Activity log

👥 Access control (IAM)

🏷 Tags

🔧 Diagnose and solve problems

ℹ️ Tags are name/value pairs that enable you to categori consolidated billing by applying the same tag to mult groups. Learn more

* Name

Environment ▼

* Value

Testing

CostCenter : DemoProject

4. **Diagnose and solve problems**: It shows you resource health, recent activity, and solutions to common problems.

5. **Networking**: It shows you the attached network interface, private and public IP addresses, virtual network and subnets. More importantly, it shows the allowed Network Security Group (NSG) rules. We have covered NSG in details in a separate section.

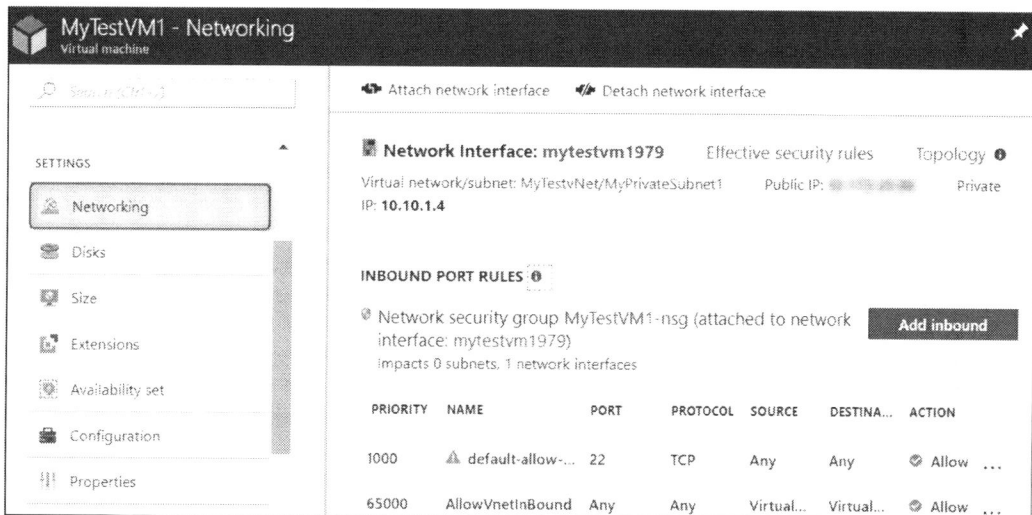

MyTestVM1 - Networking
Virtual machine

🔍 Search (Ctrl+/)

SETTINGS

🖧 Networking

💿 Disks

🖥 Size

📊 Extensions

⚙️ Availability set

⚙️ Configuration

⬛ Properties

◄► Attach network interface   ◄► Detach network interface

🖧 **Network Interface: mytestvm1979**   Effective security rules   Topology ❶

Virtual network/subnet: MyTestvNet/MyPrivateSubnet1   Public IP: ████████   Private
IP: **10.10.1.4**

INBOUND PORT RULES ❶

🔘 Network security group MyTestVM1-nsg (attached to network
   interface: mytestvm1979)
   Impacts 0 subnets, 1 network interfaces

Add inbound

PRIORITY	NAME	PORT	PROTOCOL	SOURCE	DESTINA...	ACTION
1000	⚠ default-allow-...	22	TCP	Any	Any	⊘ Allow ...
65000	AllowVnetInBound	Any	Any	Virtual...	Virtual...	⊘ Allow ...

6. **Disks**: It shows you the attached disks and their size. You can also add additional disks if required. We have covered disk management in a separate section.

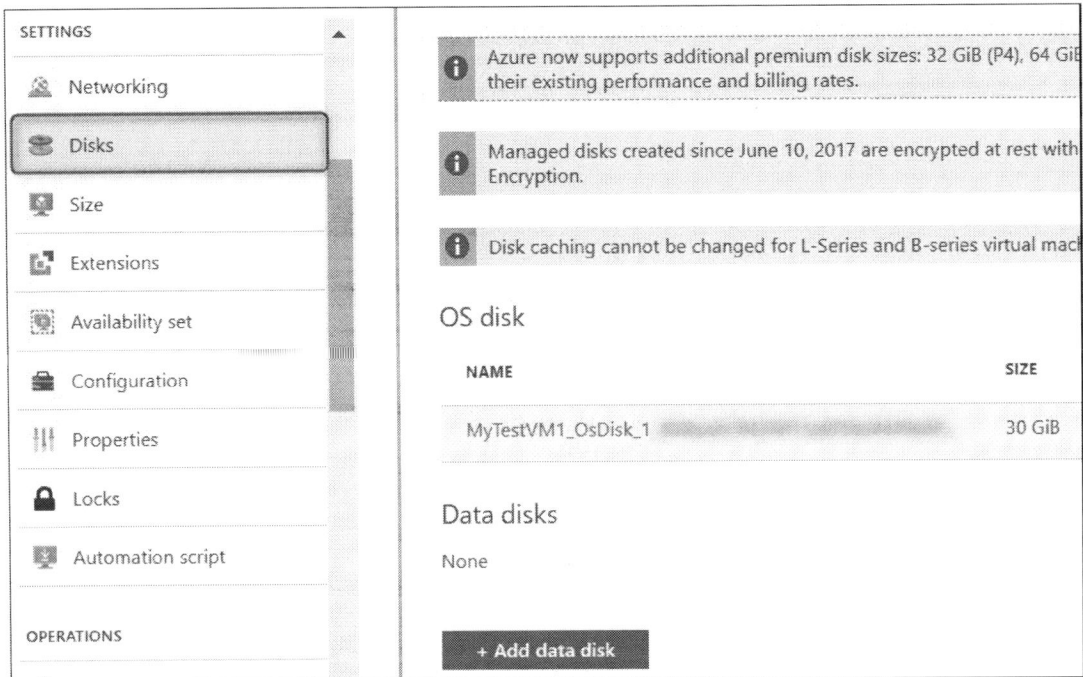

SETTINGS	
🖳 Networking	
🗄 **Disks**	
🖥 Size	
⬛ Extensions	
⬤ Availability set	
🧰 Configuration	
⌗ Properties	
🔒 Locks	
🖳 Automation script	

OPERATIONS

ⓘ Azure now supports additional premium disk sizes: 32 GiB (P4), 64 GiB
their existing performance and billing rates.

ⓘ Managed disks created since June 10, 2017 are encrypted at rest with
Encryption.

ⓘ Disk caching cannot be changed for L-Series and B-series virtual mach

OS disk

NAME	SIZE
MyTestVM1_OsDisk_1	30 GiB

Data disks

None

+ Add data disk

7. **Size**: It shows you the current VM series type and size of the selected virtual machine. You can also change the VM size if you think the current VM size is not sufficient for the application running inside the VM.

8. **Availability set**: Availability set allows you to run a group of virtual machines as a single set of application. Once a VM is launched, you cannot change the availability set. We have covered availability set with the Load Balancer section.

9. **Auto-Shutdown**: It allows you to shut down (power off) your VM automatically at the specific time.

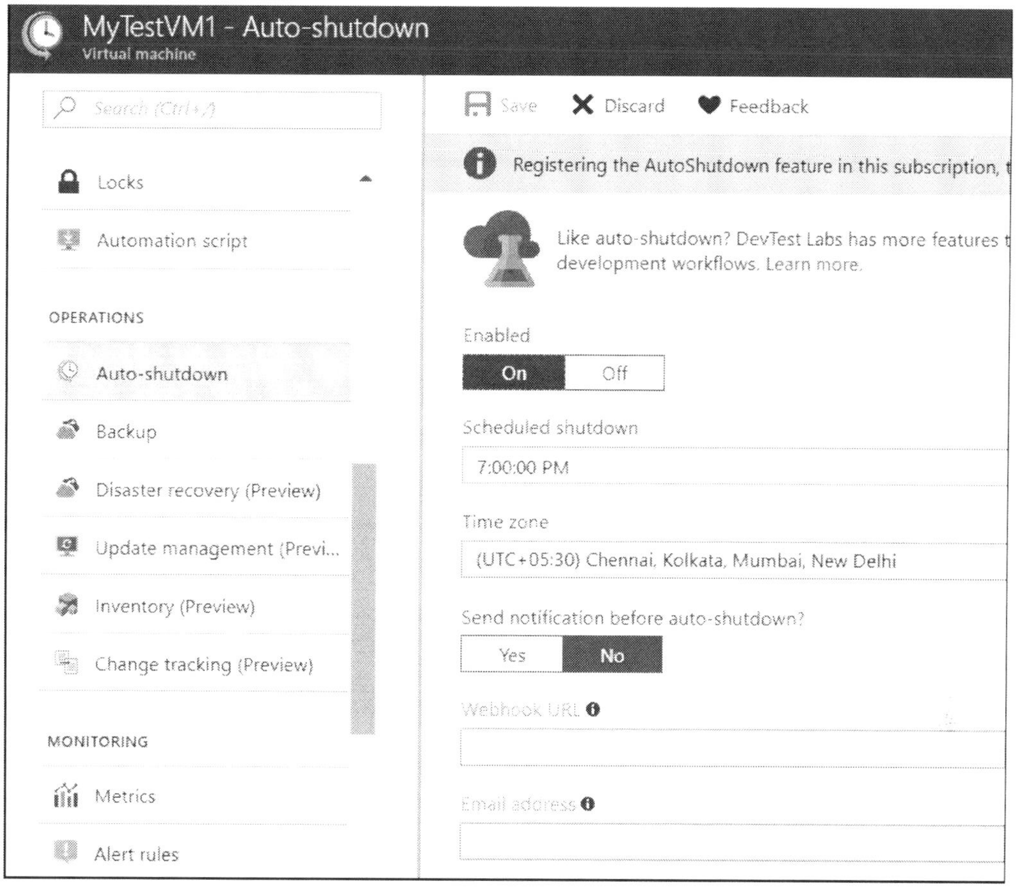

MyTestVM1 - Auto-shutdown
Virtual machine

Search (Ctrl+/)

🔒 Locks

📄 Automation script

OPERATIONS

🕐 Auto-shutdown

📀 Backup

📀 Disaster recovery (Preview)

💻 Update management (Previ...

📦 Inventory (Preview)

🗂 Change tracking (Preview)

MONITORING

📊 Metrics

🔔 Alert rules

💾 Save   ✖ Discard   ♥ Feedback

ℹ Registering the AutoShutdown feature in this subscription,

Like auto-shutdown? DevTest Labs has more features t
development workflows. Learn more.

Enabled

| On | Off |

Scheduled shutdown

7:00:00 PM

Time zone

(UTC+05:30) Chennai, Kolkata, Mumbai, New Delhi

Send notification before auto-shutdown?

| Yes | No |

Webhook URL ℹ

Email address ℹ

10. **Backup**: It allows you to take backup of your VM, so you can recover it in case of VM/Data crashes.

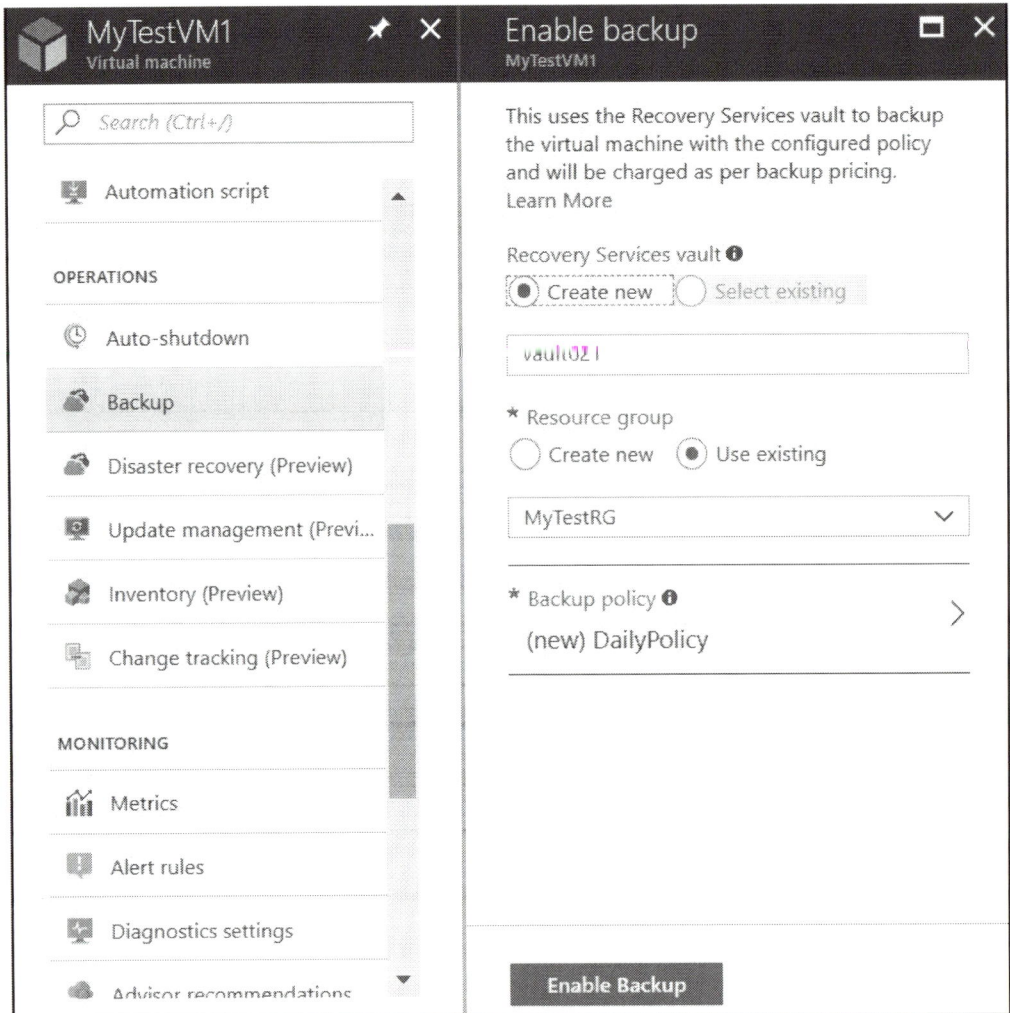

MyTestVM1
Virtual machine

Search (Ctrl+/)

Automation script

OPERATIONS

Auto-shutdown

Backup

Disaster recovery (Preview)

Update management (Previ...

Inventory (Preview)

Change tracking (Preview)

MONITORING

Metrics

Alert rules

Diagnostics settings

Advisor recommendations

Enable backup
MyTestVM1

This uses the Recovery Services vault to backup the virtual machine with the configured policy and will be charged as per backup pricing. Learn More

Recovery Services vault ⓘ
◉ Create new   ○ Select existing

vault021

* Resource group
○ Create new   ◉ Use existing

MyTestRG

* Backup policy ⓘ
(new) DailyPolicy

Enable Backup

11. **Boot diagnostics**: It allows you to take a screenshot of your running virtual machine. In case, if you are not able to take remote of your VM, you don't know what's happening inside VM? In this case, you can take inside screenshot of your VM to know the background operations that can help you to troubleshoot VM.

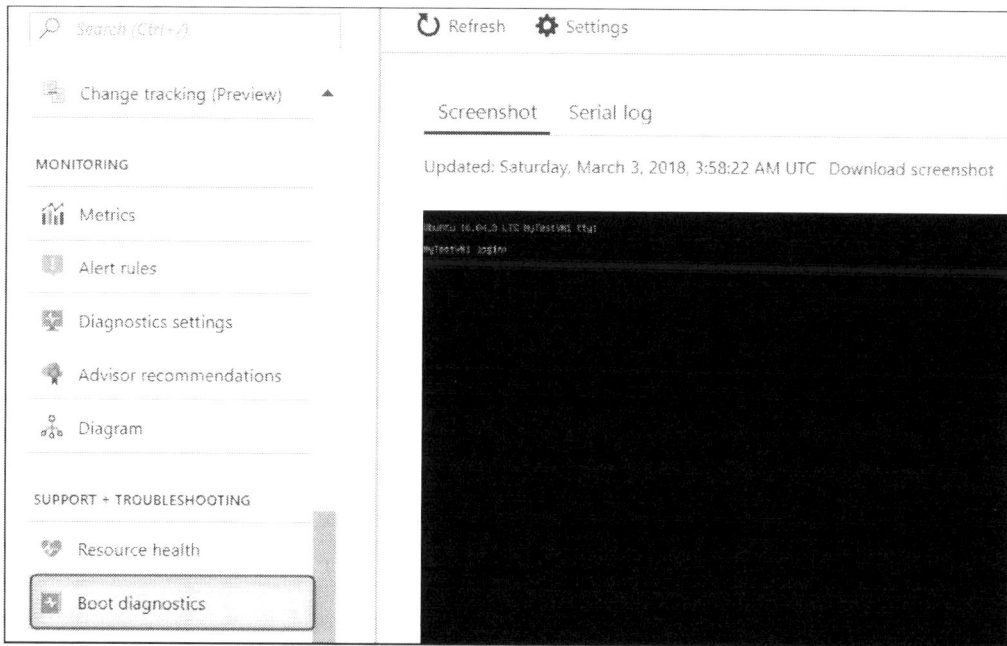

12. **Reset Password**: If you forget the credentials of your VM, you can reset using this option.

13. **New support request**: If you have any further issue and cannot solve it by yourself, you can always raise a support ticket to **Azure Help Center** to look into that.

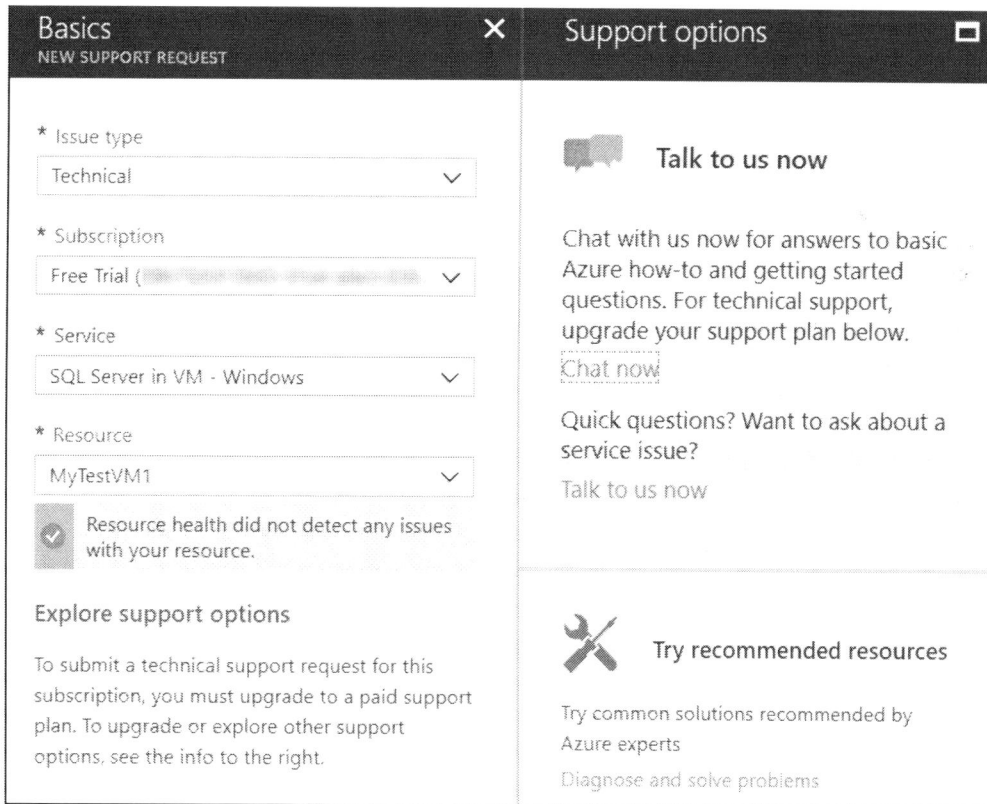

If you are interested, we also recommend you have a quick look at other few remaining VM properties options that have not been covered here.

Lab 16: Configure Disk in Azure Virtual Machine

Virtual Hard Disk (VHD) files are used to create Azure Virtual Machines. Basically, there are two types of VHDs used in Azure Virtual Machines:

1. **Image:** This type of VHD is a template for the creation of a new Azure VM.
2. **Disk**: This type of VHD can be booted and used as a mountable disk for a VM. It can be further divided into two types of disks: an OS disk and a data disk. OS disk and data disks are backed by page blobs in Azure Storage.
3. **Temporary disk**: Azure Virtual Machines also include a physical temporary disk that is not persisted to Azure Storage. The temporary disk should be used only for temporary data.

Creating and Attaching Disks to Azure VM

You can create and attach additional disks to an Azure VM. Here, we are going to show you how to create an additional disk, attach it to Azure VM, and use it to store data inside the VM. For this, you need to perform the following steps:

1. Select the Virtual Machine for which you want to attach the additional disk, select the **Disks** option and then **click Add data disk** as shown in the following figure.

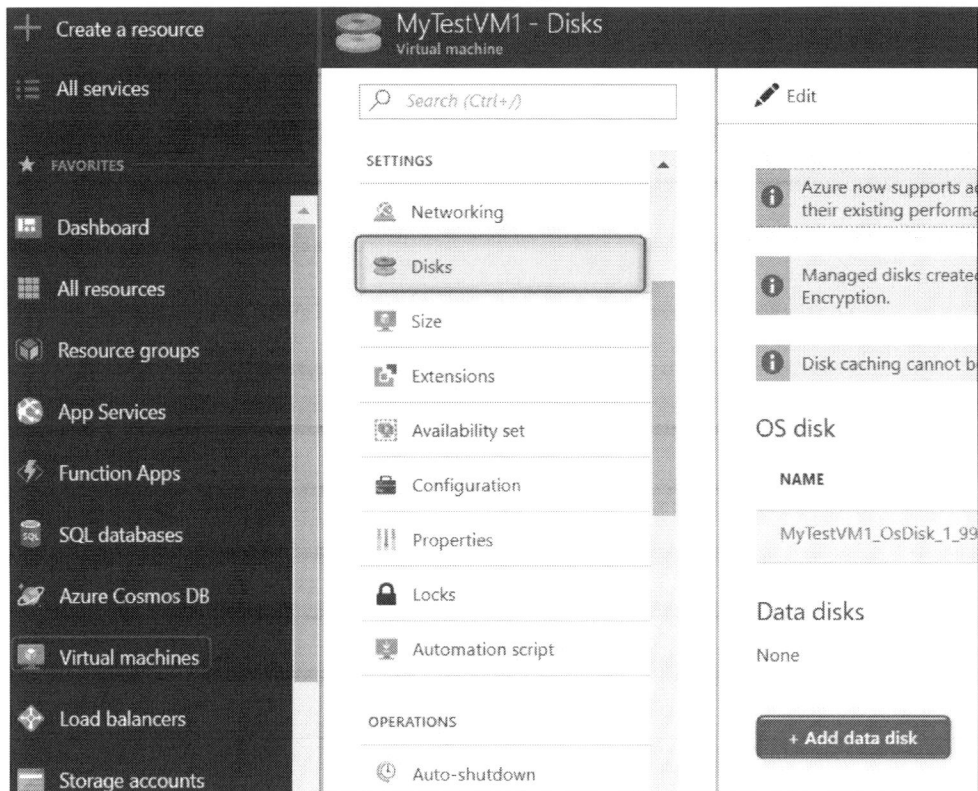

2. In the **Data disks** section, click **Create disk** as shown in the following figure.

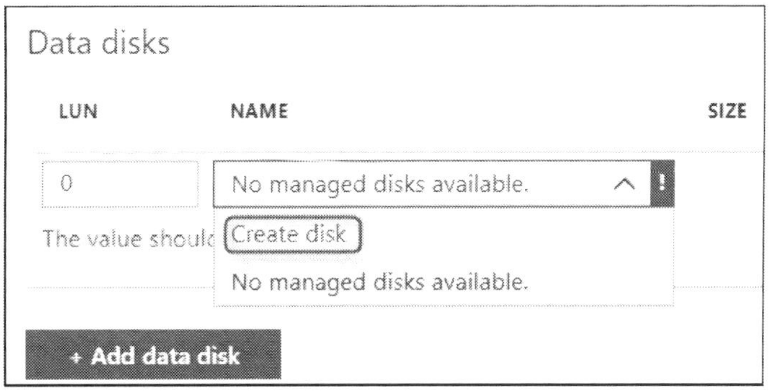

3. On the **Create managed disk** blade, specify the configuration values as mentioned below:

- Name: **MyTestDataDisk1**
- Resource group: **MyTestRG**
- Account type: **Standard HDD** or **Premium (SSD)**
- Source type: **None**
- Sie: **10**

4. Once you set the desired settings, click **Create** as shown in the following figure to proceed.

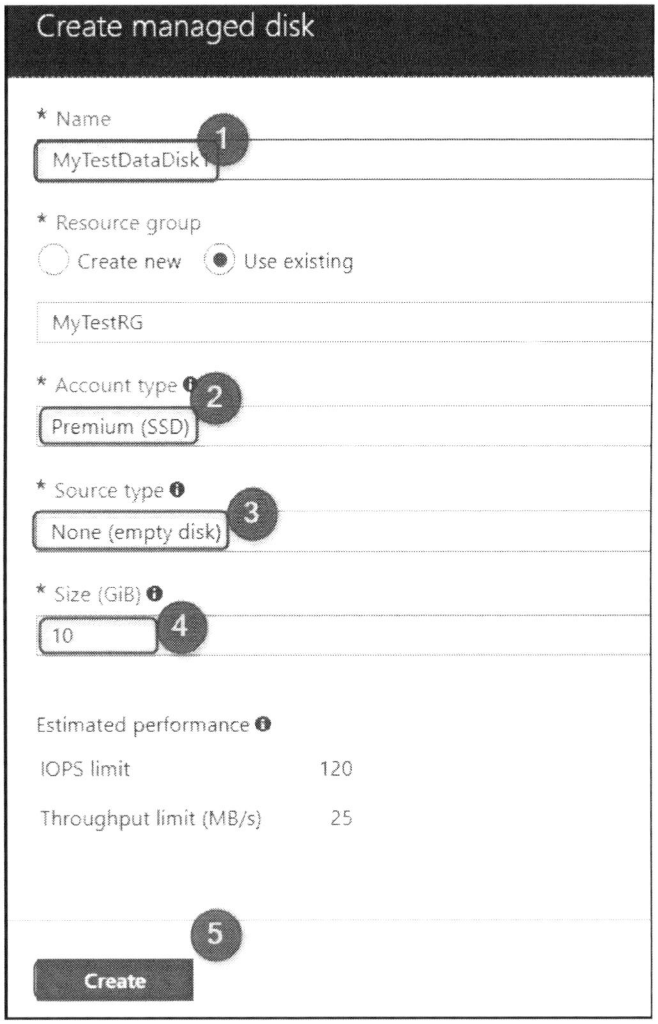

5. The disk will be created and listed it the **Disks** list. Click **Save** to save the configuration.

Using Data Disks for Azure VM

Once created, you can use the data disk to save the data on the created disk. However, first you need to format disk before you could store data on it. For this, login to your virtual machine and format the disk. Depending on the virtual machine's OS (Windows or Linux), formatting process may differ. Here, let's see how to format and use disk an a Linux virtual machine.

1. Use `sudo fdisk -l` command to know the disk name as shown in the following figure.

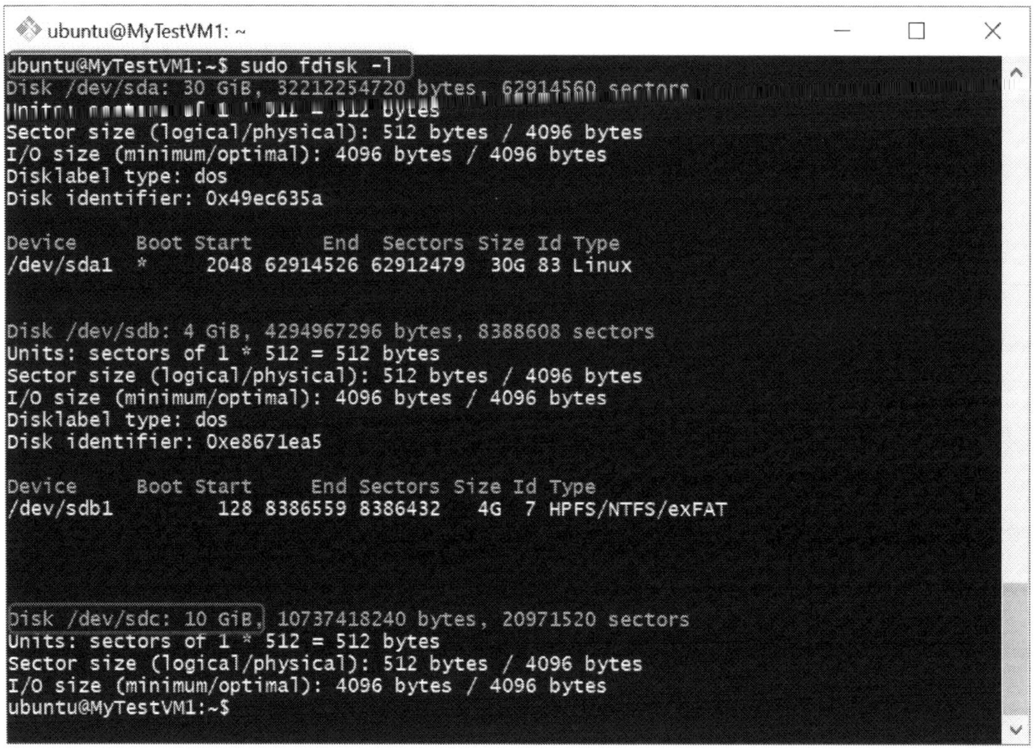

2. Now use the following command to format the disk. Replace your disk name shown in by executing the above command.

```
sudo mkfs.ext4 /dev/sdc
```

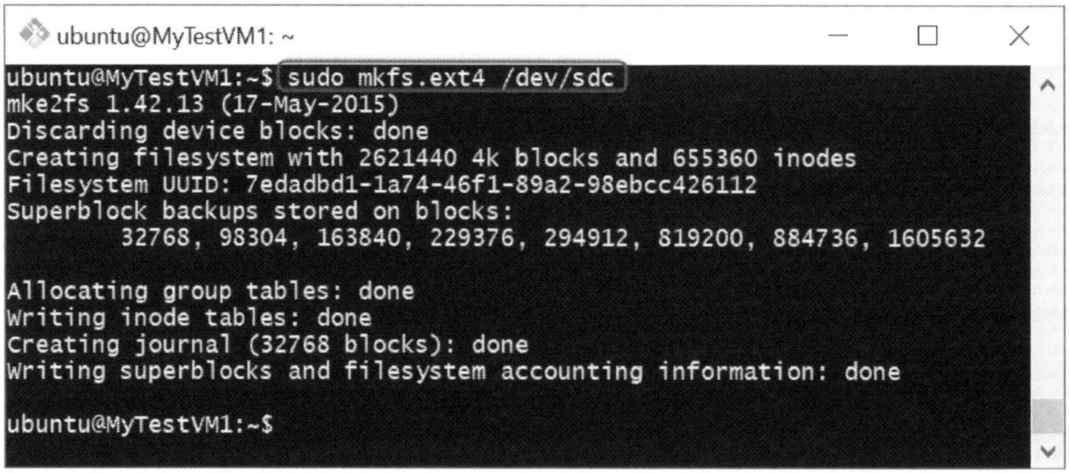

3. After formatting, create a mount point, mount the disk, and create a test directory using the following commands:

```
sudo mkdir /data
```

```
sudo mount /dev/sdc /data
cd /data
sudo mkdir MyTestDir1
```

6. If you are using Windows virtual machine, use the **disk management tool** (diskmgmt.msc) to format and use Azure data disks.

Detaching Data Disk

If you no longer need the attached data disk, or want to replace the attached data disk with another data disk, you need to perform the following steps:

1. Unmount the attached disk (Linux only) using the following command.
   ```
   sudo umount /dev/sdc /data
   ```
2. Now, click **Add data disk** in the **Data disks** section.
3. Select the disk you want to detach and then click the **Detach** icon as shown in the following figure.

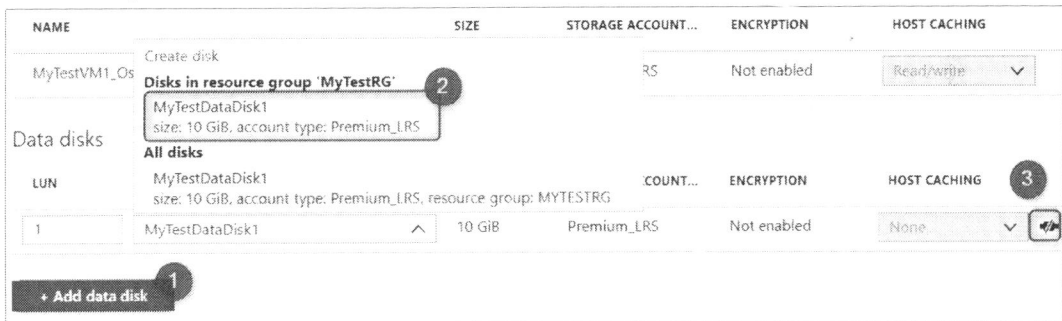

4. Click **Save** to save the configuration. The disk will be detached from the virtual machine.

Creating Snapshot of Azure Disks

Snapshots are excellent point-in-time backup solution. If you have a snapshot of a disk, you can use it to create a new disk from this snapshot and recover the lost data at the time of when it was created. To create a snapshot of Azure disk, you need to perform the following steps:

1. Select the disk in the **Disks** section of which you want to create the snapshot.

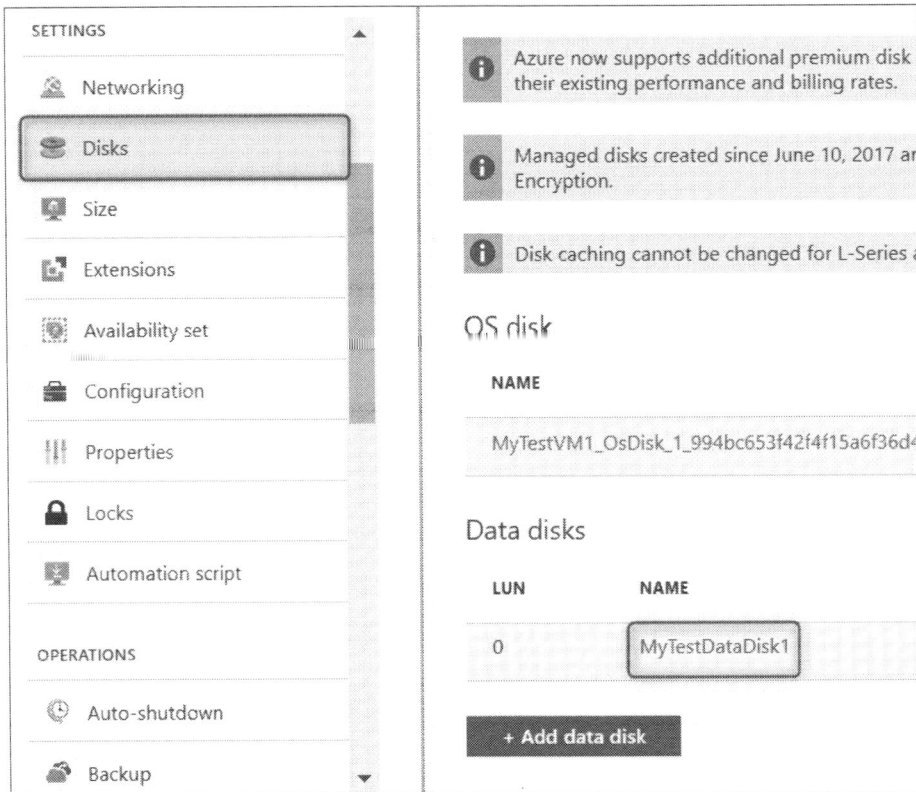

2. On the next blade, you have the following options to manage the selected disk:
   - **Save**: To save the configuration changes.
   - **Discard**: To discard the configuration changes.
   - **Create Snapshot**: To create a snapshot of the disk.
   - **Export**: To export disk
   - **Move**: To move disk in to another Azure subscription or resource group.
   - **Delete**: To delete the selected disk.
3. If the disk is currently attached to a virtual machine, few of the options will be greyed out as shown in the following figure.

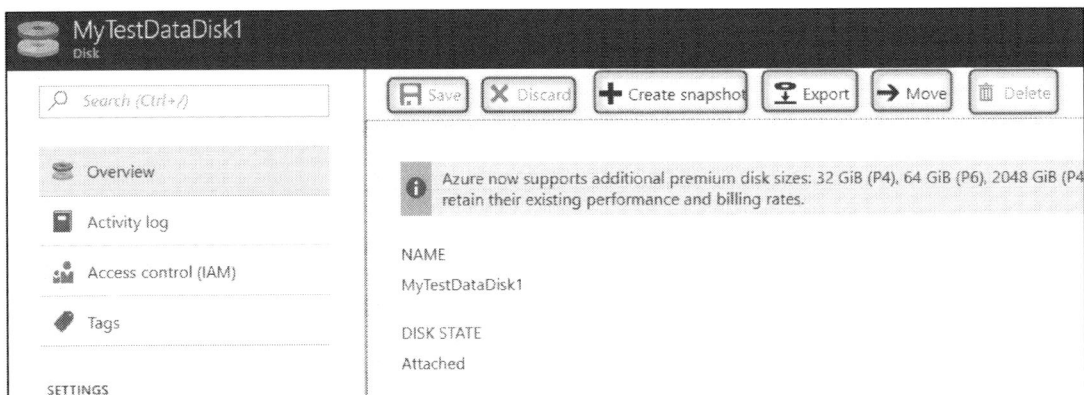

4. To create snapshot, click **Create snapshot**.

5. On the **Create snapshot** blade, specify the name, resource group, and disk account type appropriately as shown in the following figure.

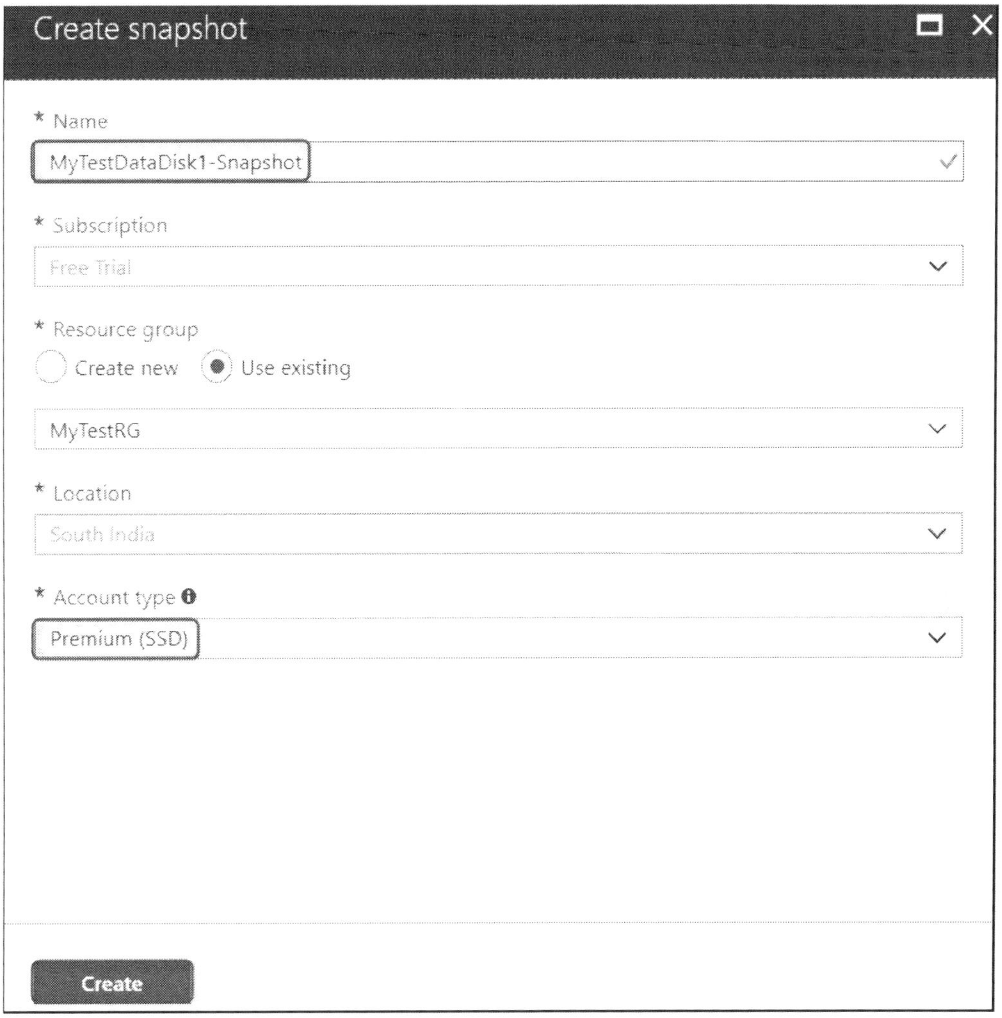

6. Click **Create** to proceed. After a few minutes, the snapshot will be created.

Creating Data Disk from Snapshot and Recover Lost Data

The snapshot you have created will hold all the data when it was created. Now let's create the disk from the taken snapshot, attach the created disk to Azure VM, and recover the lost data. For this, you need to perform the following steps:

1. Select a virtual machine and navigate to the **Disk**s blade.
2. Click **Add data disk** and then select **Create disk** option as shown in the following figure.

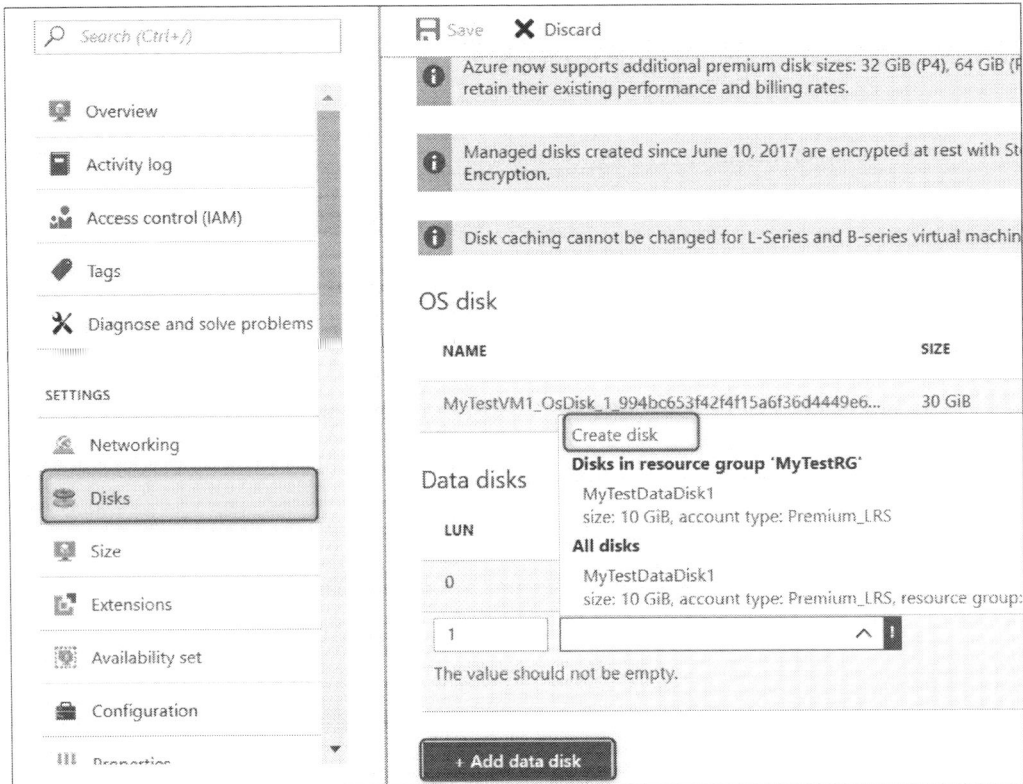

3. On the **Create disk** blade, specify the following configuration values:

- Name: **MyTestSnapDisk1**
- Resource group: **MyTestRG**
- Source type: **Snapshot**
- Account type: **Premium (SSD)**
- Source snapshot: **MyTestDataDisk1 - Snapshot**

4. After providing the appropriate values, click **Create** to create disk as shown in the following figure.

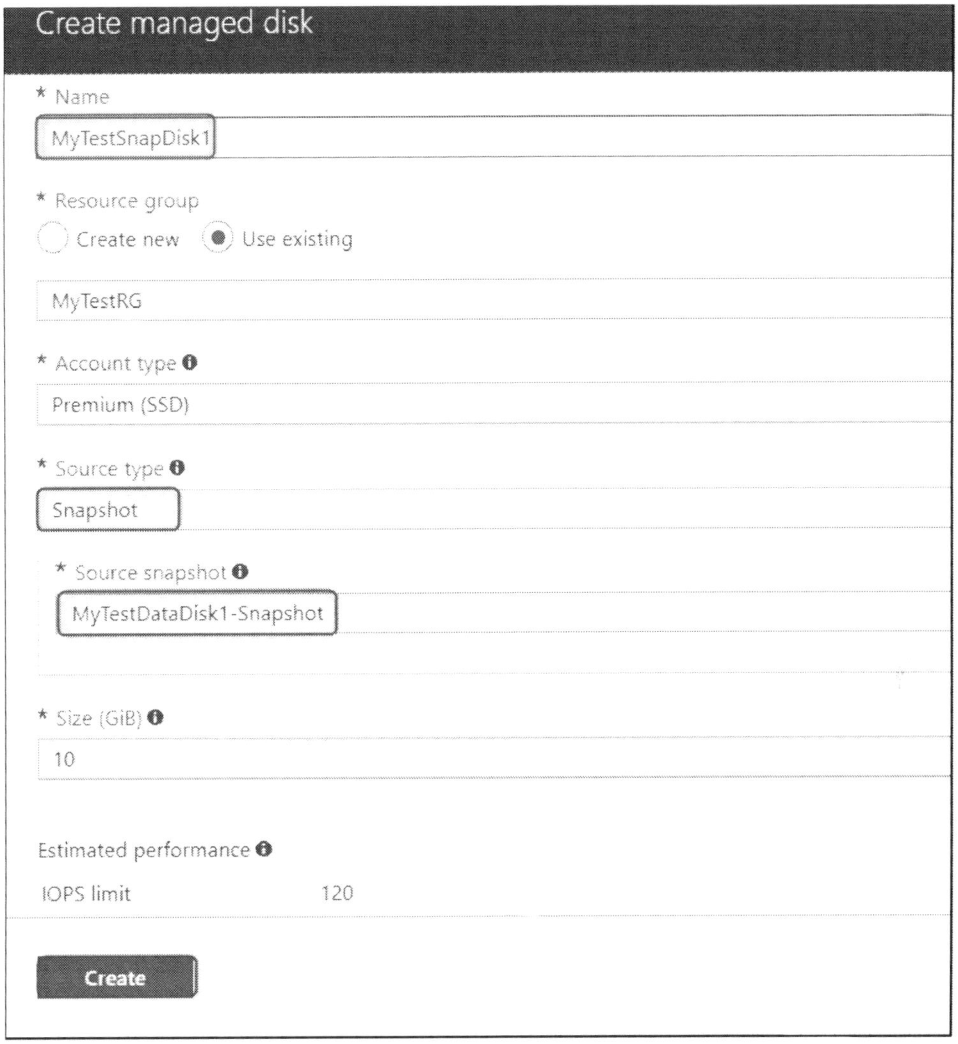

Create managed disk

* Name

MyTestSnapDisk1

* Resource group

○ Create new   ● Use existing

MyTestRG

* Account type ⓘ

Premium (SSD)

* Source type ⓘ

Snapshot

* Source snapshot ⓘ

MyTestDataDisk1-Snapshot

* Size (GiB) ⓘ

10

Estimated performance ⓘ

IOPS limit   120

Create

5. A new disk will be created from the snapshot you selected. Click **Save** to save the configuration as shown in the following disk.

6. Now, login to your virtual machine and mount the created disk (we assume you are using Linux virtual machine). You will find all the data stored on the disk when the snapshot was created.

Lab 17: Capturing VM Image in Azure Cloud

Once you have your new Azure VM configured appropriately, you can create a clone of this VM. In AWS, this is called Amazon Machine Image (AMI) creation. The captured image contains all the OS and Data disks with all the stored data.

You can use this image to launch a new VM or recover the VM if it was crashed anyhow. One more useful case of using an image is - you might want to create several more VMs using the one you just created as a template. For example, you have configured your web server on a VM and want to add four similar VMs behind a load balancer. You can use your captured image as a source VM for all these VMs rather than creating and configuring all four VMs separately. This process is called as capturing the VM, or creating a generalized VM Image.

Note: When you capture the VM to use it as a template for future VMs, you will no longer be able to use the original VM. This is because the source VM is deleted after the capture is completed.

To create a capture image, you need to perform the following steps:

1. Login to your virtual machine of which you want to capture image.
2. Depending on the virtual machine's OS platform, you need to select one of the following methods:
   a. For Windows virtual machine, navigate to the **%windir%/system32/sysprep** directory and then run **Sysprep.exe**.
   b. Select the **Generalize** check box, select **Shutdown** from Shutdown Options, and then click **OK** as shown in the following figure. The VM will be generalized and powered off when the process completes.

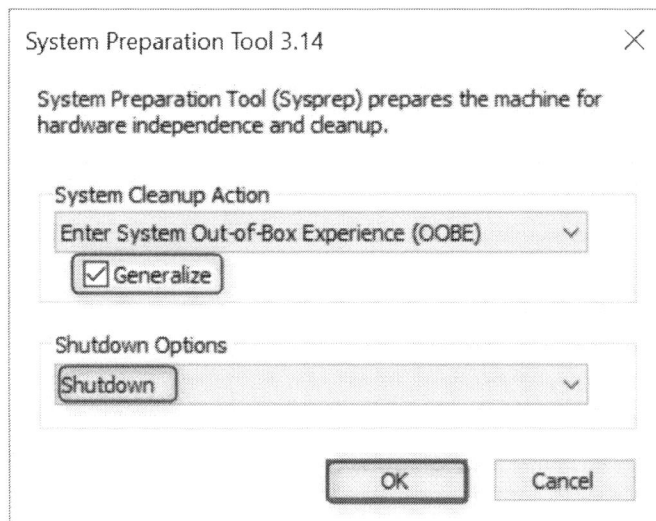

   c. If you are using a Linux virtual machine, execute the following commands as shown in the following figure.
```
sudo waagent -deprovision
```

```
sudo shutdown now
```

3. Once the generalized process is completed, you can capture the image. For this, select the virtual machine, and then click **Capture** as shown in the following figure.

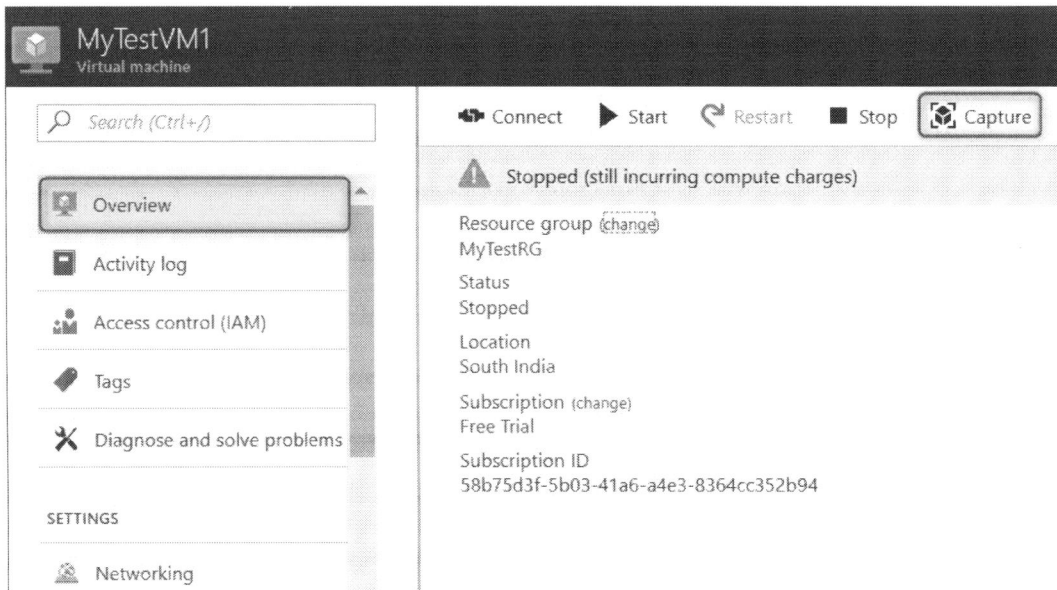

4. On the **Create image** blade, specify the image name and select resource group.
5. Select the **Automatically delete** check box and then click **Create** as shown in the following figure.

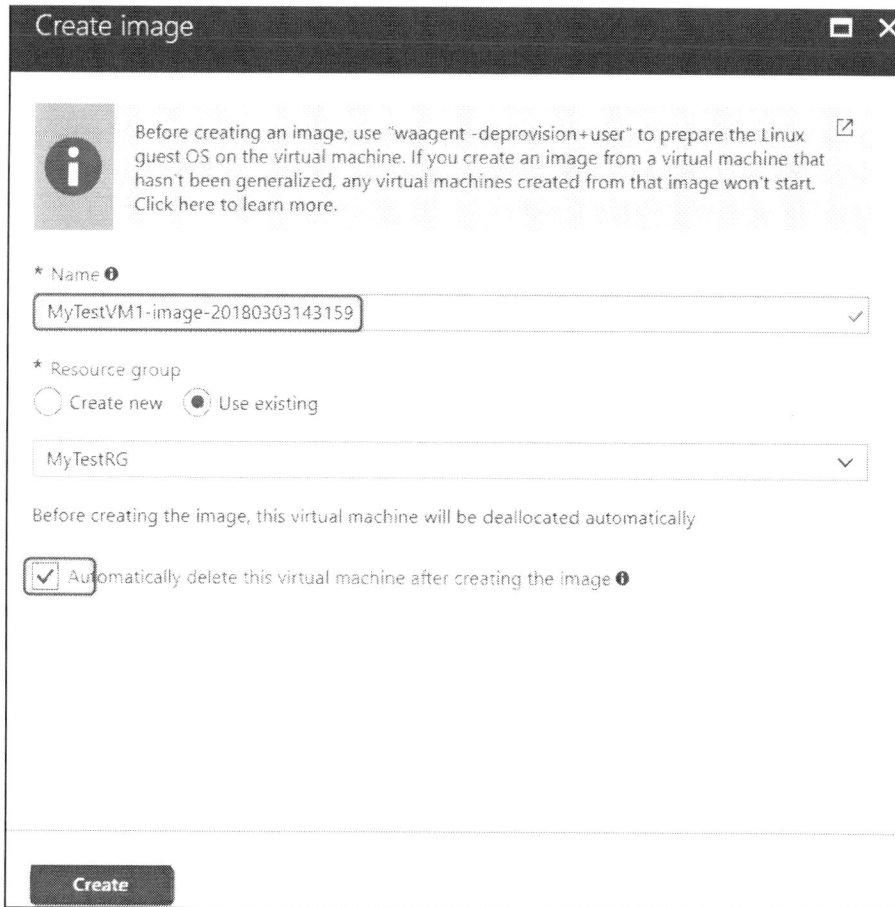

Create image ☐ ✕

ⓘ Before creating an image, use "waagent -deprovision+user" to prepare the Linux ⧉ guest OS on the virtual machine. If you create an image from a virtual machine that hasn't been generalized, any virtual machines created from that image won't start. Click here to learn more.

* Name ❶

MyTestVM1-image-20180303143159 ✓

* Resource group
○ Create new ◉ Use existing

MyTestRG ⌄

Before creating the image, this virtual machine will be deallocated automatically

☑ Automatically delete this virtual machine after creating the image ❶

Create

6. If all the process goes as expected, you will see the following success message in the notification bell as shown in the following figure.

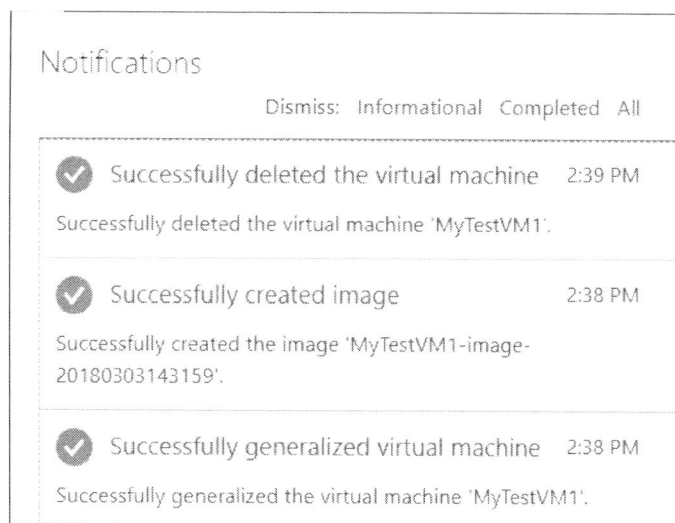

Notifications

Dismiss: Informational Completed All

✓ **Successfully deleted the virtual machine**   2:39 PM
Successfully deleted the virtual machine 'MyTestVM1'.

✓ **Successfully created image**   2:38 PM
Successfully created the image 'MyTestVM1-image-20180303143159'.

✓ **Successfully generalized virtual machine**   2:38 PM
Successfully generalized the virtual machine 'MyTestVM1'.

7. Once the image is captured, you can find it under the **All resources** section as shown in the following figure.

All resources
protechgurusgmail (Default Directory)

NAME	TYPE
MyTestDataDisk1	Disk
MyTestDataDisk1-Snapshot	Snapshot
mytestrgdiag272	Storage account
MyTestSnapDisk1	Disk
MyTestVM1_OsDisk_	Disk
mytestvm1979	Network interface
MyTestVM1-image-20180303143159	Image
MyTestVM1-ip	Public IP address
MyTestVM1-nsg	Network security group
MyTestvNet	Virtual network

That's all you need capture Azure VM images.

Lab 18: Creating Azure VM from Captured Image

As explained in the previous exercise, you can create an Azure VM from the captured image. The captured image will be used as a source template for the creating VM and will hold all the VM's data when the image was captured.

To create an Azure VM from the captured image, you need to perform the following steps:

1. Select the captured image from the **All resources**.
2. On the **Overview** blade, click **Create VM** as shown in the following figure.

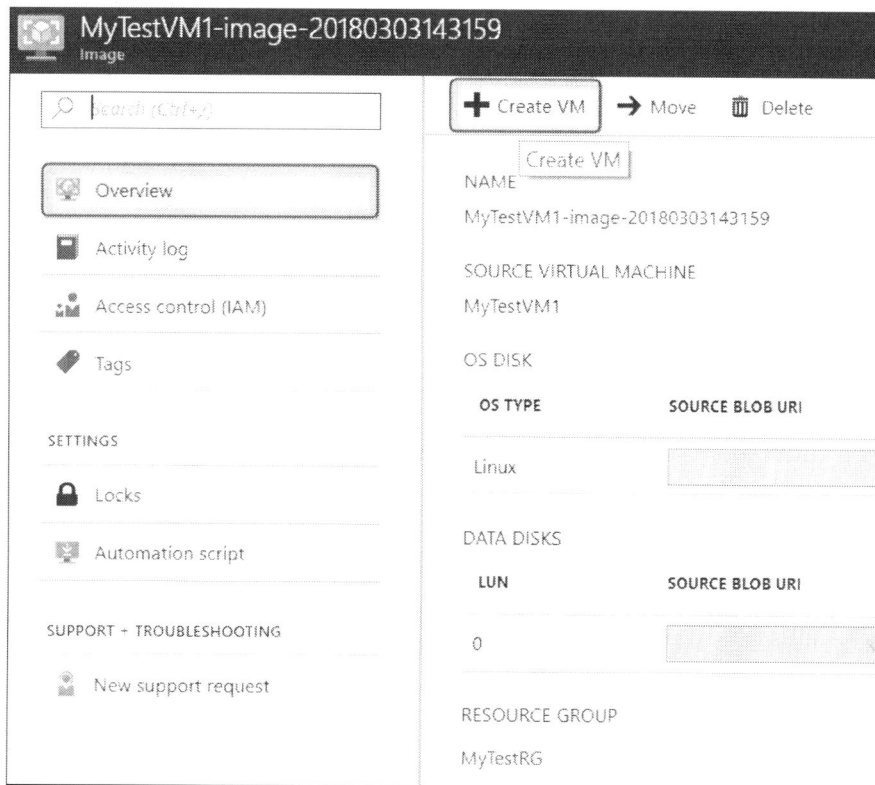

3. On the **Basics** blade, specify the VM name such as MyTestVM2, username, password, resources group, etc. and then click **OK** as shown in the following figure.

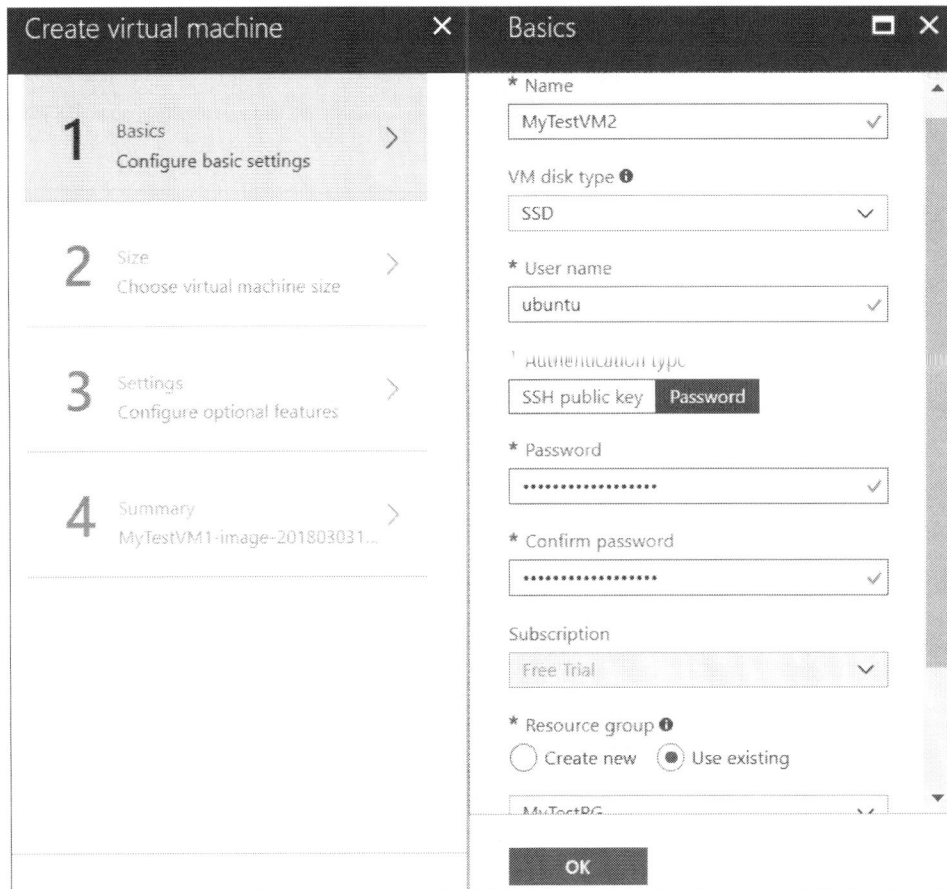

Create virtual machine

1 Basics
Configure basic settings

2 Size
Choose virtual machine size

3 Settings
Configure optional features

4 Summary
MyTestVM1-image-201803031...

Basics

* Name

MyTestVM2

VM disk type ❶

SSD

* User name

ubuntu

᾿ Authentication type

SSH public key **Password**

* Password

················

* Confirm password

················

Subscription

Free Trial

* Resource group ❶
  ◯ Create new   ⦿ Use existing

MyTestRG

OK

4. On the **Choose a size** blade, choose the appropriate VM size. For the Free Trial, be stuck with **B1S** size.

5. On the **Settings** blade, select the appropriate settings such as virtual network, subnet, public IP, NSG, and then click **OK** as shown in the following figure.

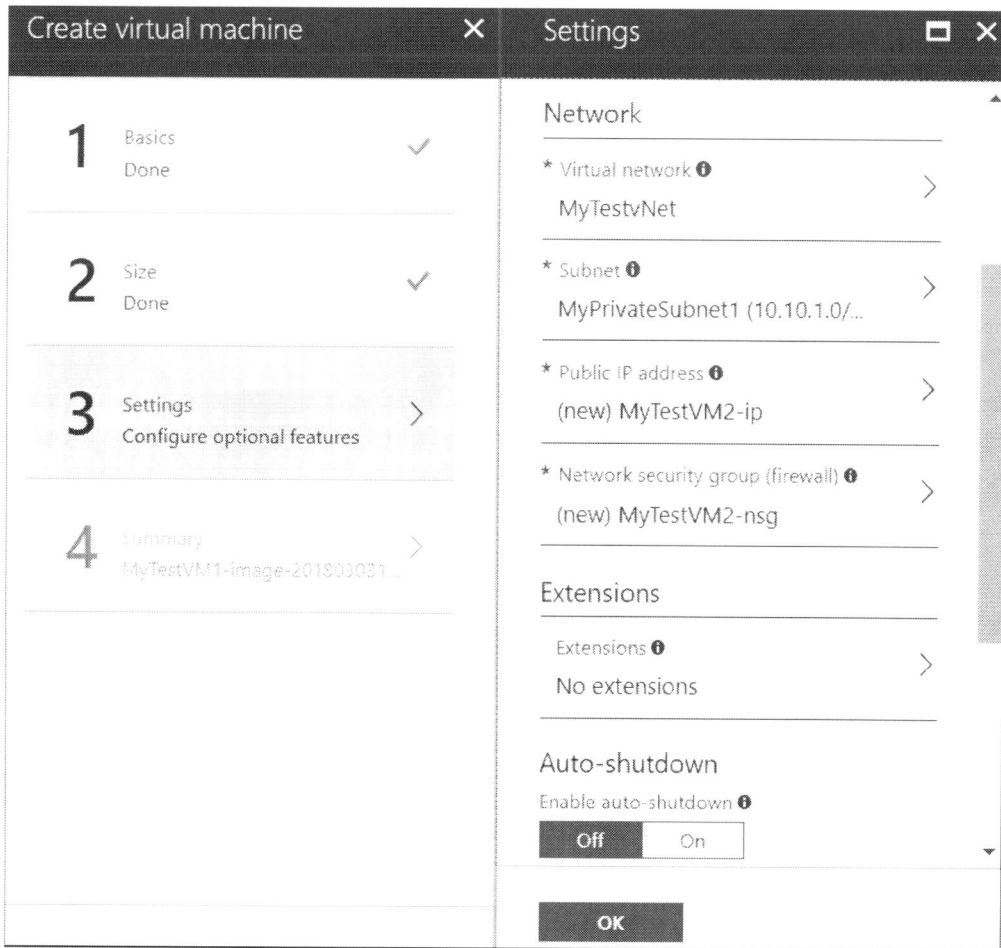

6. On the **Summary** blade, review the VM settings and click **OK** to proceed. After a few minutes, a new VM from the captured image will be created and available to use in Azure cloud.

Lab 19: Importing and Exporting Azure Virtual Machine

In Azure Cloud, you can export your virtual machine and then can run on your on-premise Hyper-V host. As discussed earlier, VMs in Azure cloud use disks as a place to store an operating system, applications, and other data. Basically, all Azure VMs have at least two disks: one for Windows operating system disk and other for temporary disk storage. VMs in Azure cloud are stored as VHDs.

In order to export an Azure VM to your local system, you need to perform the following steps:

Stopping Running Virtual Machine

Before you could export an Azure VM, first you must stop the VM if it is running. For this, select the virtual machine you want to export and then click **Stop** to stop it as shown in the following figure.

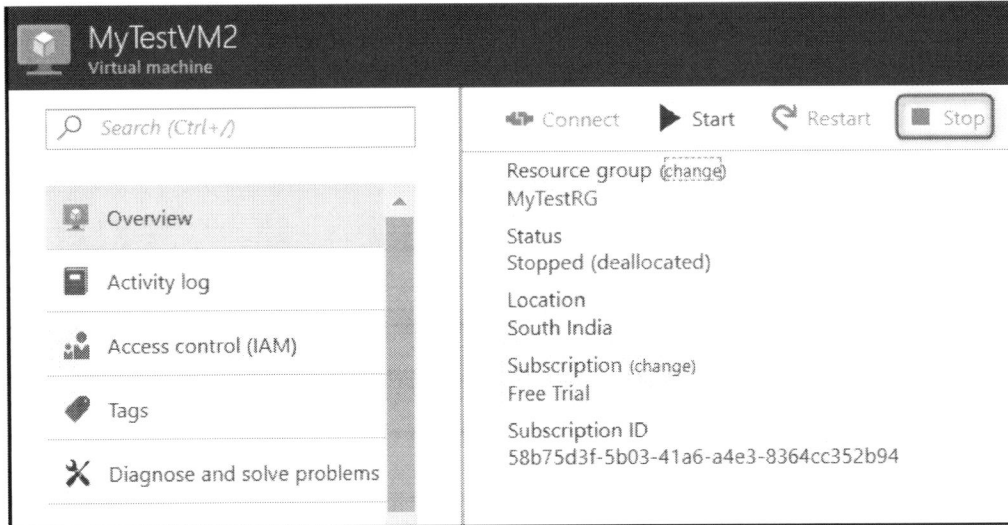

Generating SAS URL and Downloading VHD

After stopping your virtual machine, next you need to generate a SAS URL. The SAS URL is a temporary URL valid for a specific time. After the defined time, the URL becomes invalid and cannot be used later. To generate SAS URL, select the **Disks** blade of your desired VM and click system disk that contains the operating system.

Click **Export** to export the system VHD as shown in the following figure.

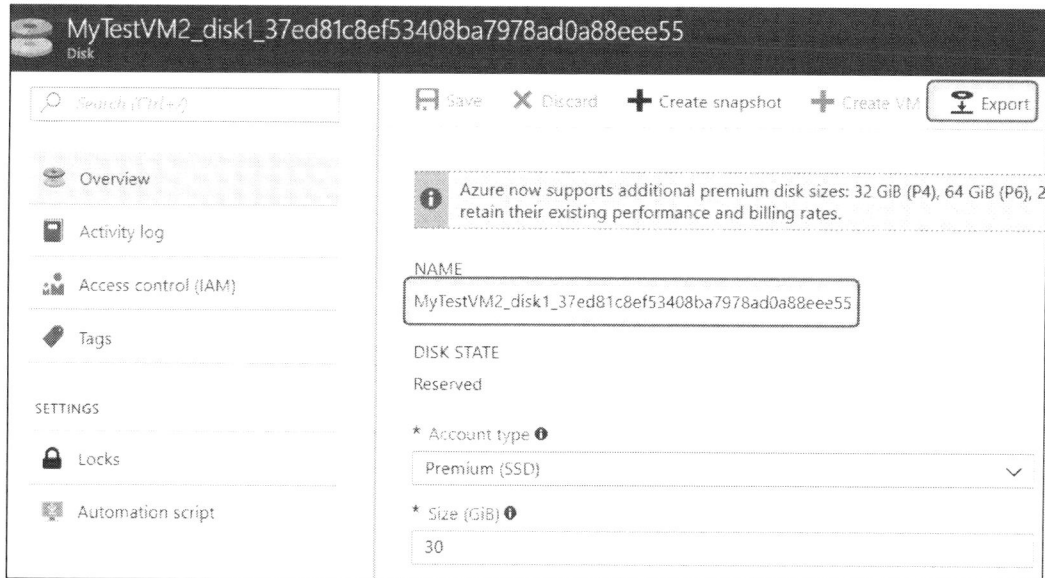

In the **Export disk** section, specify the time in seconds within which VHD is downloadable. Usually, we found that the time of downloading may vary from 5-10 hours depending on the speed of your Internet connection. So, adjust the timing as accordingly.

Click **Generate URL** as shown in the following figure.

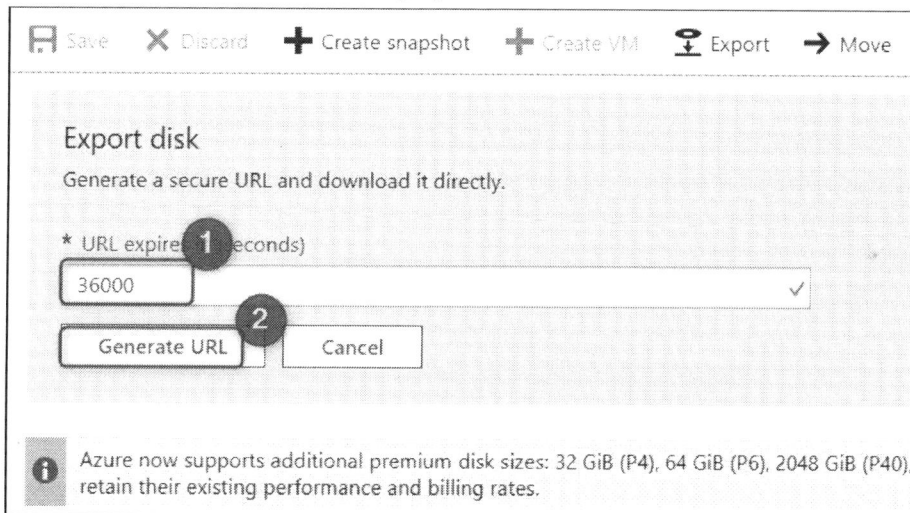

A SAS URL will be generated. Either copy and paste the SAS URL in your browser or click **Download the VHD file** link as shown in the following figure.

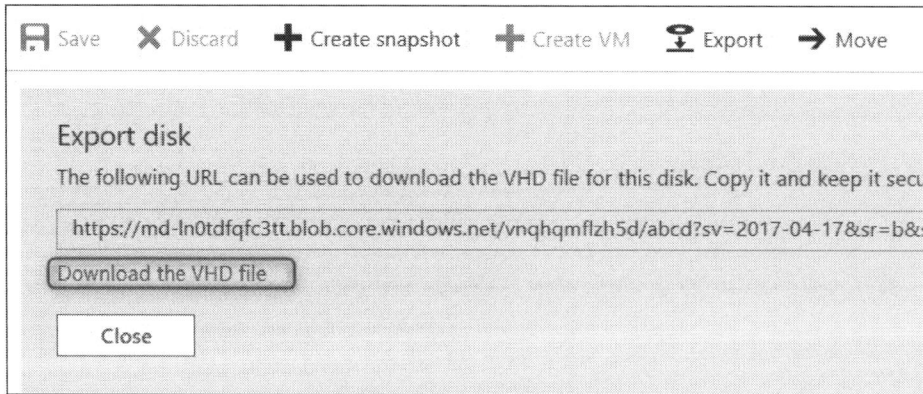

Once the VHD file is downloaded, you can import it to your on-premise or local Hyper-V host and run as a virtual machine. If your hypervisor is different than Hyper-V, use the VHD converter tool to convert VHD into appropriate supported disk format depending on the type of hypervisor you are using.
The imported VM will have all the configuration that was available in the Azure Cloud. If your virtual machine is Linux based and you were used SSH key authentication to login this Azure VM, first you should set the password for your Linux VM user, so you could login into VM imported in your local hypervisor.

Uploading your local virtual machine to Azure Cloud

If you have a virtual machine running on your Hyper-V host, you can upload it to Azure Cloud. This can be done using the Windows PowerShell. We have not covered this in detail here. If you are interested to know more about uploading VM to Azure Cloud, please have a look at the following article.

- Uploading Virtual Machine to Azure Cloud
  https://docs.microsoft.com/en-us/azure/virtual-machines/windows/upload-generalized-managed

Lab 20: Azure Network Security Group (NSG)

A NSG contains a list of security rules which allow or deny network traffic to resources connected to Azure Virtual Networks (VNet). You can associate NSGs to subnets, individual VMs, or individual NICs attached to VMs. When you associate an NSG to a subnet, the rules apply at the subnet level and to all resources connected to the subnet. Additionally, the traffic can be restricted by associating an NSG to a VM or NIC.

Subnet NSG vs NIC NSG

NSG applied to subnet: If an NSG applied on subnet has a matching rule to deny traffic, the packet is dropped.

NSG applied to NIC (Resource Manager): If an NSG applied at NIC has a matching rule that denies traffic, packets are dropped at the NIC, does not matter if the NSG applied at the subnet level has a matching rule to allow that traffic.

NSG Properties

When you create an NSG, you need to define the following properties:

- **Name**: Name of the NSG
- **Region**: Azure region in which NSG will be created
- **Resource group**: Resource group in which NSG will be created
- **Rules**: Inbound or outbound rules to define what traffic is allowed or denied

NSG rules

Along with NSG properties, you also need to specify the NSG rule options. The NSG rule options consist the following values:

- **Name**: Name of the rule.
- **Protocol**: Protocol to match for the rule.
- **Source port range**: Source port range to match for the rule.
- **Destination port range**: Destination port range to match for the rule.
- **Source address prefix**: Source address prefix to match for the rule.
- **Destination address prefix**: Destination address prefix to match for the rule.
- **Direction**: Direction of traffic to match for the rule. (Inbound or Outbound)
- **Priority**: Rules are checked in the order of priority. (Value range from 100 - 4096)
- **Access**: Type of access to apply if the rule matches. (Allow or Deny)

Default NSG Rules

When you create an NSG, there are few default rules already created for you. The default rules have the following characteristics:

- **Virtual network**: All inbound and outbound traffic is allowed within a virtual network.
- **Internet**: Outbound traffic is allowed, but inbound traffic is blocked.
- **Load balancer**: Allow Azure Load Balancer to probe the health of your VMs and role instances.

Now let's get some hands-on practice on NSG. Let's play with the NSG attached to your VM. In the previous exercise, we have created MyTestVM2 from the captured image.

Since, we didn't apply any NSG manually, hence a default is created and applied on the NIC attached to this VM. Let's see what all rules are applied by default. For this, select MyTestVM2 VM, and open the **Networking** blade as shown in the following figure.

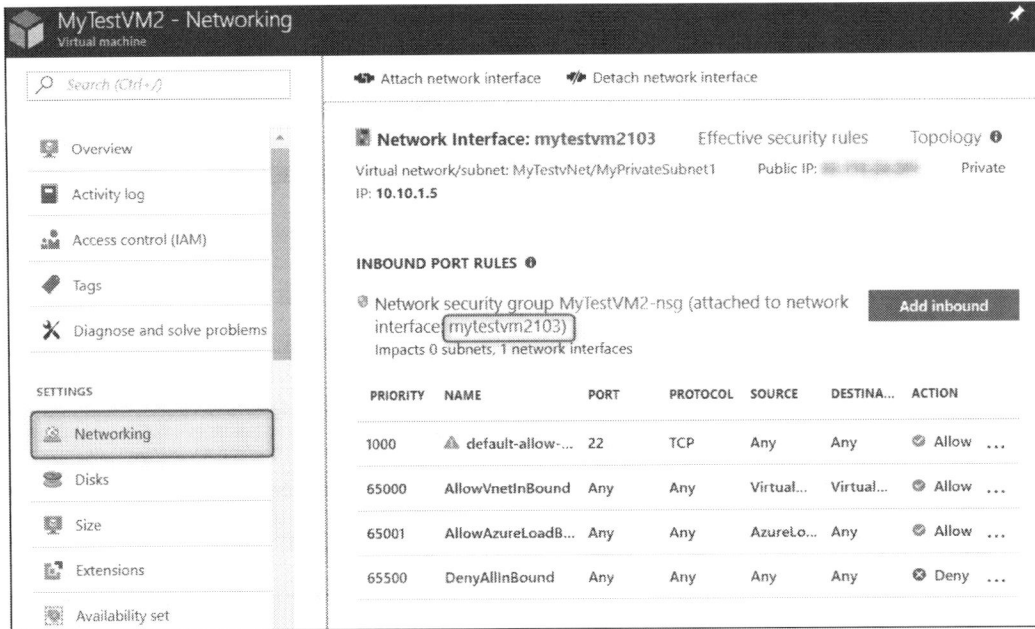

You can see in the above figure that the following four rules are currently applied to this NSG.

- **Default-allow-ssh** (priority - 1000): Allows SSH connection from anywhere.
- **AllowVnetInBound** (priority – 65000): Allows all incoming traffic between resources within the same virtual network.
- **AllowAzureLoadBalancer** (priority - 65001): Allows load balancer traffic to probe health check.
- **DenyAllInBound** (priority - 65500): Denies any traffic apart from the above-mentioned.

Getting Hands-on with NSG Rules

Since the NSG applied on your VM currently allows SSH connection from anywhere, lets delete it and create a more secure NSG rule for SSH connection.

1. To delete an NSG, just click **Eclipsis (…)** and then click **Delete**.
2. Click **Yes** to delete. The NSG will be deleted. Since you have deleted the SSH NSG rule, you will not be able to connect your MyTestVM2 remotely. You can try SSH connection to validate it.
3. To create a new NSG rule, click **Add inbound port** rule.
4. On the **Add inbound security rule** blade, click **Advanced** at the top of the blade and specify the following values (also shown in the following figure):
   - Select **IP Address** from the **Source** drop-down list.
   - Specify your **public IP address** in the **Source IP addresses/CIDR ranges** text box. (you can get your public IP by clicking https://www.whatismyip.com).
   - Type asterisk **(*)** in the **Source port ranges** text box.

- Select **Any** in the **Destination** drop-down list.
- Type **22** in the **Destination port ranges** text box.
- In the **Protocol** section, make sure that **Any** is selected.
- In the **Action** section, make sure that **Allow** is selected.
- Set the priority for the NSG rule, e.g. **100**.
- Specify the rule name as **SSH_Port_22** or any other meaningful name.
- Provide a meaningful description about the NSG.
- Finally, click **Create** to create your NSG rule.

5. Once NSG is created, it applies immediately, so you can try again to connect SSH of MyTestVM2 virtual machine. You should be able to establish SSH connection successfully.

Configure NSG Rule for Web Server

Now, let's configure MyTestVM2 as a simple web server and create an NSG rule that allows public users to access your web server. For this, you need to perform the following steps:

1. Connect and execute the following command on the MyTestVM2 virtual machine.

```
sudo apt-get update
```

```
sudo apt-get install apache2
sudo service apache2 start
sudo service apache2 status
```

```
ubuntu@MyTestVM2: ~                                                        —

ubuntu@MyTestVM2:~$ sudo service apache2 start
ubuntu@MyTestVM2:~$ sudo service apache2 status
● apache2.service - LSB: Apache2 web server
   Loaded: loaded (/etc/init.d/apache2; bad; vendor preset: enabled)
  Drop-In: /lib/systemd/system/apache2.service.d
           └─apache2-systemd.conf
   Active: active (running) since Sat 2018-03-03 12:51:07 UTC; 20s ago
     Docs: man:systemd-sysv-generator(8)
   CGroup: /system.slice/apache2.service
           ├─15204 /usr/sbin/apache2 -k start
           ├─15208 /usr/sbin/apache2 -k start
           └─15209 /usr/sbin/apache2 -k start
```

2. Now, your MyTestVM2 is configured and running as an Apache web server. Open a Web browser, type the public IP address of your virtual machine, and check whether you can access Apache home page or not. What happens? No, you should not, because you have not created any NSG rule for your web server.

3. Create an NSG rule for your web server as per the following configuration values.

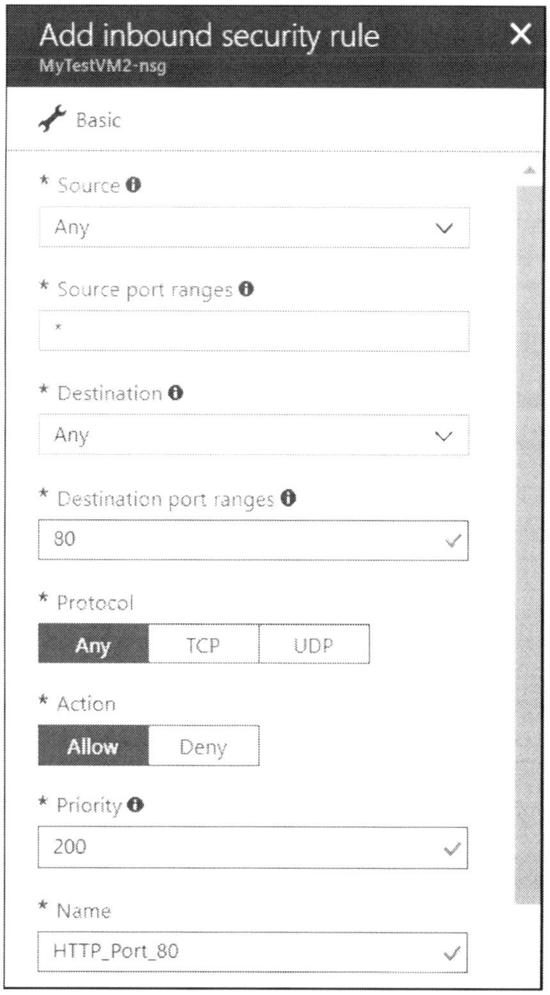

Add inbound security rule
MyTestVM2-nsg

🔧 Basic

* Source ❶

Any ⌄

* Source port ranges ❶

×

* Destination ❶

Any ⌄

* Destination port ranges ❶

80 ✓

* Protocol

| **Any** | TCP | UDP |

* Action

| **Allow** | Deny |

* Priority ❶

200 ✓

* Name

HTTP_Port_80 ✓

4. Once the above NSG rule is created, refresh your browser. You should be able to access the Apache home page of your configured Web server (MyTestVM2).

Lab 21: Creating and Applying NSG for Azure Virtual Network

We have created and tested NSGs that apply on Network Interface Cards (NICs) attached to the virtual machines. As discussed earlier, you can also apply NSGs at the virtual network (vNet) level. Virtual network NSGs are applicable to all the resources belong to that virtual network including, VMs, Subnets, NICs, frontend servers, backend servers etc.

In the following exercise, we are going to create an NSG, make some inbound/outbound NSG rules, and apply them on vNet and subnets.

1. In **Azure Portal**, click **All services**, type **network security** in the search box, and select **Network security groups** as shown in the following figure.

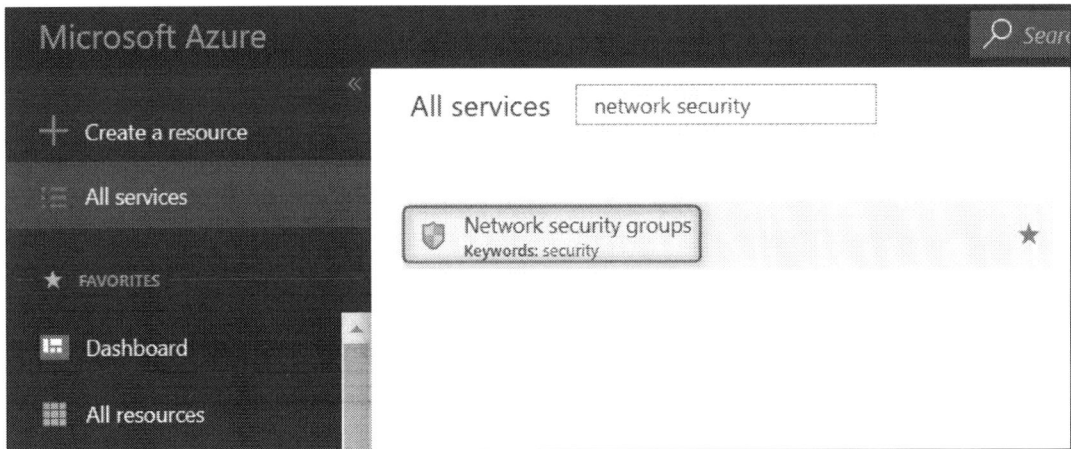

2. On the **Network security groups** blade, click **Add**, specify the Name as **MyTestvNet-NSG1**, Resource group as **MyTestRG**, and Location as **South India** as shown in the following figure.

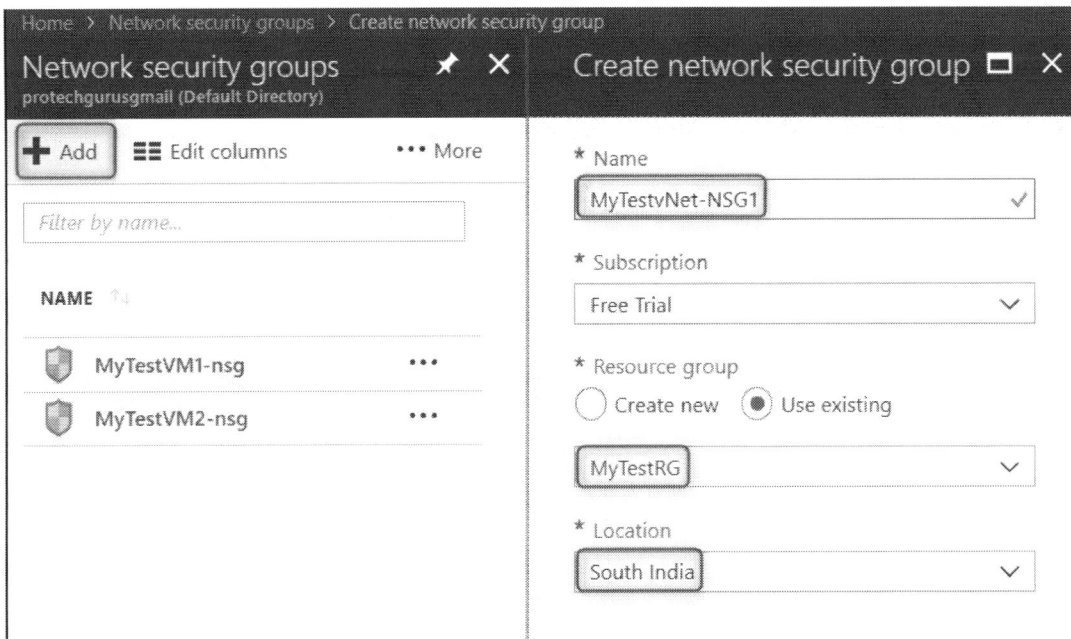

3. Click **Create** to create the NSG. The NSG will be created and listed in the **Network security group** list.

4. Open the created NSG and review the NSG rules created by default.
5. From the available NGS properties options, select **Subnets**. You can see in the following figure that there are no subnets are associated with this NSG.

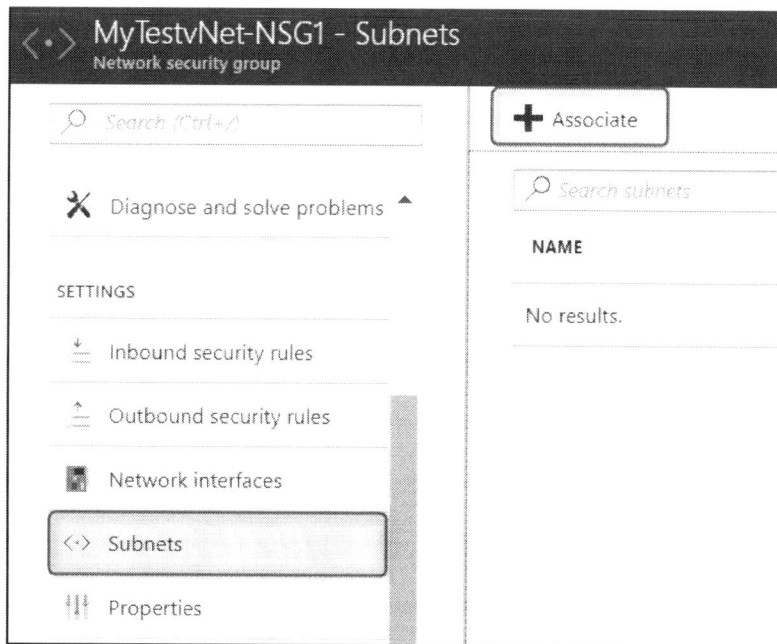

6. Click **Associate** to associate this NSG with desired vNet and subnets.
7. In the **Associate subnet** blade, select **MyTestvNet** as the virtual network.
8. Click **Subnet** in the left blade and select **MyPrivateSubnet1** in the **Choose subnet** blade as shown in the following figure.

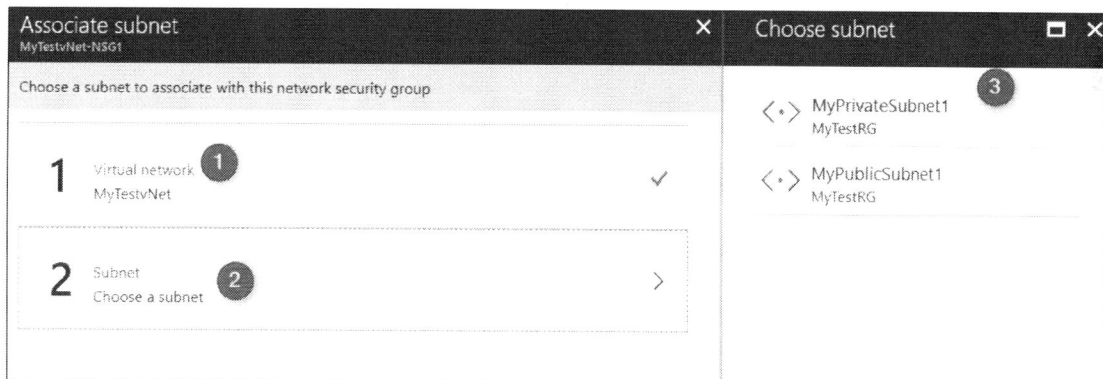

9. Click **OK** to associate the selected subnet.

Testing vNet NSG Rules

Once the NSG is associated to MyTestPrivateSubnet1. Disconnect and reconnect SSH connection of MyTestVM2. You should not be able to establish the SSH connection, even the NSG applied at MyTestVM2 VM's NIC allows the SSH inbound connection. This is because subnet level NSG is denying the SSH connection and Deny always take preference over the Allow action.

Configure Virtual Network NSG Rules

Now, let's a create an inbound rule for this NSG as per the following figure. Replace your public IP address in the **Source IP address** box.

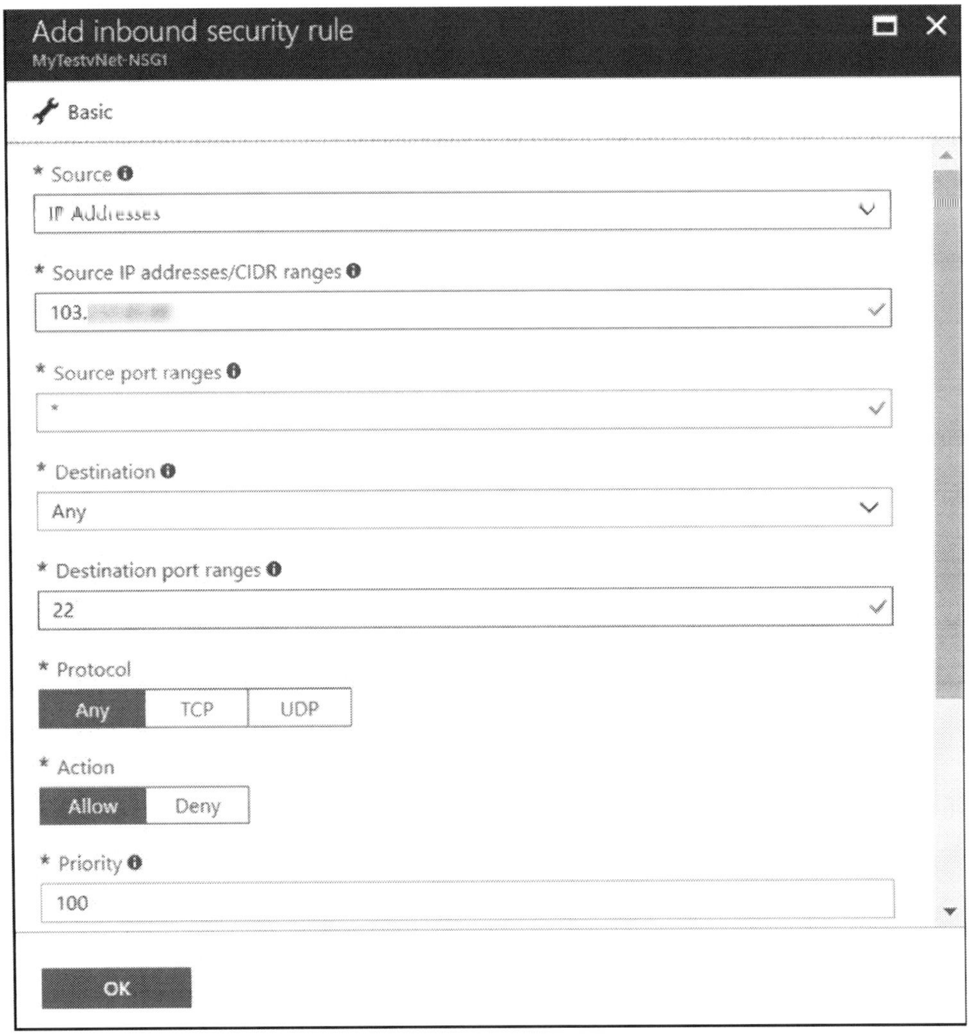

Once the inbound rule is created, retry to connect SSH of MyTestVM2 virtual machine. This time, you should be able to access SSH connection successfully, because the inbound SSH connection to your public IP address is allowed in both NSGs: NIC level NSG as well as vNet level NSG.

NICs Level NSG vs vNet Level NSG

Now, let us deny the SSH connection at NIC level NSG (MyTestVM2-NSG) as shown in the following figure.

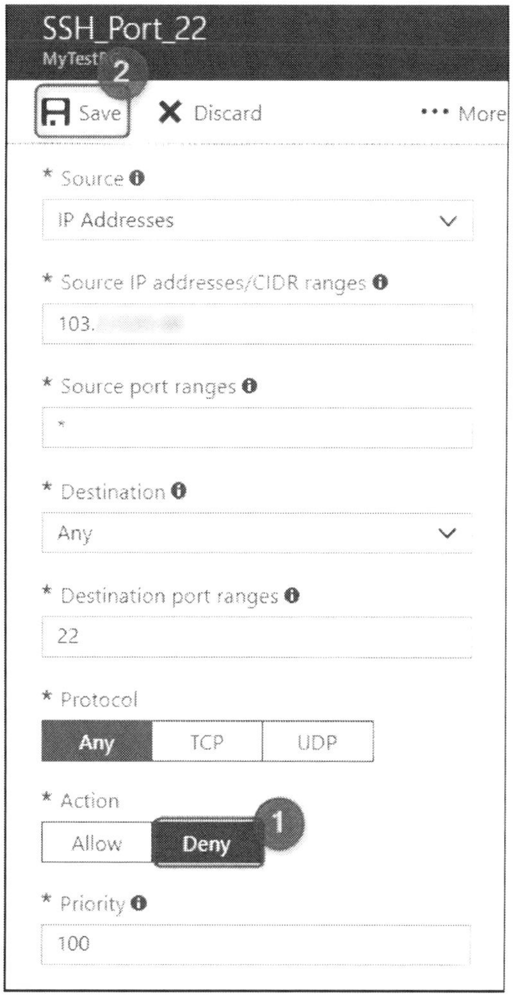

Disconnect and try to reconnect the SSH connection of MyTestVM2. What happens? You should not be able to access SSH connection of your virtual machine. Because you have denied SSH port at NIC level NSG. However, vNet level NSG is still allowing SSH inbound connection. But deny action always take preference if the priority of both NSG rules are same.

NSG Rule Priority Preference Testing

Now create one more inbound NSG rule for MyTestVM2-NSG, allow SSH port 22 for your public IP address, but set the priority of this NSG rule as 110 (greater than NSG deny rule) as shown in the following figure.

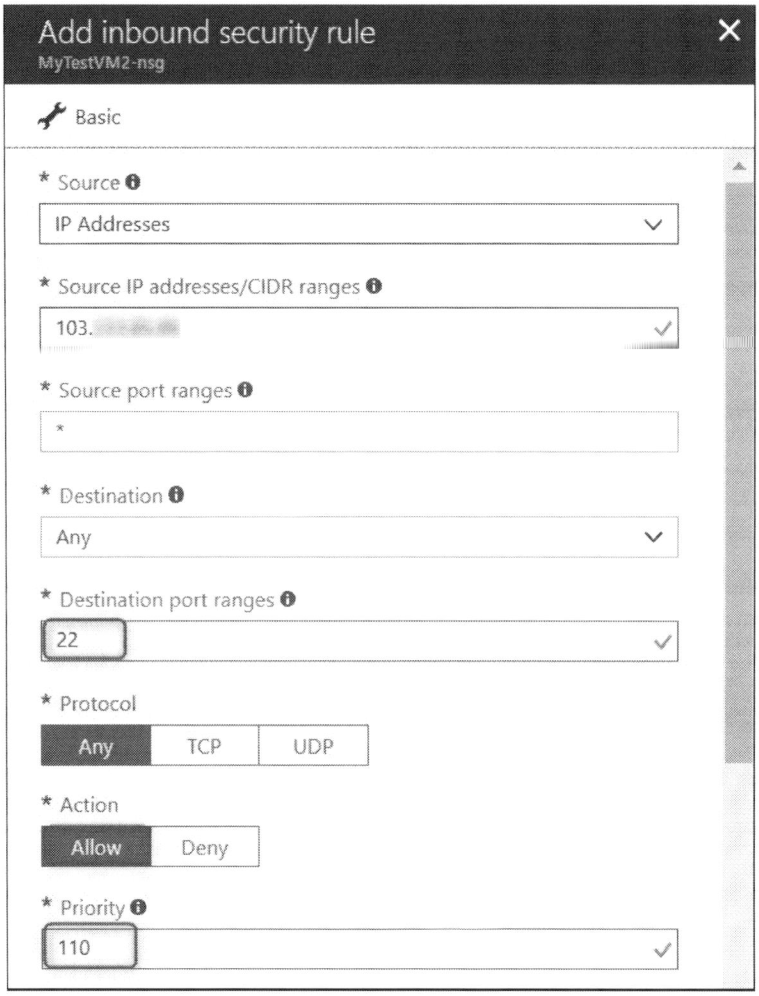

Add inbound security rule
MyTestVM2-nsg

🔧 Basic

* Source ❶

IP Addresses ⌄

* Source IP addresses/CIDR ranges ❶

103. ✓

* Source port ranges ❶

*

* Destination ❶

Any ⌄

* Destination port ranges ❶

22 ✓

* Protocol

Any | TCP | UDP

* Action

Allow | Deny

* Priority ❶

110 ✓

Try again to connect SSH of MyTestVM2. What happens this time? Are you able to connect MyTetsVM2 VM? If not, then why?

No – you should not be able to access SSH connection. Because, you have two NSG inbound rules: One is denying the SSH port with priority 100 and another is allowing SSH port with priority 110. The lower priority always takes preference (which is denying the SSH port) irrespective of whether other NSG rules are allowing the same port (SSH in this case) or not.

Now, open the NSG rule that is denying SSH port and set its priority as 120 (more than allowing NSG rule) as shown in the following figure.

SSH_Port_22
MyTestRG

💾 Save ✕ Discard ••• More

* Source ❶

IP Addresses ⌄

* Source IP addresses/CIDR ranges ❶

103.233.85.88

* Source port ranges ❶

*

* Destination ❶

Any ⌄

* Destination port ranges ❶

22

* Protocol

| Any | TCP | UDP |

* Action

| Allow | Deny |

* Priority ❶

120 ✓

Now, try again to connect MyTestVM2 using SSH, what happens this time? Are you able to connect?

Yes, brother, you should be able to connect this time. Because, the denying SSH port NSG rule has a less priority preference than the NSG rule that is allowing SSH port.

This is how Network Security Groups (NSGs) work in the Azure cloud. Hope, you get the basic ideas about Azure NSGs. You can continue to add, modify, delete, and test more NSGs inbound and outbound rules to get more familiar with Azure NSGs.

Lab 22: Managing Azure Storage Services

Storage is one of the main services of any Cloud service provider. Microsoft Azure Storage is a Microsoft-managed service which provides durable, scalable, and redundant storage solutions. You just store your data in Azure storage and Microsoft takes care of all backups and maintenance for you. Let's have a quick look on a few of the key storage Azure cloud factors:

- In Azure cloud, you can host 50 storage accounts, each of which can hold 500 TB data.
- In Azure cloud, there are various types of storage services: such as Blob service, File Share service, Table service, and Queue service.

Azure Storage Replication Strategies

While creating an Azure storage account, you also need to select the appropriate data replication strategy. You can select one of the following replication options for Azure Storage:

- **Locally redundant storage (LRS):** Provides minimum 99.999999999 % (11 9's) durability of objects over a given year. Stores multiple copies of your data in one data center.
- **Zone-redundant storage (ZRS):** Provides minimum 99.9999999999 % (12 9's) durability of objects over a given year. Stores multiple copies of your data across multiple data centers or regions.
- **Geo-redundant storage (GRS):** Provides minimum 99.99999999999999 % (16 9's) durability of objects over a given year. Stores multiple copies of the data in one region, and asynchronously replicating to a second region.
- **Read-access geo-redundant storage (RA-GRS)**: Provides at least 99.99999999999999 % (16 9's) durability of objects over a given year. Provides 99.99 % read availability from the second region used for GRS.
- Click here to know more about the Azure Storage Replication Strategies

Azure Storage Pricing

As a Solutions Architect, you should have a complete pricing idea and model of any Cloud service you may wish to deploy. The pricing for Azure storage depends on the various factors. Different applications and businesses require different types of storage features, availability, durability, etc. To calculate the cost of your desired storage option, please follow the following steps:

1. Visit the **Azure Cloud storage pricing** page using the following link.
   - Microsoft Azure Storage Pricing
     https://azure.microsoft.com/en-us/pricing/details/storage/blobs/
2. On the **Azure pricing** page, select the **desired storage types**. For example, let's select **Block Blobs** as shown in the following figure.

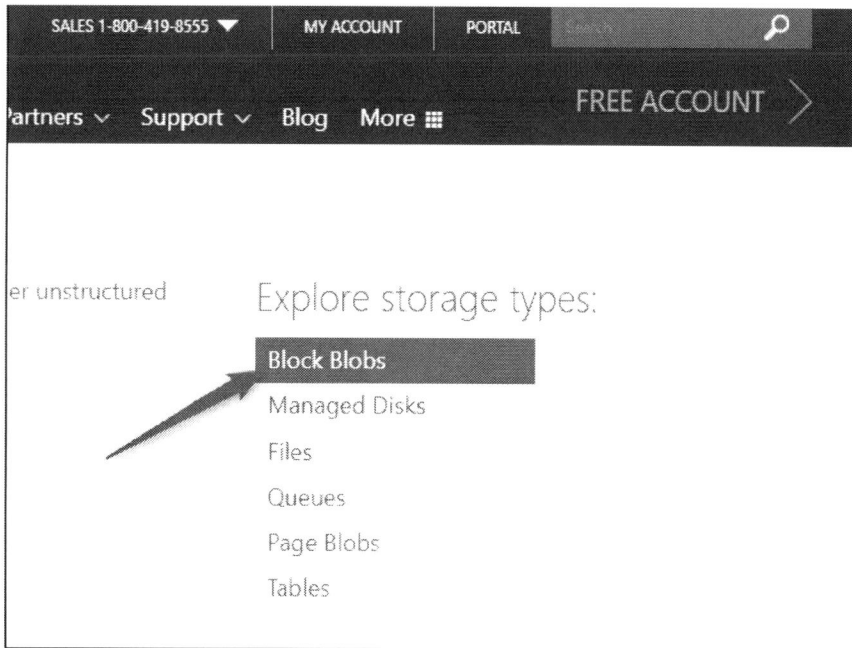

3. Scroll-down to the **Explore storage options** section.
4. Select the desired **Storage account type**, **redundancy model**, **region**, and **currency,** as shown in the following figure.

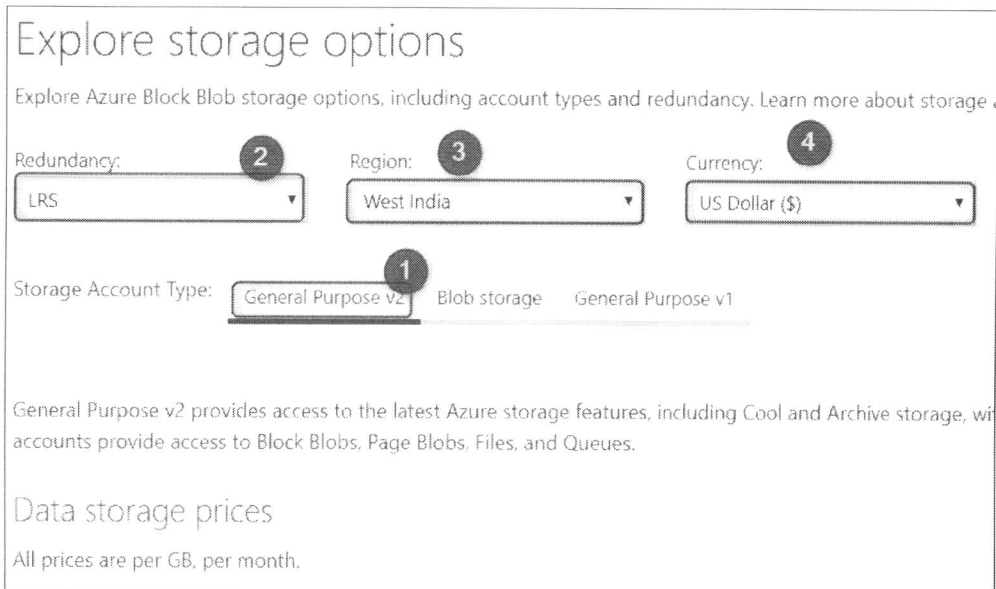

5. On the **Data storage prices** section, you will see the pricing for your selected storage options as shown in the following figure.

Data storage prices

All prices are per GB, per month.

	HOT	COOL
First 50 terabyte (TB) / month	$0.02 per GB	$0.0152 per GB
Next 450 TB / Month	$0.0192 per GB	$0.0152 per GB
Over 500 TB / Month	$0.0184 per GB	$0.0152 per GB

Azure Blob Storage

The Azure Blob storage provides you the ability to store files and access them from anywhere using URLs, REST API, and Azure SDK storage client libraries. Before using the Blob service, you need to create a storage account. After that, you can create containers, which are like folders, and then put blobs in the containers.

You can create an unlimited number of containers in a storage account and an unlimited number of blobs in each container. But the maximum size of a storage account is limited to 500 TB.

Block Blobs vs Page Blobs

Azure storage supports two kinds of blobs: **block blobs** and **page blobs**. Block blobs are used to store ordinary files (such as media or image files for websites) up to 200 GB in size. Whereas, page blobs are used to store random-access files such as VHDs up to 1 TB in size.

The format of Blobs URL is as follows:

http://[**storage account name**]/blob.core.windows.net/[**container**]/[**blob name**]

Creating Azure Blob Storage

To create a Blob Storage and store your data, you need to perform the following steps:

1. In **Azure Portal**, select **Storage**, and then select **Storage account – blob, file, table, queue** option as shown in the following figure.

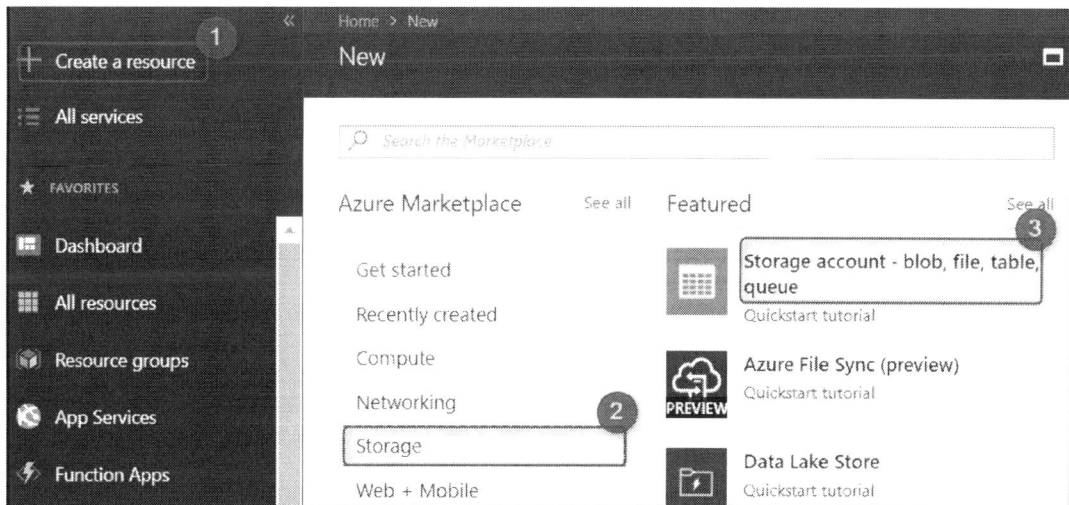

2. On the **Create storage account** page, specify the following configuration values:
   - **Name**: Provide a globally unique storage account name
   - **Deployment model**: Select Resource manager for latest Azure accounts and classic for the old Azure accounts
   - **Account kind**: The type of Azure storage account such as **Blob storage**
   - **Performance**: Select **Standard** for low performance and **Premium** for high performance storage access.
   - **Replication**: Select the desired replication strategy such as **Locally-redundant storage (LRS)**
   - **Access tier**: Select **Cool** for the infrequent access data and **Hot** for the frequent access data
   - **Subscription**: Select the subscription type such as **Free trial** or **pay-as-you-go**
   - **Resource group**: Select the resource group which will include this storage account
   - **Location**: Select the region where you want to create tour storage account
   - **Virtual network**: If you want this storage account to be accessible only from specific subnets of a specific virtual network, click **Enabled** and select the desired vNet and subnets.

3. For the testing purpose, you can create the Blob Storage account with the settings shown in the following figure.

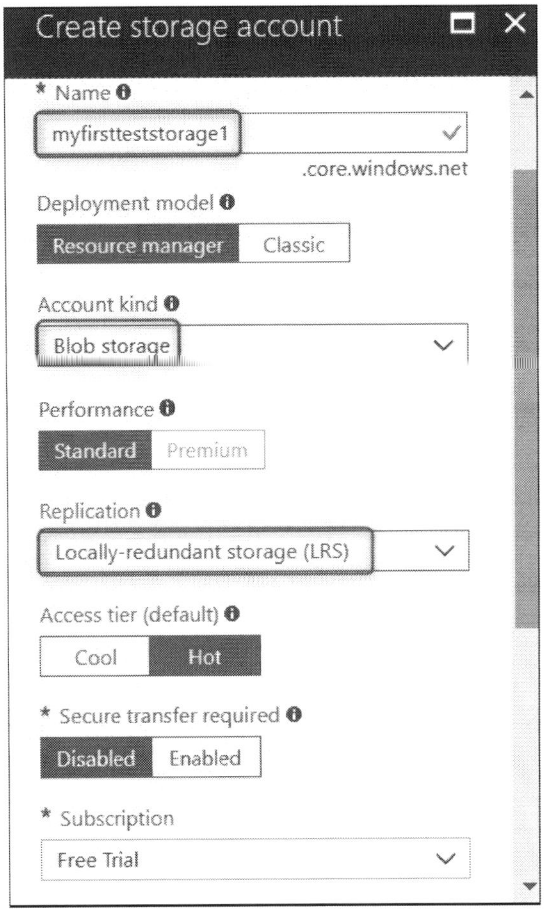

4. Once you selected the desired storage account settings as per your requirements, click **Create** to proceed. The storage account for the Blob files will be created.

Creating Container and Blobs

After creating a blob storage account, next you need to create Containers and Blobs. But before creating the containers and blobs, let's see the public level access for containers and blobs:

- **Private (no anonymous access):** Allows only storage owner to access the files.
- **Blob (read access for blobs only)**: Allows only blobs to be accessed as read only anonymously.
- **Container (anonymous read access for container and blobs):** Allows container and blobs both as anonymously read access.

To create a container and upload files, you need to perform the following steps:

1. In **Azure Portal**, select **All resources**, select your blob storage account, select **Containers**, and click **+Container** to add a container as shown in the following figure.

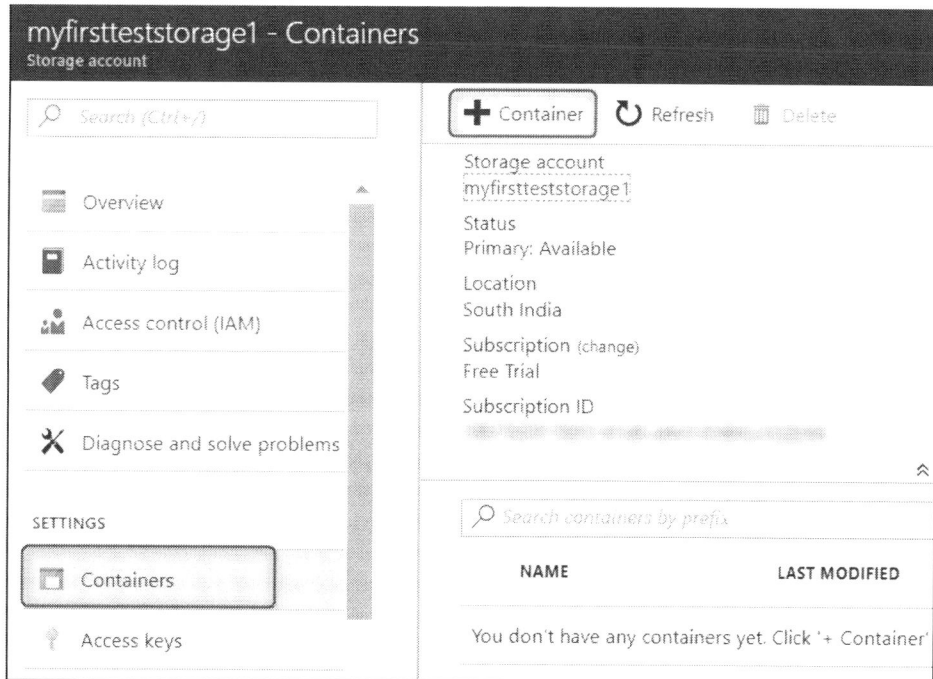

2. On the **New container** dialog box, specify the container name and select **Public access level** as **anonymous read access** as shown in the following figure.

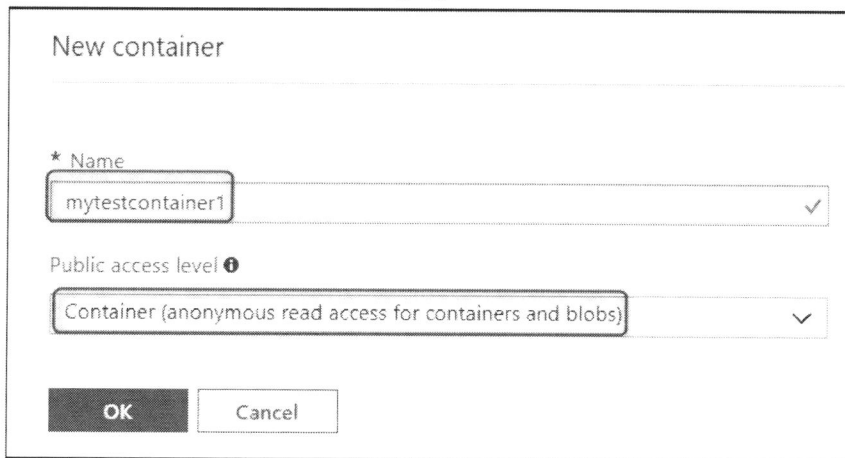

3. Click **OK** to create a container. The container will be created.
4. To upload data in this container, click **Upload**, browse the file you want to upload and click **Upload** as shown in the following figure to finish.

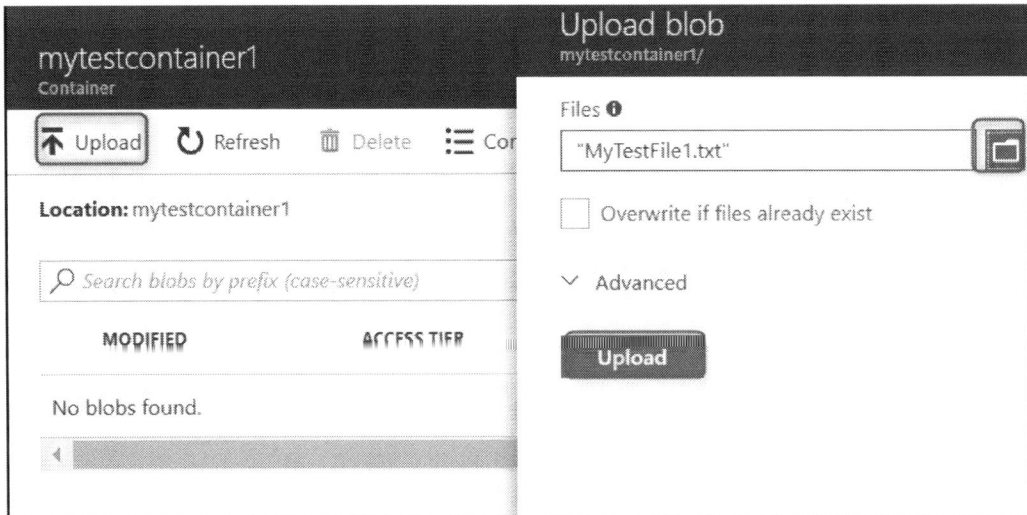

5. Once the file is uploaded, click the **Ellipsis** (...) to see the available options as shown in the following figure.

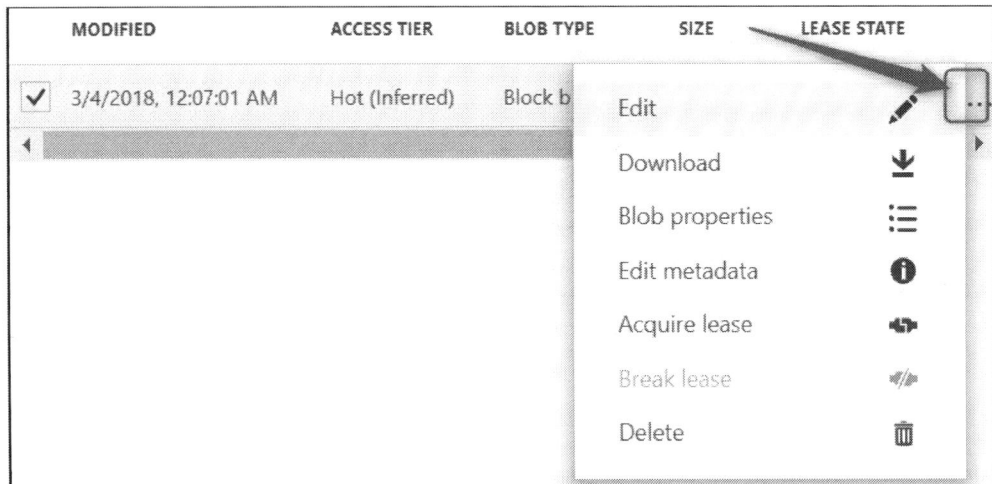

6. For example, select **Blob properties** and see what properties options are available within it as shown in the following figure.

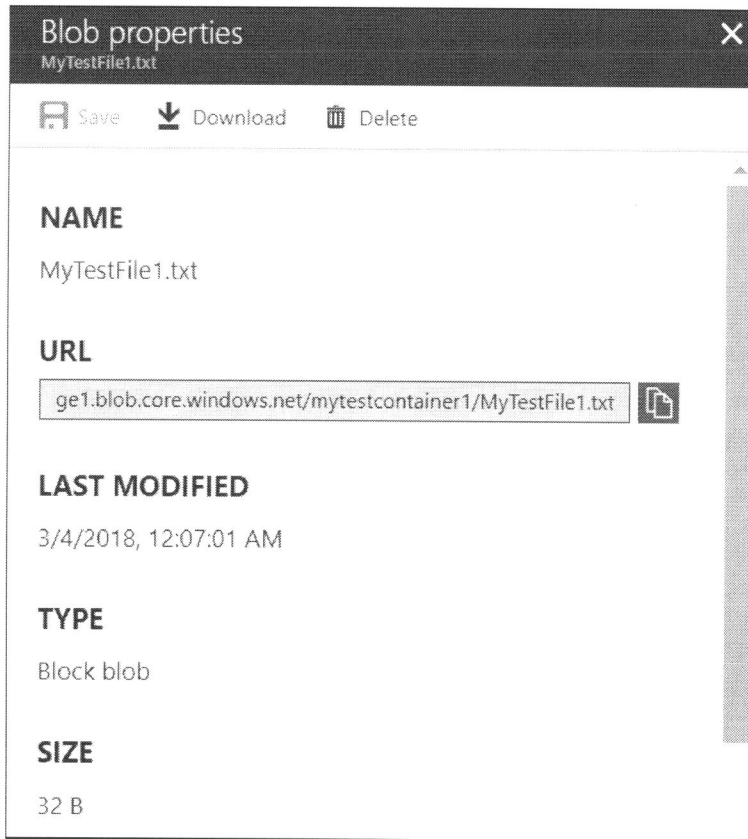

Blob properties
MyTestFile1.txt

💾 Save   ⬇ Download   🗑 Delete

NAME

MyTestFile1.txt

URL

ge1.blob.core.windows.net/mytestcontainer1/MyTestFile1.txt

LAST MODIFIED

3/4/2018, 12:07:01 AM

TYPE

Block blob

SIZE

32 B

7. Copy the blob URL and paste into your Web browser, you should see the content written in the file as you have selected anonymous read access while creating the container.

Lab 23: Working with Azure Storage Explorer

There are various nice tools that you can use to manage Azure Storage. One of the most popular and trusted is **Microsoft Azure Storage Explorer**. The download and installation process of Microsoft Azure Storage Explorer is a simple process.

1. Download Microsoft Azure Storage Explorer using the following link.
   - https://azure.microsoft.com/en-us/features/storage-explorer/
2. Once downloaded, double click the setup file and install it using the default selections.

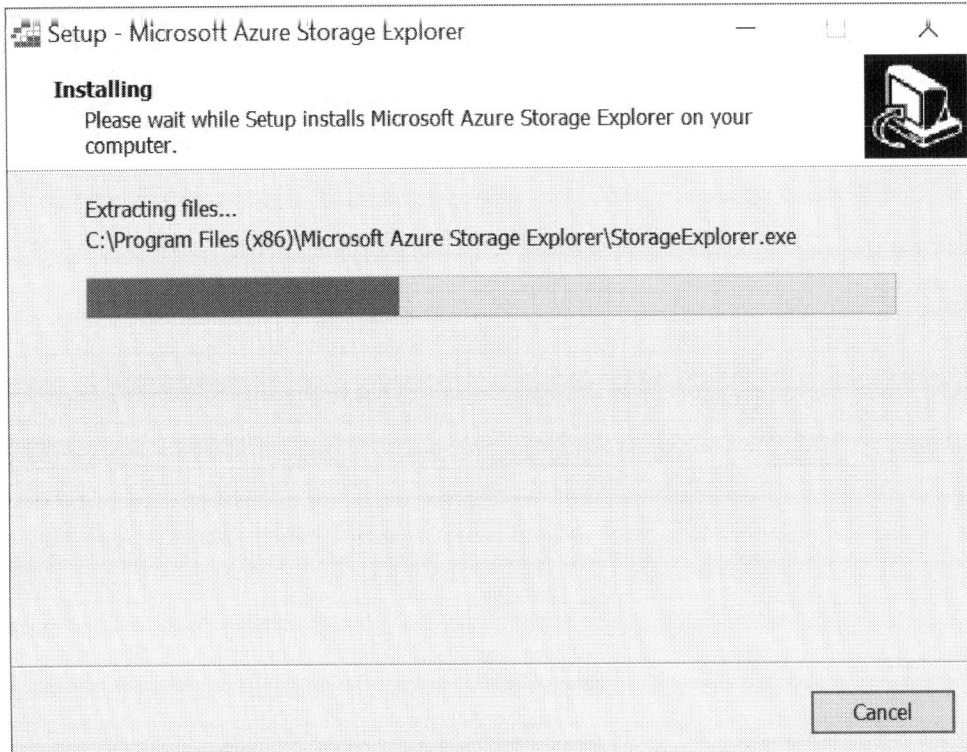

3. Once the Azure Storage Explorer is installed, open it, select **Azure** in the **Azure environment** drop-down list as shown in the following figure.

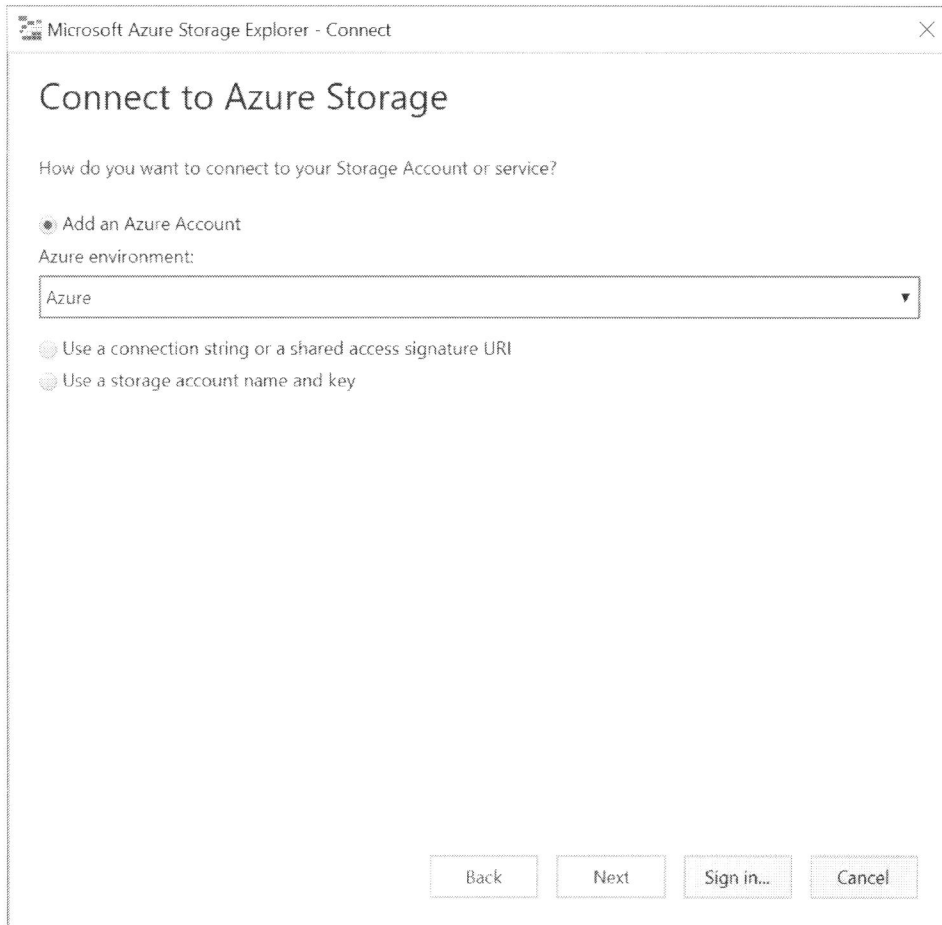

Microsoft Azure Storage Explorer - Connect

Connect to Azure Storage

How do you want to connect to your Storage Account or service?

◉ Add an Azure Account

Azure environment:

Azure ▾

○ Use a connection string or a shared access signature URI
○ Use a storage account name and key

Back   Next   Sign in...   Cancel

*Note: If you want to use only a specific storage account (not all Azure storage accounts), select **Use a storage account name and key** option and provide the appropriate storage account name and access key. You can find the storage access keys from the created Storage Account properties options.*

4. Click the **Sign in** button and use your login credentials to sign in. Once signed in, you will see all the storage accounts you have in your Azure account as shown in the following figure.

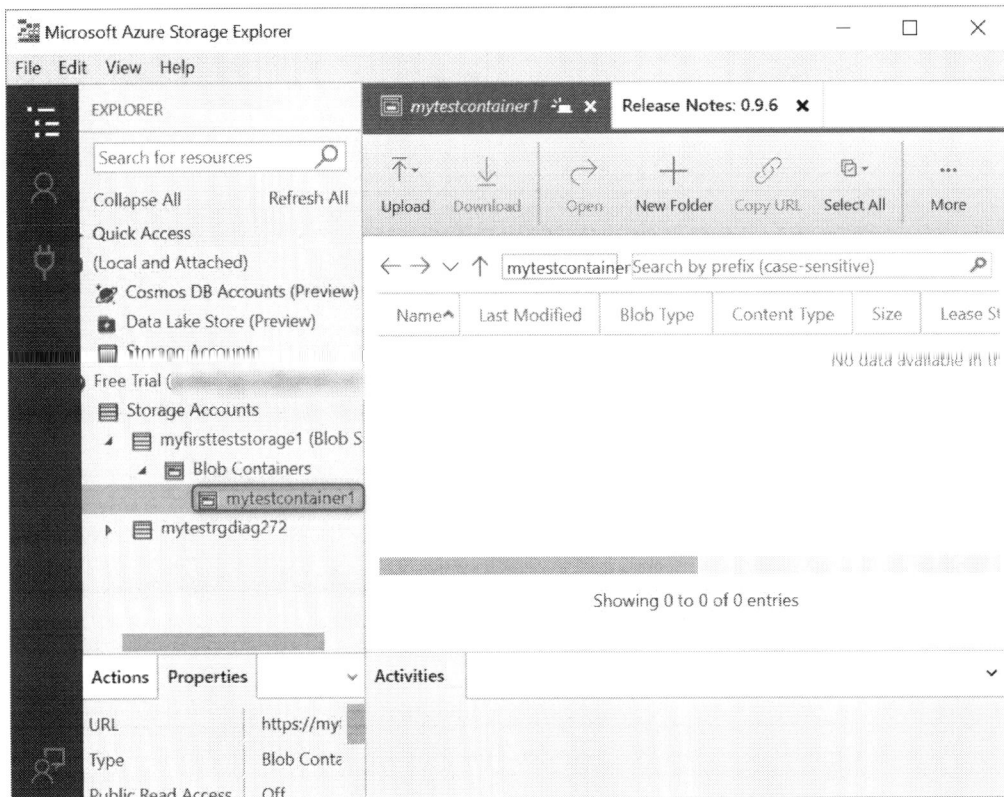

5. Once signed in, you can perform download, upload, delete, create, etc. storage actions as per your choice and need.

Lab 24: Managing Azure Storage Using Azure CLI

The Azure CLI is a command-line tool to manage Azure cloud services. If you have worked with AWS cloud, it is similar to AWS CLI tool. Azure CLI provides a great experience for managing Azure cloud resources. Depending on the OS platform you are using, you may use the appropriate link to explore Azure CLI installation.

- Install Azure CLI on Windows
  https://docs.microsoft.com/en-us/cli/azure/install-azure-cli-windows?view=azure-cli-latest
- Install Azure CLI on Mac OS
  https://docs.microsoft.com/en-us/cli/azure/install-azure-cli-macos?view=azure-cli-latest
- Install Azure CLI on RHEL or Cent OS
  https://docs.microsoft.com/en-us/cli/azure/install-azure-cli-yum?view=azure-cli-latest
- Install Azure CLI on Ubuntu or Debian
  https://docs.microsoft.com/en-us/cli/azure/install-azure-cli-apt?view=azure-cli-latest

Installing Azure CLI on Ubuntu Linux

For this exercise, we will install Azure CLI on MyTestVM2 (Ubuntu Linux). To do this, you need to perform the following steps:

1. Connect and login to MyTestVM2 virtual machine.
2. First you need to add the apt repository for Azure CLI. For this, execute the following commands.

```
AZ_REPO=$(lsb_release -cs)
echo "deb [arch=amd64]
https://packages.microsoft.com/repos/azure-cli/ $AZ_REPO main" |
sudo tee /etc/apt/sources.list.d/azure-cli.list
```

3. Now add the apt-key using the following command.

```
sudo apt-key adv --keyserver packages.microsoft.com --recv-keys
52E16F86FEE04B979B07E28DB02C46DF417A0893
```

4. Now install the required packages and install Azure CLI using the following commands

```
sudo apt-get install apt-transport-https
sudo apt-get update && sudo apt-get install azure-cli
```

5. The following figure shows how to install Azure CLI on a Ubuntu machine.

6. Once the Azure CLI is installed, you can manage Azure Storage containers and blobs using the various commands.

7. To manage Azure storage using Azure CLI, you need to provide authentication. As well This is done by using the following command:

```
az login
```

8. The above command will display a URL and a code to verify your identity as shown in the following figure. Open the given URL in your browser such as Google Chrome and provide the validation code.

```
ubuntu@MyTestVM2:~$ az login
To sign in, use a web browser to open the page https://aka.ms/devicelogin and e
r the code GC2JGA6US to authenticate.
[
  {
    "cloudName": "AzureCloud",
    "id": "58b75d3f-5b03-41a6-a4e3-8364cc352b94",
    "isDefault": true,
    "name": "Free Trial",
    "state": "Enabled",
    "tenantId": "cc367500-01ca-418d-90f4-d9cc71ccfe1f",
    "user": {
      "name": "                              ",
      type :  user
    }
  }
]
```

9. Once validated successfully, the following message will be displayed.

Microsoft Azure Cross-platform Command Line Interface

You have signed in to the Microsoft Azure Cross-platform Command Line Interface application on your device. You may now close this window.

10. Before you could connect and use Azure storage using Azure CLI, you also need the storage account name and a storage access key as authentication. To know the storage access keys, select your **Storage account** in Azure Portal and navigate to **Access keys** section as shown in the following figure.

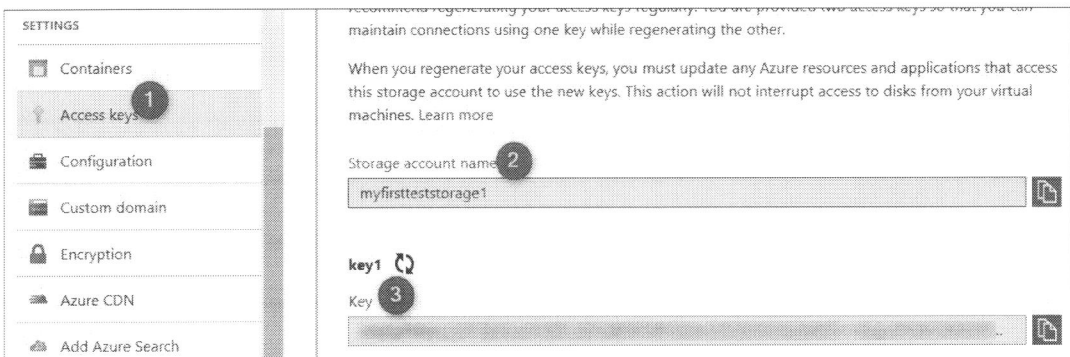

11. Note down the storage account name and access key somewhere as we will use these later.
12. On the Linux terminal, execute the following command to add storage account and key as a variable environment for Azure CLI.

```
export AZURE_STORAGE_ACCOUNT="<your-storage-account-name>"
export ZURE_STORAGE_ACCESS_KEY="<your-storage-access-key>"
```

Working with Azure Storage using Azure CLI

Now you are ready to manage Azure storage accounts using Azure CLI. Let's do few hands-on practices.

1. Execute the following command to create an Azure storage container named as mytestconatiner2.
```
az storage container create --name mytestcontainer2
```
2. Execute the following commands to create a file named as mytestfile2 and upload it to the created container (mytestcontainer2).

```
ubuntu@MyTestVM2: ~                                             —    □    ×

ubuntu@MyTestVM2:~$ az storage container create --name mytestcontainer2
{
  "created": true
}
ubuntu@MyTestVM2:~$ echo "My Test File" > mytestfile2
ubuntu@MyTestVM2:~$ az storage blob upload --container-name mytestcontainer2 \
> --name mytestfile2 \
> --file /home/ubuntu/mytestfile2
Finished[#####################################################]  100.0000%
{
  "etag": "\"0x8D5819072234403\"",
  "lastModified": "2018-03-04T05:26:13+00:00"
}
ubuntu@MyTestVM2:~$ |
```

3. Execute the following command to verify that the file has been uploaded successfully in mytestcontianer2 container.

```
ubuntu@MyTestVM2: ~                                             —    □    ×

  "etag": "\"0x8D5819072234403\"",
  "lastModified": "2018-03-04T05:26:13+00:00"
}
ubuntu@MyTestVM2:~$ az storage blob list \
> --container-name mytestcontainer2 \
> --output table
Name            Blob Type    Blob Tier    Length   Content Type              Last Mo
fied                         Snapshot
----------      -----------  -----------  -------- ------------------------  -------
----------      ----------
mytestfile2     BlockBlob    Hot                13 application/octet-stream  2018-03
4T05:26:13+00:00
ubuntu@MyTestVM2:~$ |
```

4. To download a blob file named as **mytestfile2** stored in **mytestcontainer2** container and assign its name as **mytestblob** under **/home/ubuntu** directory, execute the following command. In the following command, replace your azure storage account name and access key appropriately.

```
sudo az storage blob download --container-name mytestcontainer2 -
-name mytestfile2 --file /home/ubuntu/mytestblob --account-name
myfirstteststorage1 --account-key <your-access-key-id>
```

```
ubuntu@MyTestVM2: ~                                              —    □    ×

ubuntu@MyTestVM2:~$
ubuntu@MyTestVM2:~$ sudo az storage blob download --container-name mytestcontainer2 \
> --name mytestfile2 \
> --file /home/ubuntu/mytestblob \
> --account-name myfirstteststorage1 \
> --account-key

Finished[###############################################################]   100.0000%
{
    "content": null,
    "deleted": false,
    "metadata": {},
    "name": "mytestfile2",
    "properties": {
        "appendBlobCommittedBlockCount": null,
        "blobTier": null,
        "blobTierChangeTime": null,
```

5. Your blob file be downloaded into the mentioned local directory.

Note: You can explore Azure CLI more in details here.

https://docs.microsoft.com/en-us/cli/azure/get-started-with-azure-cli?view=azure-cli-latest

---

Lab 25: Working with Azure Files Share

The Azure Files service enables you to set up a highly available network file shares that can be accessed by using the standard Server Message Block (SMB) protocol. It is similar to on-premise NFS servers. In AWS, Elastic Files System (EFS) provides the same functionalities as provided by Azure Files Share.

Azure Files Share can be accessed by multiple virtual machines and multiple users/application can simultaneously read and write in to Azure Files Shares. To access Azure Files Share from VMs, just mount it as you would any other file share, and then you can access it through the network URL or the drive letter to which it was assigned.

The Azure Files Share URL has the format **\\[storage account name].file.core.windows.net\[share name].** Once the Azure Files Share is mounted, you can access it and work as you work with local drives and directories.

Apart from Azure Portal, you can also use PowerShell cmdlets and Azure CLI to create, mount, and manage Azure File shares.

If you are interested, please visit the following link for more details about Azure Files Share.

- https://docs.microsoft.com/en-us/azure/storage/files/storage-files-scale-targets

Creating Storage Account for Azure Files Share

Now let's create an Azure Files Share, mount it on a virtual machine, and create some files under it to get hands-on skills for Azure Files Share. Azure Files Share requires a General-purpose storage account. To create an Azure storage account for Azure Files Share, you need to perform the following steps:

1. In **Azure Portal**, open **Storage Accounts** blade.
2. On the **Storage Accounts** blade, click **Add** to add a storage account.
3. In the **Name** text box, type the name of your storage such as **mytestazureshare1**.
4. In the **Account kind** drop-down list, select **Storagev2**.
5. In the **Replication** drop-down list, select the desired replication strategy such as Locally-redundant storage (LRS).
6. In the **Resources group** section, select **MyTestRG** resources group.
7. In the **Location** section, select the desired location, such as **South India**.

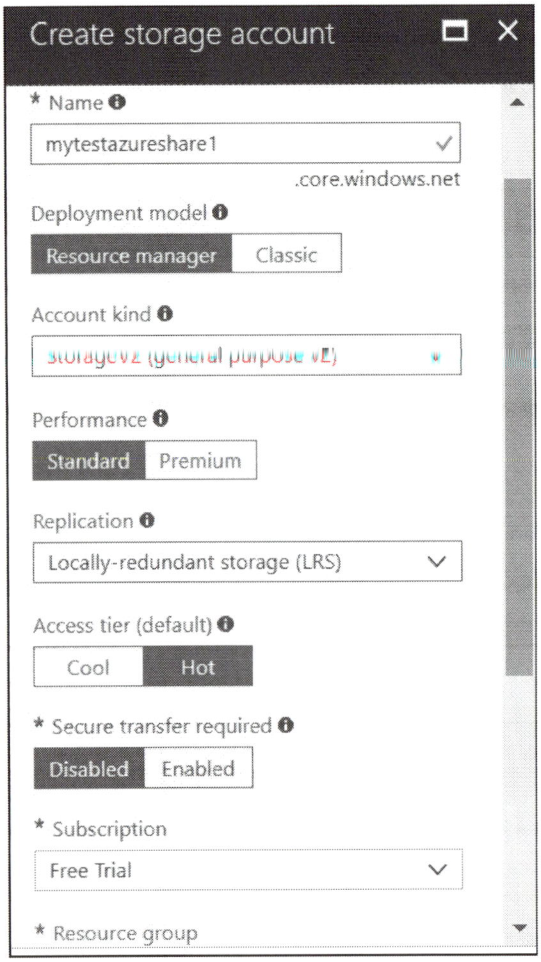

Create storage account □ ✕

* Name ❶

| mytestazureshare1 | ✓ |

.core.windows.net

Deployment model ❶

| **Resource manager** | Classic |

Account kind ❶

| storagev2 (general purpose v2) | ▾ |

Performance ❶

| **Standard** | Premium |

Replication ❶

| Locally-redundant storage (LRS) | ⌄ |

Access tier (default) ❶

| Cool | **Hot** |

* Secure transfer required ❶

| **Disabled** | Enabled |

* Subscription

| Free Trial | ⌄ |

* Resource group

8. Finally, click **Create** to create the storage account. After a few minutes, the storage account will be created and listed in the **Storage Accounts** list.

Creating Azure Files Share

After creating a storage account, you need to perform the following steps to create an Azure Files Share.

1. Select the created storage account, select **Overview** option and then select **Files** in the right blade as shown in the following figure.

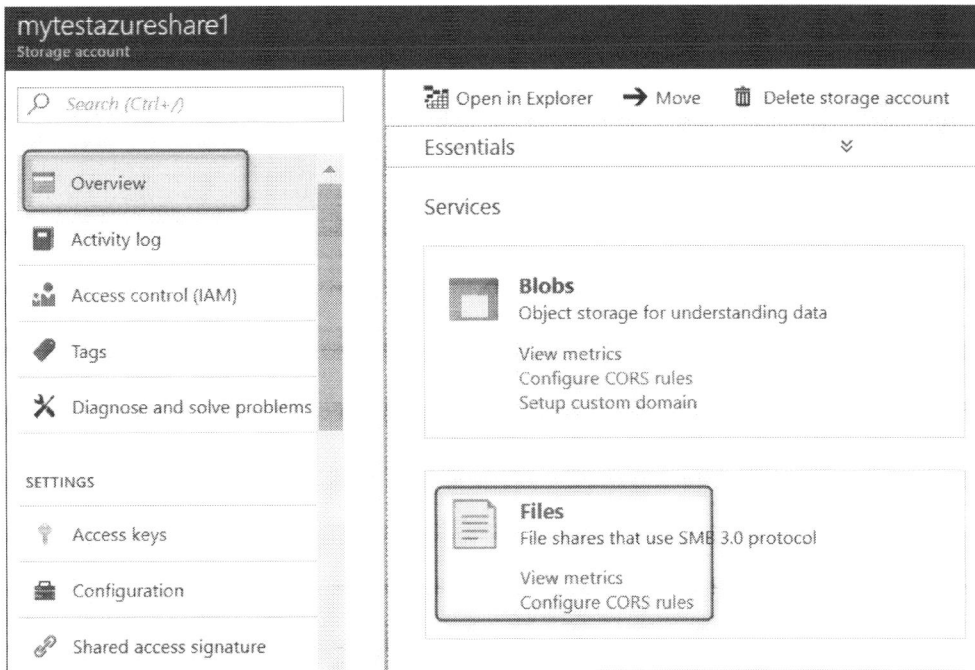

2. On the **File share** blade, click **+File share** to add a new file share.

3. Specify a unique share name (in this case **mytestshare1**) and the desired **Quota** (e.g. 10 GB) limit for your Azure Files Share as shown in the following figure.

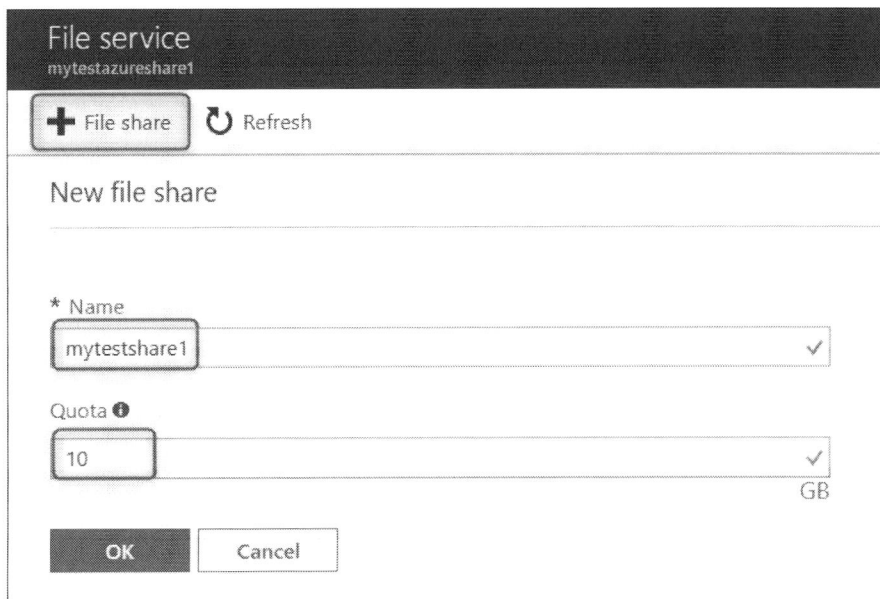

4. Click **OK** to complete the process. Your new Azure Files Share will be created and available to mount and use on required clients and virtual machines.

Lab 26: Mounting Azure Files Share

As discussed earlier, Azure Files Share is used as network shares on the clients. For this, you need to mount the Azure Files Share before to use. Depending on the operating system platform used by the client, on which you want to mount, you need to use the appropriate commands (method) to mount. Before you could mount Azure Files Share on any client, you would require the following details:

- **Storage account name**: Name of your Azure storage account (in this case – mytestazureshare1)
- **Files Share name**: Name of the Files Share name you want to mount (in this case - mytestshare1)
- **Storage Access Key**: A secret access key of the storage account (can be found under access keys option).

Mount Azure Files Share on Windows Machine

1. To mount Azure Files Share on a Windows machine, right-click on **My Computer** (This PC) and then select **Map network drive** as shown in the following figure.

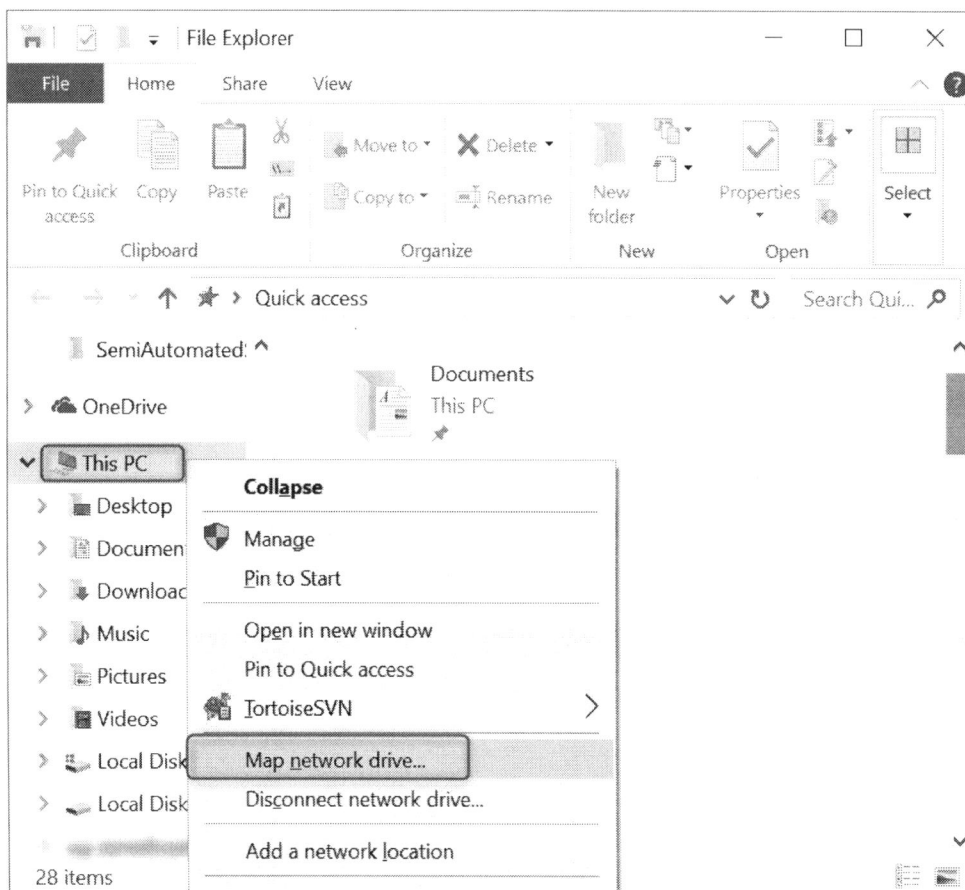

2. On the **Map Network Drive** window, use the following format to mount Azure Files Share.
   - **\\<storage account name>**.file.core.windows.net**<file-share-name>**
3. In our case, the following format will be used as shown in the following figure.
   - \\mytestazureshare1.file.core.windows.net\mytestshare1

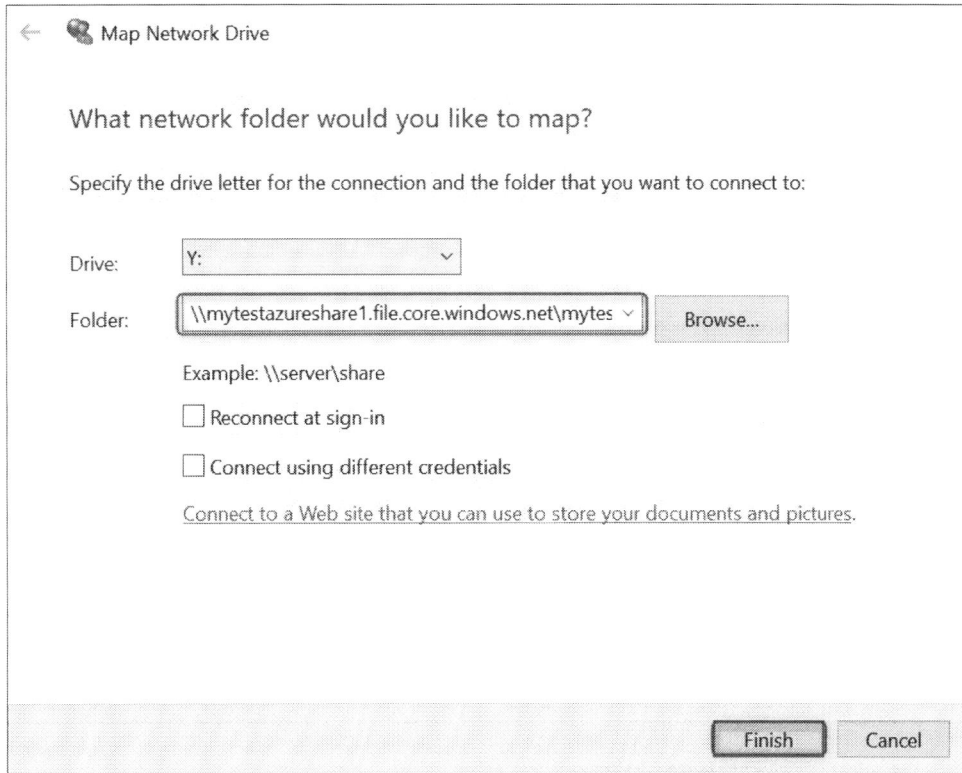

4. Click **Finish** to proceed.
5. You will be asked to enter a username and password. Type the **storage account name** as username and **storage access key** as a password. The network drive will be mounted and available to use for you as shown in the following figure.

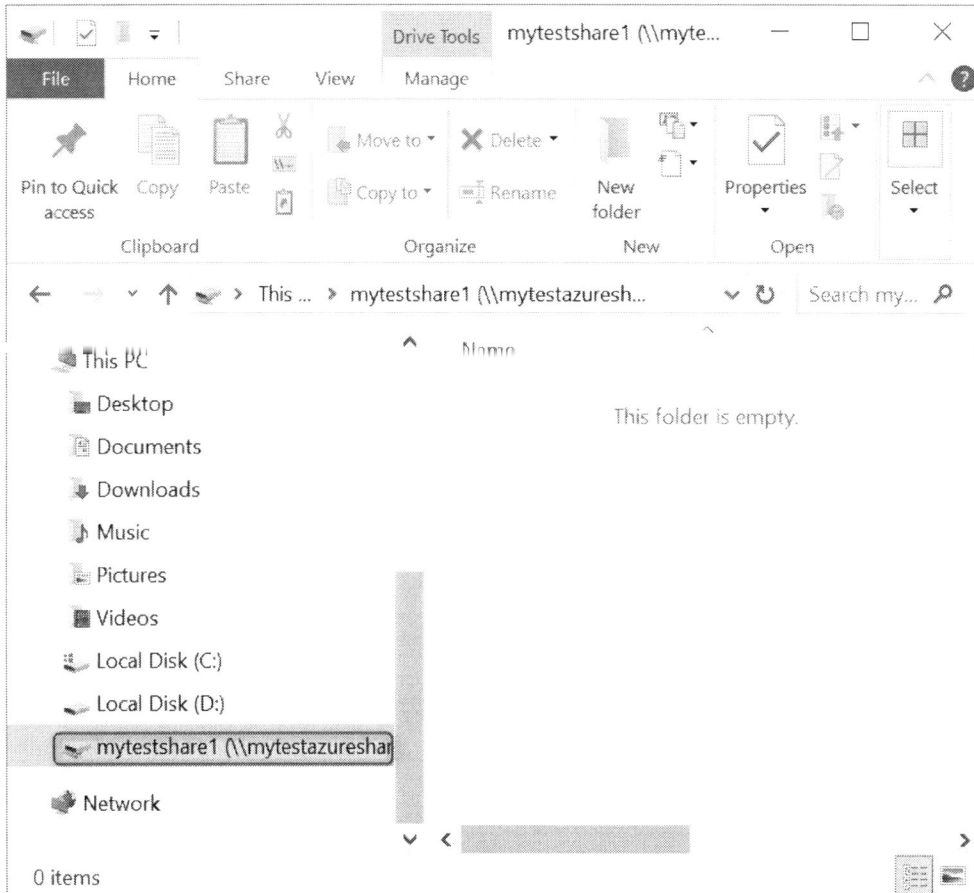

6. Now you can use this drive as your local drive. You can disconnect the mapped network drive at any time.

Mount Azure Files Share on Linux Machine

If you are using a Linux system, you can use the Common Internet File System (CIFS) protocol to mount and use Azure Files Share. Let's see how to mount and use the Azure Files share on our Linux virtual machine (MyTestVM2).

1. On a Ubuntu Linux virtual machine, execute the following command to install cifs utility packages.
   ```
   sudo apt-get update
   sudo apt-get install cifs-utils
   ```
2. For RHEL or CentOS based Linux virtual machine, use the following commands to install samba and cifs utility packages.
   ```
   sudo yum install samba-client samba-common cifs-utils
   ```
3. Once the samba/cifs utility packages are installed, you can use the following command to mount the Azure Files Shares on Linux machines.
   ```
   sudo mount -t cifs //<storage-account-
   name>.file.core.windows.net/<file-share-name> <mount-point> -o
   vers=3.0,username=<storage-account-name>,password=<storage-
   account-key>,dir_mode=0777,file_mode=0777,serverino
   ```

4. Let's create a mount point named as **/azureshare**, mount the azure files share, and create a test directory to test whether everything working or not. For this, you need to execute the following commands as shown in the following figure as well.

```
sudo apt-get update
sudo apt-get install cifs-utils
sudo mkdir /azureshare
sudo mount -t cifs
//mytestazureshare1.file.core.windows.net/mytestshare1
/azureshare -o
vers=3.0,username=mytestazureshare1,password=<your-account-
access-key>,dir_mode=0777,file_mode=0777,serverino
cd /azureshare/
sudo mkdir testdir1
```

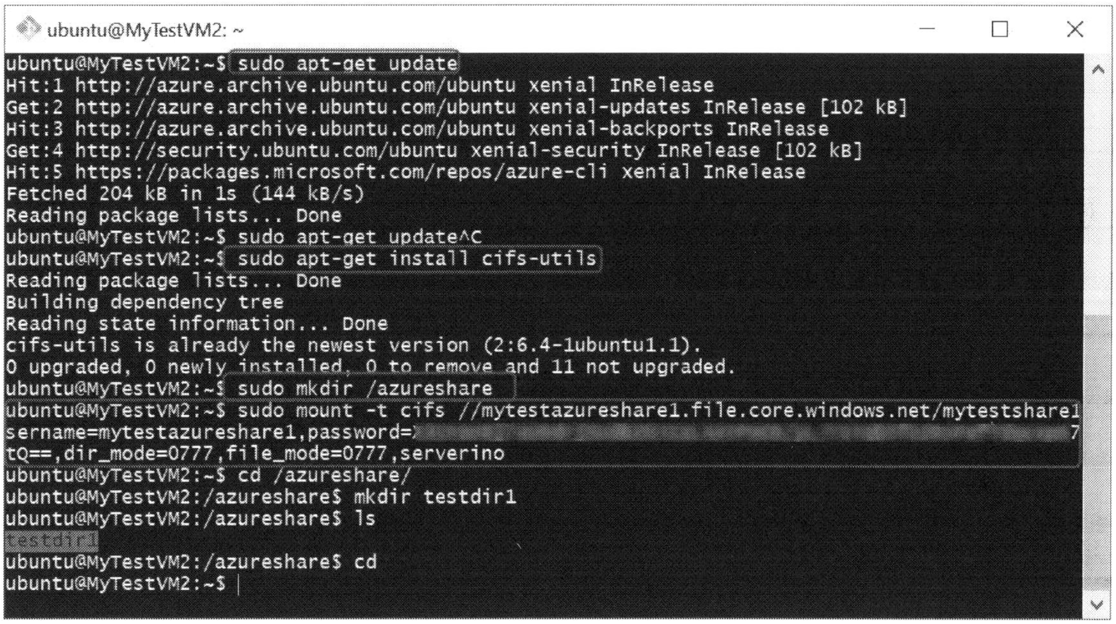

5. For the persistent mount on a Linux machine, you need to modify the **/etc/fstab** file, which is beyond the scope of this guide. If you are interested, you can visit the following link for more details.

- Using Azure Files Share on Linux
  https://docs.microsoft.com/en-us/azure/storage/files/storage-how-to-use-files-linux

Mount Azure Files Share on Mac OS Machine

You can also mount Azure Files Share on Mac OS. For this, use the following command syntax:

```
mount_smbfs //<storage-account-name>@<storage-account-
name>.file.core.windows.net/<share-name> <desired-mount-point>
```

You will be asked for password, provide the storage account key as password.

That's all you need to create, mount, and use Azure Files Share in Azure cloud.

Lab 27: Azure Database Storage Services

A persistent data store is the heart of many applications. You can choose a relational database engine such as Azure SQL Database, SQL Server running in Azure Virtual Machines, or non-Microsoft databases such as Oracle or MySQL. If your application needs a non-relational, NoSQL databases, you can choose DocumentDB and Azure Table Storage options.

Azure SQL Database

The Azure SQL Database provides a relational database-as-a-service, which is typically used for Online Transaction Processing workloads. The Azure SQL Database provides various attractive PaaS features. These include elastic scale, predictable performance, business continuity, near-zero maintenance, and the use of familiar development languages and tools. However, with Azure SQL database, you will not get physical server access to manage by own.

Depending on your need, Azure SQL Database provides three tiers: Basic, Standard, and Premium.

Each tier differs from each other based on the performance, database size limit, and Database Throughput Units (DTUs). The maximum database size in tiers varies from 2 GB to 500 GB. Further, each tier has its own performance levels such as S0, S1, P1, and P2. Each performance level supports a different number of DTUs.

Azure Database Tiers

Let's have a quick look at different types of Azure database tiers:

Basic
- Used for small databases with minimal operations at a given time such as development and testing
- Supports up to 2 GB database size
- Supports maximum 5 DTUs

Standard
- Used for applications that require multiple concurrent transactions
- Supports up to 250 GB database size
- Supports 10-100 DTUs

Premium
- Used for mission-critical, enterprise-grade applications that require high transaction rates and advanced business continuity features
- Supports up to 500 GB database size
- Supports 100-800 DTUs

Which database tier and their performance level you should choose? It depends on the workload and potential future growth of the application. For the getting started with Azure database, it's good to choose the basic tier. One more good thing here is that you can change the database tier whenever needed without any downtime.

Lab 28: Creating and Using Azure SQL Database

When you create an Azure SQL Database server, you create a logical server. That logical Azure SQL Database server is essentially a Tabular Data Stream endpoint. TDS is a communication protocol between the client and SQL Server.

Creating an Azure SQL Database

To create an Azure SQL database, you need to perform the following steps:

1. In **Azure Portal**, select **Create resources**, select **Databases** and then select **SQL Database** as shown in the following figure.

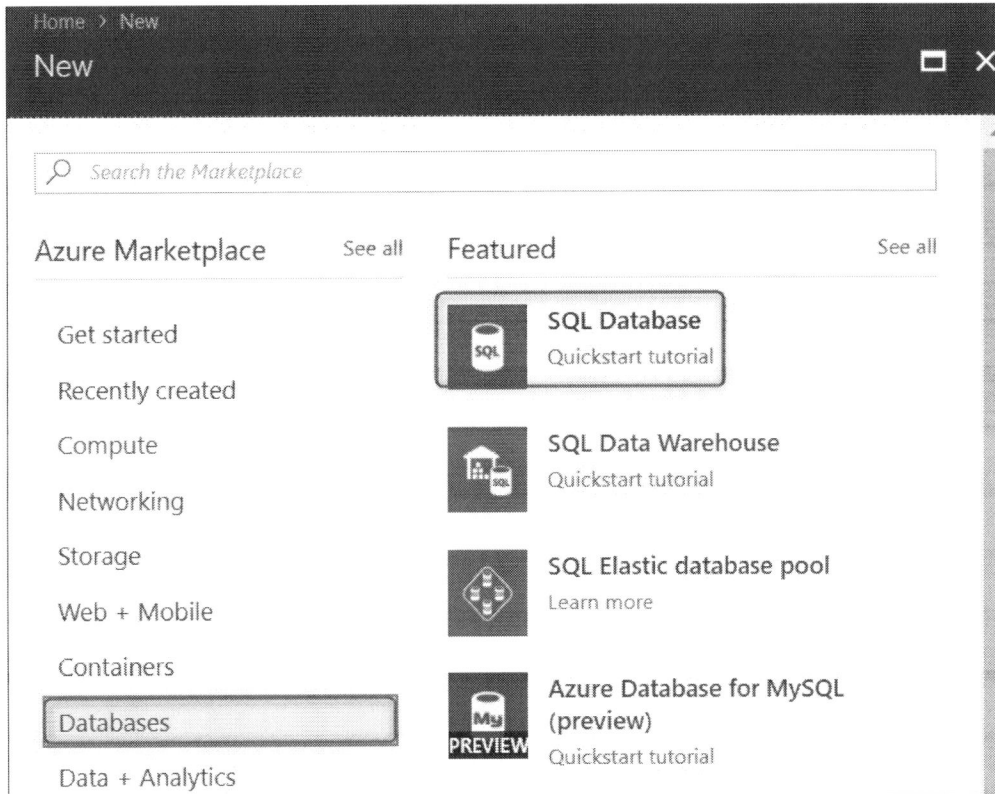

2. On the **SQL Database** blade, specify appropriate database name and resource group.
3. In the **Select source** drop-down list, select **Blank database**.
4. In the **Server** section, click **Configure required settings** and create a new database as shown in the following figure.

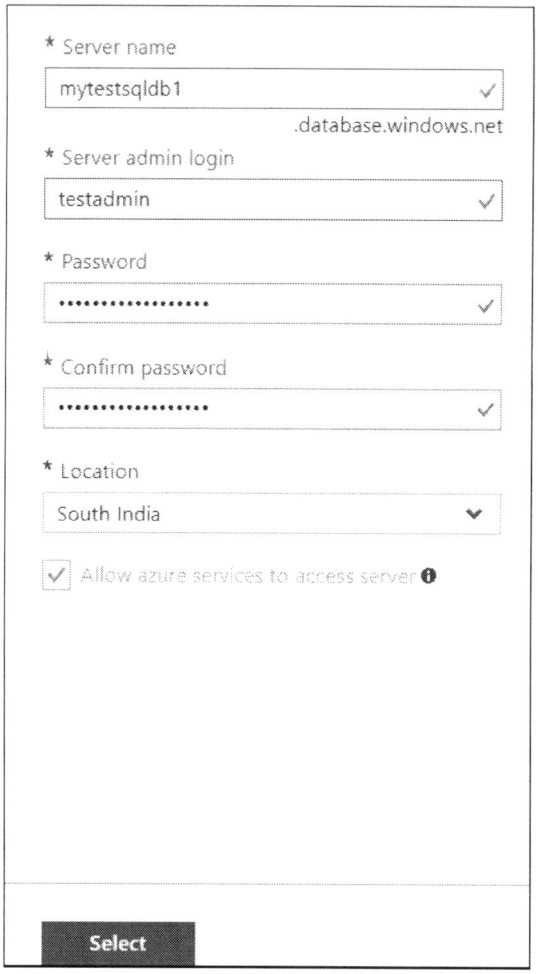

* Server name

mytestsqldb1   ✓

.database.windows.net

* Server admin login

testadmin   ✓

* Password

••••••••••••••••   ✓

* Confirm password

•••••••••••••••   ✓

* Location

South India   ⌄

☑ Allow azure services to access server ❶

Select

5. In the **Pricing tier**, select the **Basic Tier**, click **Apply** and then click **Create** as shown in the following figure.

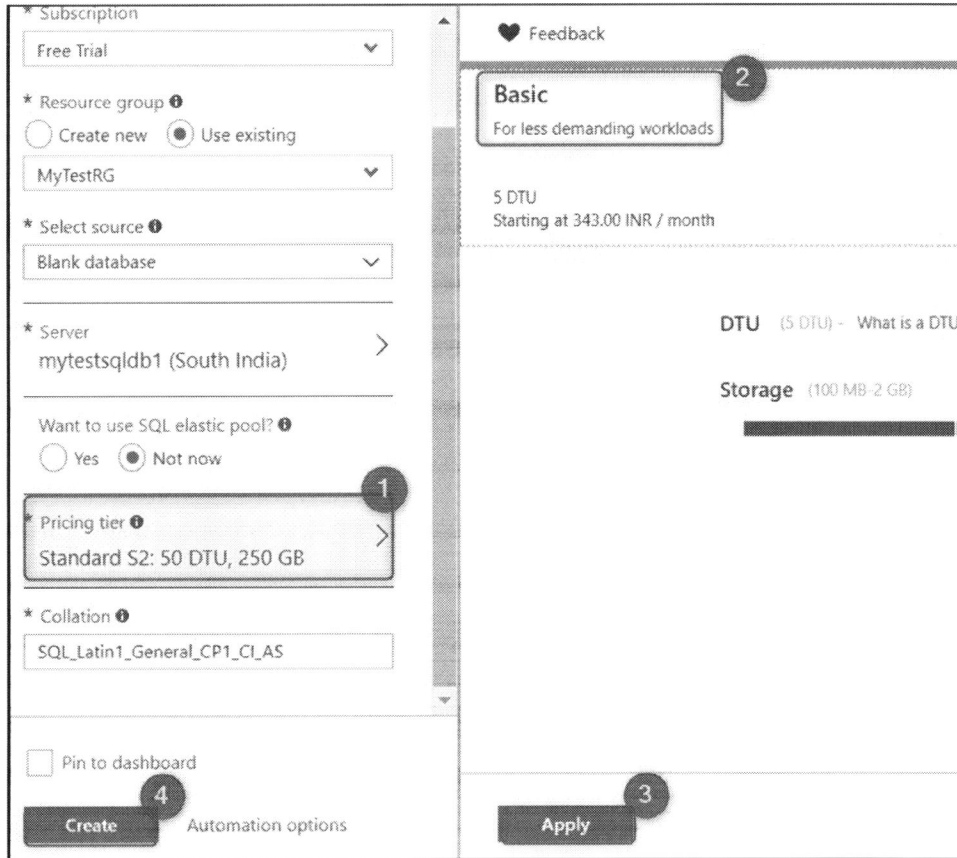

6. The **Azure SQL database** server will be created and available in the SQL database servers list.
7. You can find the server name by navigating the **Overview** section of the created SQL database.
8. By default, firewall rules explicitly deny access from any IP address. So, you cannot connect your SQL database. To change or modify SQL firewall rules as per your needs, click **Set server firewall** as shown in the above figure.

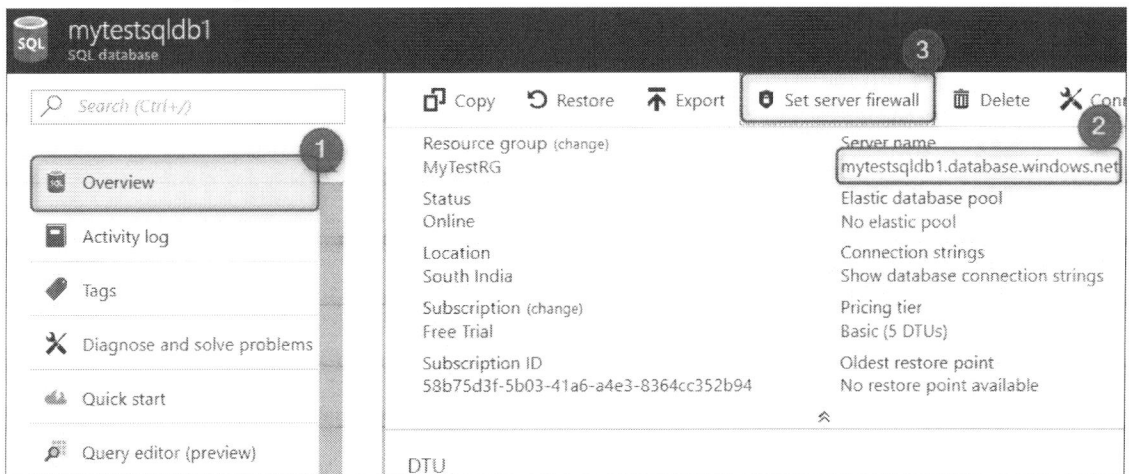

9. On the **Firewall settings** blade, click **Add client IP** (or any other IPs from where you want to connect) and then click **Save** to save the firewall rules as shown in the following figure.

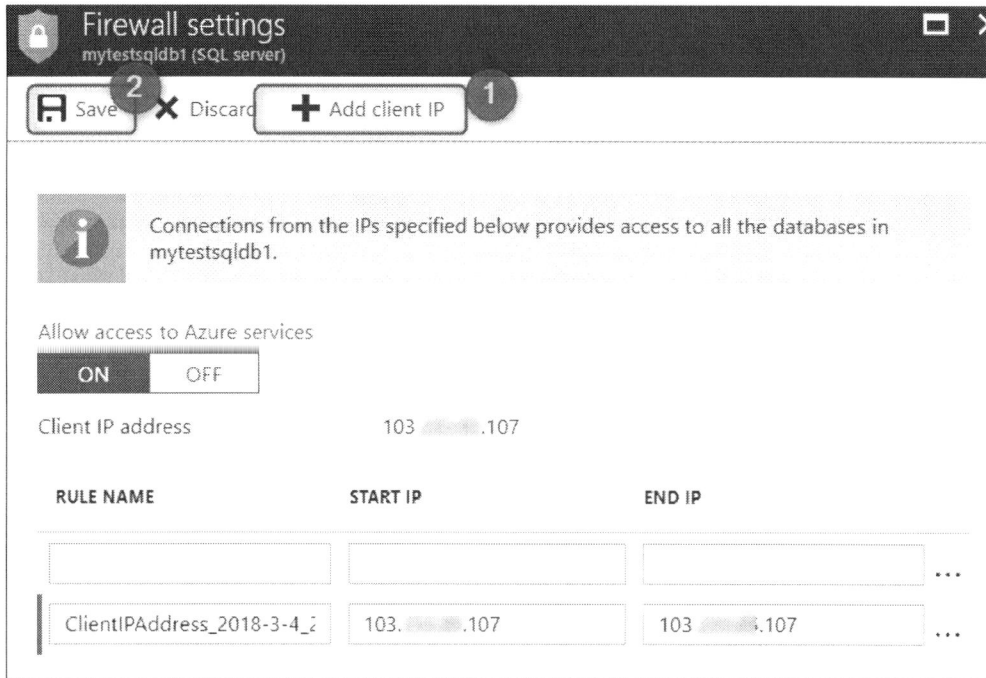

Connecting Azure SQL Database

To connect Azur SQL database, you need to download and install SQL Server Management Studio (SSMS) for windows. You can download SSMS using the following link.

- Download SQL Server Management Studio
  https://docs.microsoft.com/en-us/sql/ssms/download-sql-server-management-studio-ssms

Open the SSMS tool, specify the connection settings as shown in the following figure.

- Server name: **Name of Azure SQL Server**
- Authentication: **SQL Server Authentication**
- Login: **Azure SQL server user name**
- Password: **Azure SQL server password**

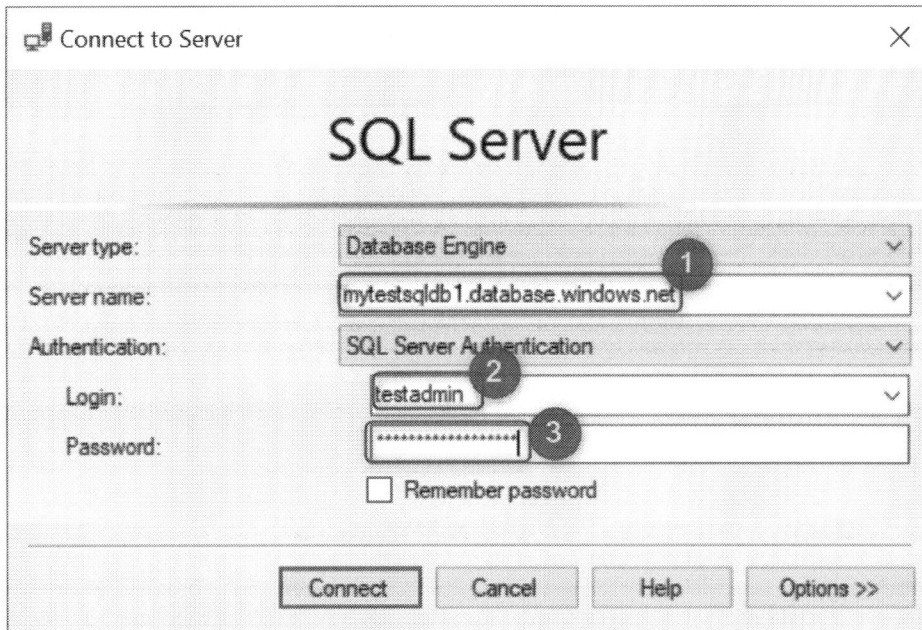

Finally, click **Connect** to connect the Azure SQL database. You should be able to connect your SQL database as shown in the following figure.

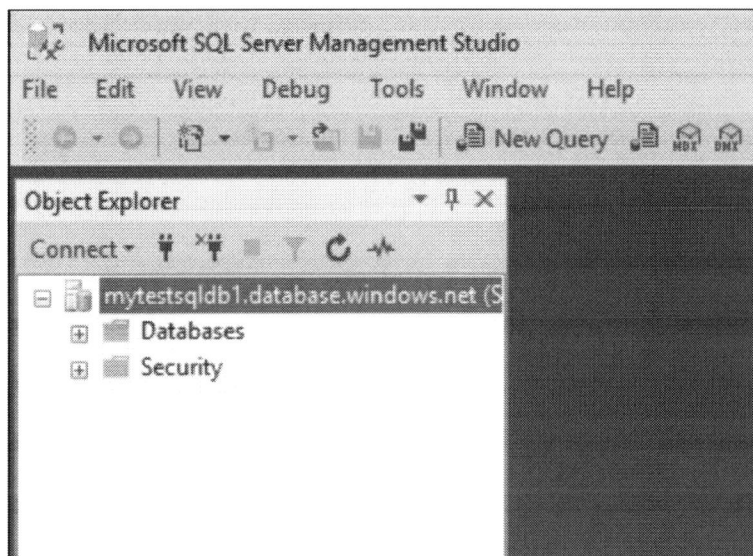

Application Connection Strings

The SQL databases are used by a wide range of applications. These applications may have different language platforms such as .Net, PHP, etc. When you create a SQL database, it gives you options for all the supported application's strings that you may like to connect SQL database from an application side.

1. To check the SQL database application strings, select your SQL database server and navigate to the **Connection strings** section.
2. Here, you can see the various connections string syntaxes for the different types of applications as shown in the following figure.

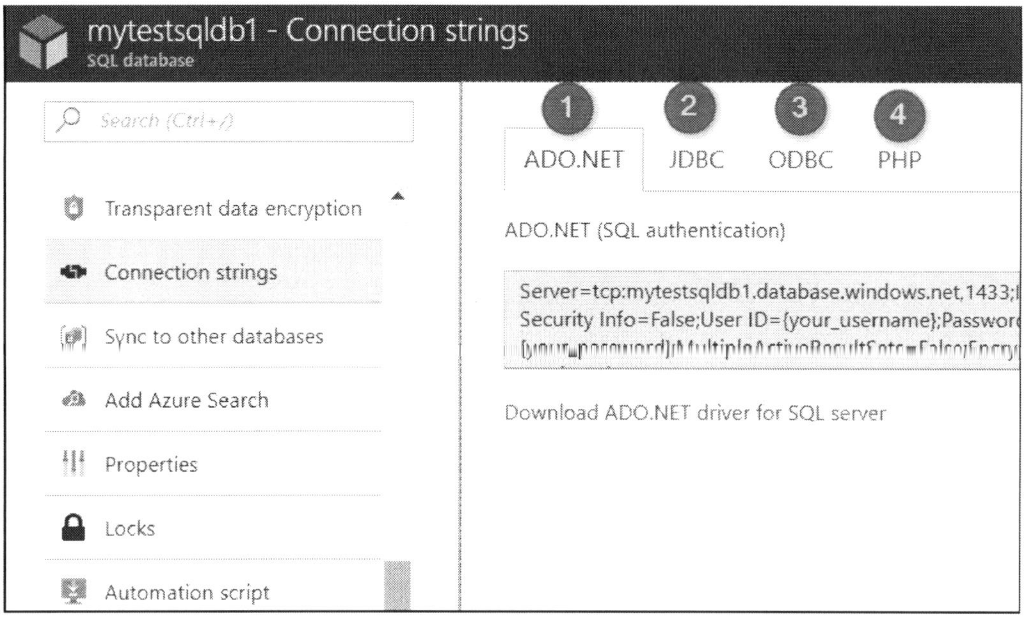

mytestsqldb1 - Connection strings
SQL database

Search (Ctrl+/)

① ADO.NET ② JDBC ③ ODBC ④ PHP

Transparent data encryption

Connection strings

Sync to other databases

Add Azure Search

Properties

Locks

Automation script

ADO.NET (SQL authentication)

Server=tcp:mytestsqldb1.database.windows.net,1433;
Security Info=False;User ID={your_username};Password
{your_password};MultipleActiveResultSets=False;Encry

Download ADO.NET driver for SQL server

Lab 29: Restoring Azure SQL Database

If something goes wrong with your SQL database, you can restore the database from an older point-in-time snapshot taken by Microsoft. In the background, Microsoft keeps three copies (one writes and two read only) of your SQL databases for a specific timeframe. The timeframe from which you can restore varies based on your Azure SQL Database tier: 7 days for Basic, 15 days for Standard, and 35 days for Premium.

To restore SQL database, you need to perform the following steps:

1. In **Azure Portal**, select your SQL database you want to restore.
2. Select **Overview** and then click **Restore** as shown in the following figure.

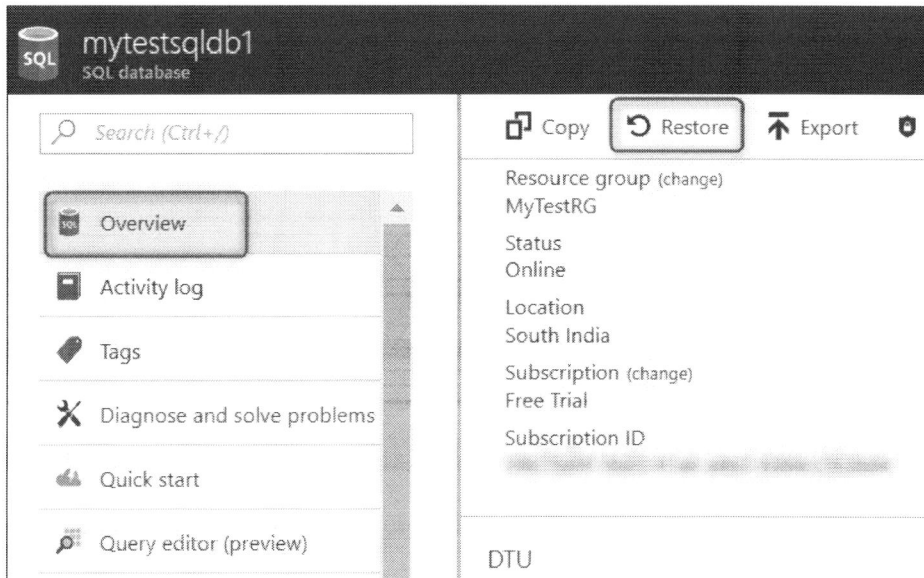

3. On the **Restore** blade, specify the restoring database name, select the date and time you want to restore, and then click **OK** as shown in the following figure.

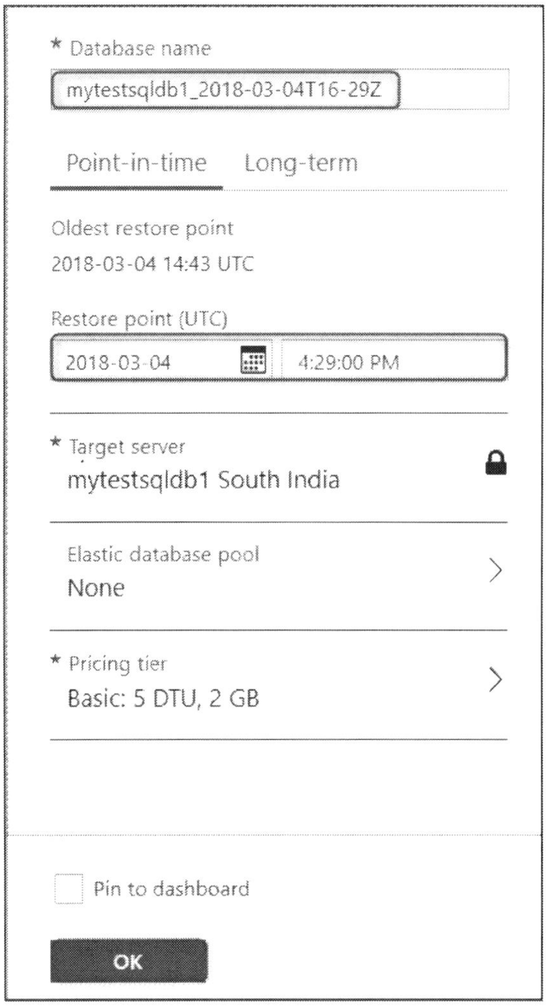

* Database name

mytestsqldb1_2018-03-04T16-29Z

Point-in-time   Long-term

Oldest restore point

2018-03-04 14:43 UTC

Restore point (UTC)

2018-03-04   🔲   4:29:00 PM

* Target server   🔒

mytestsqldb1 South India

Elastic database pool   ⟩

None

* Pricing tier   ⟩

Basic: 5 DTU, 2 GB

☐ Pin to dashboard

OK

4. The database restoration process will start and may take several minutes depending on the tier and size of the database.

Lab 30: Exporting, Importing SQL Databases

Another useful method to alternative of backup and restore is **Export and Import SQL databases**. The Import and export feature enables you to export an Azure SQL database as a **BACPAC** file. The BACPAC file is saved to Azure Blob storage. Once exported, you can then import the BACPAC file to a new server. BACPAC file creates a copy of the source from the point when it was created. However, the export process does not provide surety for a transactionally consistent copy of the source database. Therefore, it is recommended that you first create a copy which does provide transactional consistency and then perform the export.

To export SQL database, you need to perform the following steps:

1. In **Azure Portal**, select SQL database you would like to export.
2. In the **Overview** section, click **Export** as shown in the following figure.

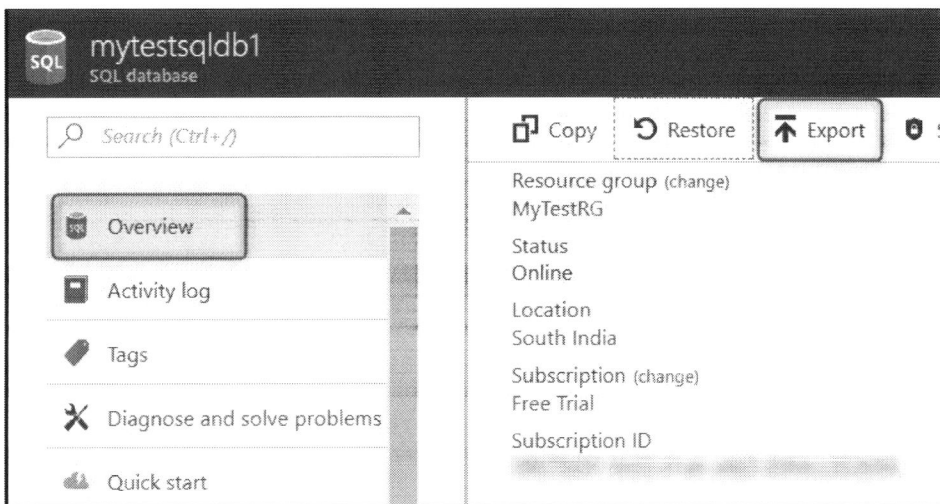

3. In the **Export** blade, specify the database name and navigate to **Configure required settings** options as shown in the following figure.

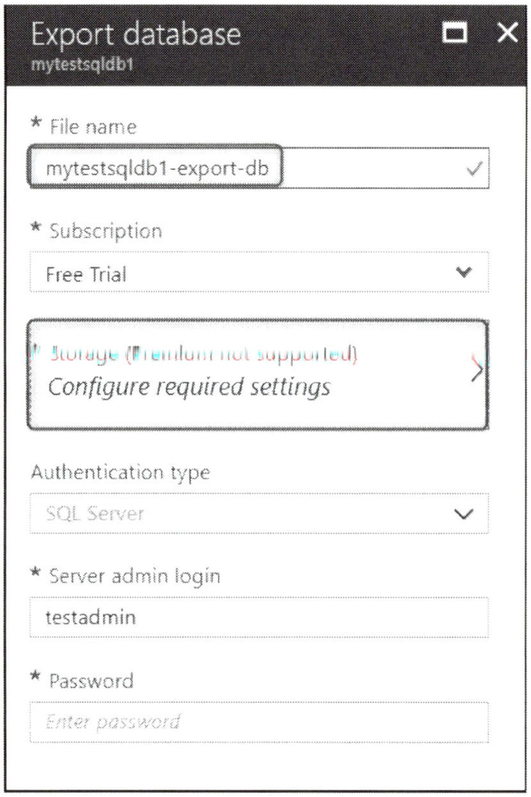

4. In the **Storage accounts** blade, select the desired **Blob storage account** and a **container** where the database will be exported as shown in the following figure.

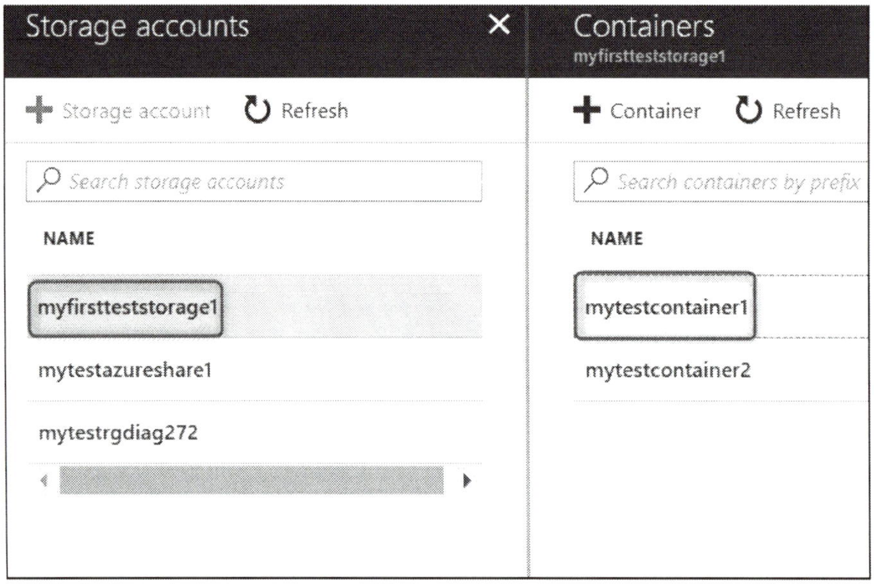

5. Specify the database password and click **OK** to finish. Once the export process is completed, you will see the BACPAC file in the selected storage account and container.

Lab 31: Azure Active Directory

Identity access management provides a mechanism to know who used the application and what actions the user can perform. The identity mechanism in the Azure Cloud platform is served by Azure Active Directory (Azure AD). However, Azure AD is not a fully replacement of Windows Server Active Directory.

Azure AD is a multitenant directory service, in which, each tenant has a dedicated instance of Azure AD.

Azure AD Editions

Azure Active Directory comes in four editions—Free, Basic, Premium P1, and Premium P2.

1. **Free**: Provides the ability to manage users, synchronize with on-premises Active Directory, establish SSO across Azure and Office 365, and access SaaS applications in the Azure AD application gallery.
2. **Basic**: Provides all the features provided by the Free tier, and some additional features such as self-service password resets, group-based application access, customizable branding, and a 99.9 percent availability SLA.
3. **Premium P1 and P2**: Provides all the features provided by the Free and Basic tiers, and some additional features such as self-service group management, advanced security reports and alerts, Multi-Factor Authentication, licenses for Microsoft Forefront Identity Manager (Microsoft Identity Manager), and future enterprise features.
   You can explore different Azure AD editions in details using the below link.
   - https://azure.microsoft.com/en-in/pricing/details/active-directory

Creating Azure AD

When you sign up for an Azure cloud subscription, a default Azure AD is created for you by default. To view the default created Azure AD, you need to perform the following steps:

1. Login to **Azure Portal** and navigate to the **Azure AD** as shown in the following figure.

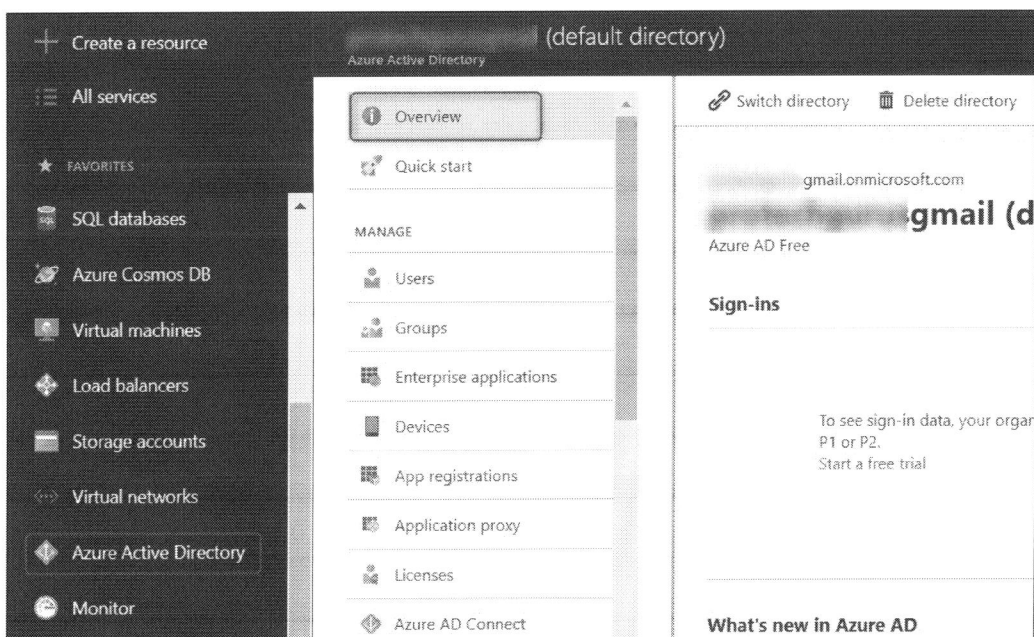

2. Under the **Overview** blade, click the **Create a directory** link as shown in the following figure.

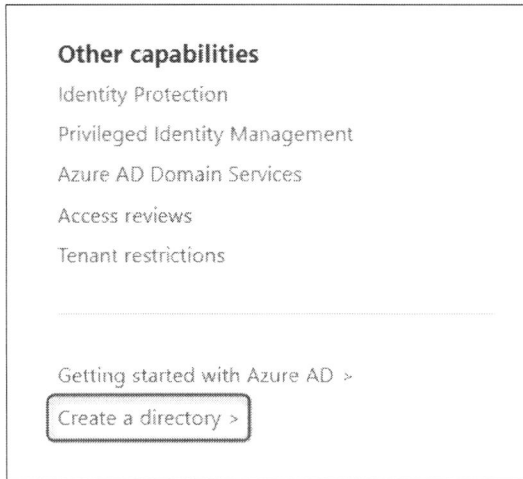

Other capabilities

Identity Protection

Privileged Identity Management

Azure AD Domain Services

Access reviews

Tenant restrictions

Getting started with Azure AD ≫

Create a directory ≫

3. On the **Create directory** blade, specify the organizational name, initial domain name, and select the region as shown in the following figure.

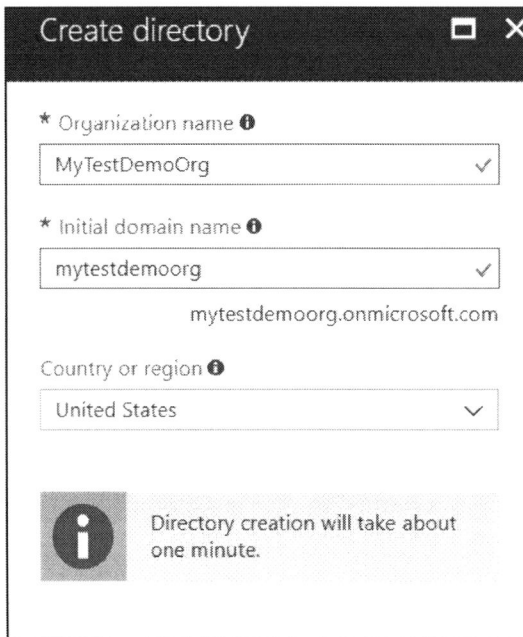

Create directory □ ✕

* Organization name ❶

MyTestDemoOrg ✓

* Initial domain name ❶

mytestdemoorg ✓

mytestdemoorg.onmicrosoft.com

Country or region ❶

United States ⌄

ℹ Directory creation will take about one minute.

4. Finally, click **Create** to proceed. After a few minutes, your Azure AD will be created.
5. To switch to the created Azure AD, click your account settings and select your directory under the Directory section as shown in the following figure.

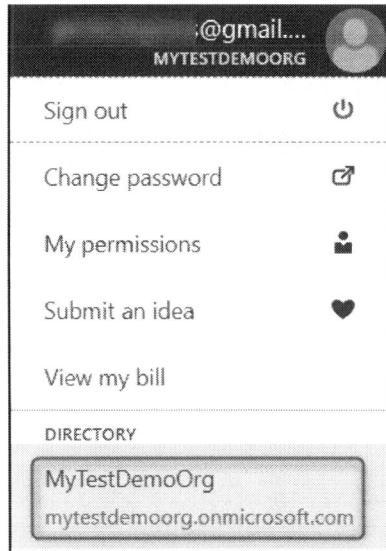

```
                    :@gmail....
                    MYTESTDEMOORG

    Sign out                           ⏻

    Change password                    ☑

    My permissions                     👤

    Submit an idea                     ♥

    View my bill

    DIRECTORY

    MyTestDemoOrg
    mytestdemoorg.onmicrosoft.com
```

6. Once created, you can add users, groups, devices and can perform few other related tasks as shown in the following figure.

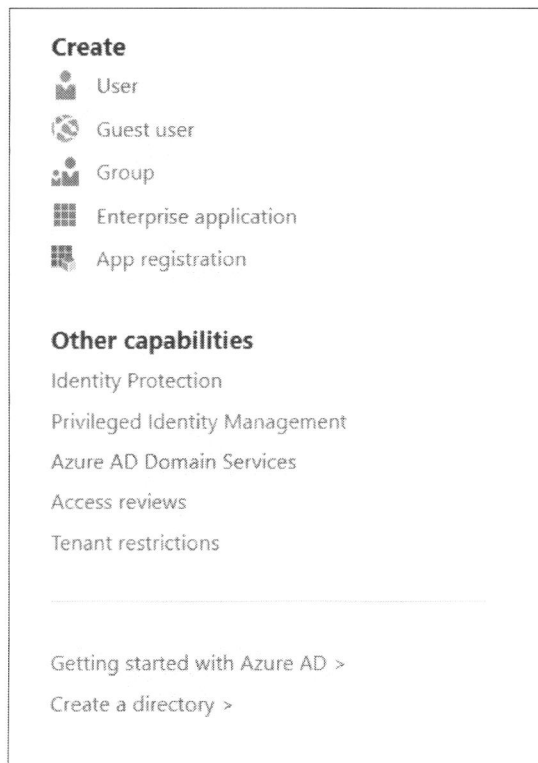

```
    Create
    👤  User
    ◎  Guest user
    👥  Group
    ▦  Enterprise application
    ▦  App registration

    Other capabilities
    Identity Protection
    Privileged Identity Management
    Azure AD Domain Services
    Access reviews
    Tenant restrictions


    Getting started with Azure AD >
    Create a directory >
```

Deleting Azure AD

1. To delete an Azure AD, switch to the directory that you want to delete and click **Delete directory** as shown in the following figure.

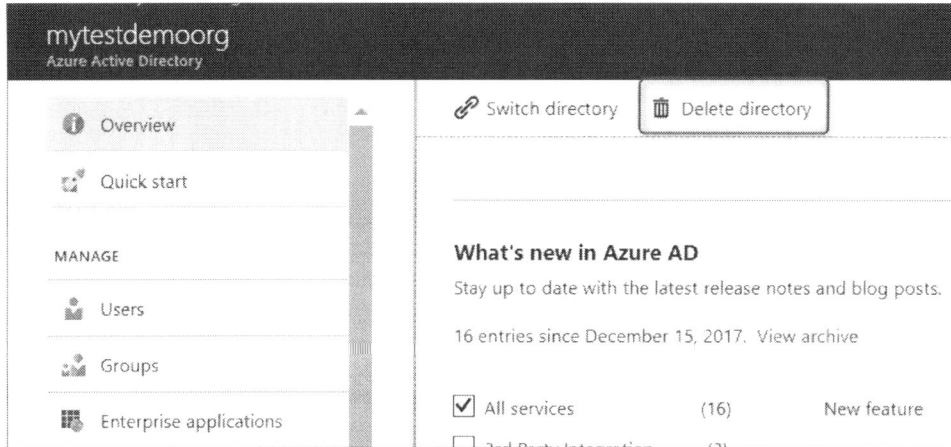

2. On the **Delete directory** blade, click the **Delete** button. The directory will be deleted.

Azure AD Domain Names

The default domain name for Azure AD has the following format:

- **<directory_name>.**onmicrosoft.com

When you create a user in Azure AD, the user has the following login format:

- user**@directory_name.**onmicrosoft.com

For example, let's assume that your user name is **testuser** and your Azure AD name is **mytestdemoorg**, then the user login format would be like the following.

- testuser**@mytestdemoorg.**onmicrosoft.com

However, if you already own a domain, you can use your custom domain name as well.

Adding Custom Domain Names in Azure AD

To add a custom domain name in Azure AD, you need to perform the following steps:

1. In Azure Portal, select the Azure AD for which you want to use custom domain name and select **Custom domain names**.
2. In the **Custom domain names** section, click **Add custom domain** as shown in the following figure.

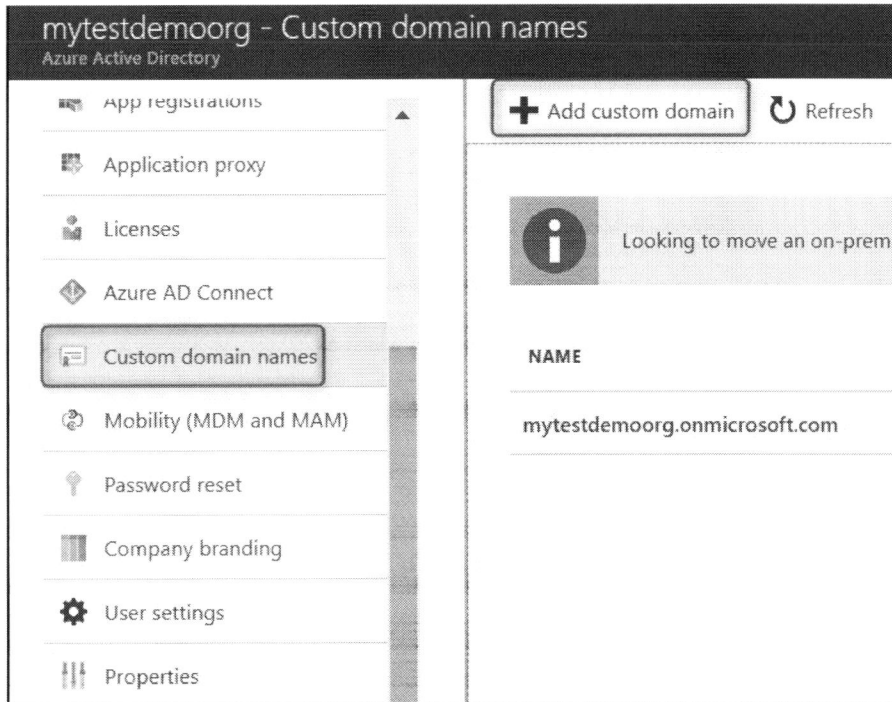

3. Specify your custom domain name and click **Add Domain** as shown in the following figure

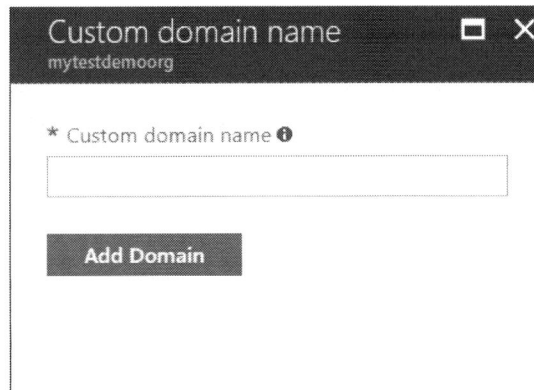

4. Now, you will require to prove that you own this custom domain. For this, you will require to add **MX DNS records** in your owned domain name.
5. Once you added the MX record into your DNS registrar click **Verify**. Your custom domain will be ready to use.
6. Depending on your DNS registrar, domain records adding process may differ. Please follow the DNS registrar documentation for more details.

For more details about how to add and verify custom domains in Azure AD, please have a look at the following link.

- https://docs.microsoft.com/en-us/azure/active-directory/add-custom-domain

Lab 32: Azure Marketplace

Sometimes you may need tools to use for your projects, but you may not have sufficient time to study and then setup from the scratch. But, you do not need to worry in the Cloud era. Most of the tools come with preconfigured in each Cloud provider marketplaces such as AWS marketplace, Azure Marketplace. Azure Marketplace is the premier destination for most of your software needs - certified and optimized to run on Azure.

Most of the software come with a free trial for a specific time limit, so you can work and test them before to decide to go for production. Few of them are also available without any additional cost, but for a few of them you may need to pay an additional cost apart from the virtual machine cost.

To launch a preconfigured resource from Azure marketplace, you need to perform the following steps:

1. In Azure Portal, navigate to **All resources** > **Marketplace** as shown in the following figure.

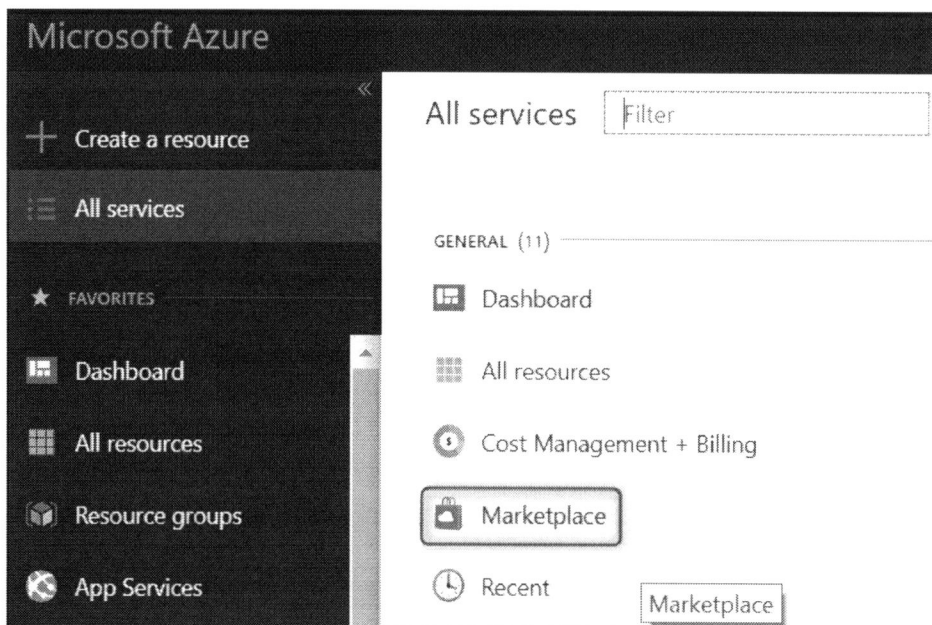

2. In the **Marketplace** blade, you can select the desired category, such as **Security**, **Storage**, **Compute** etc. depending on your need of resource you want to use from the marketplace.

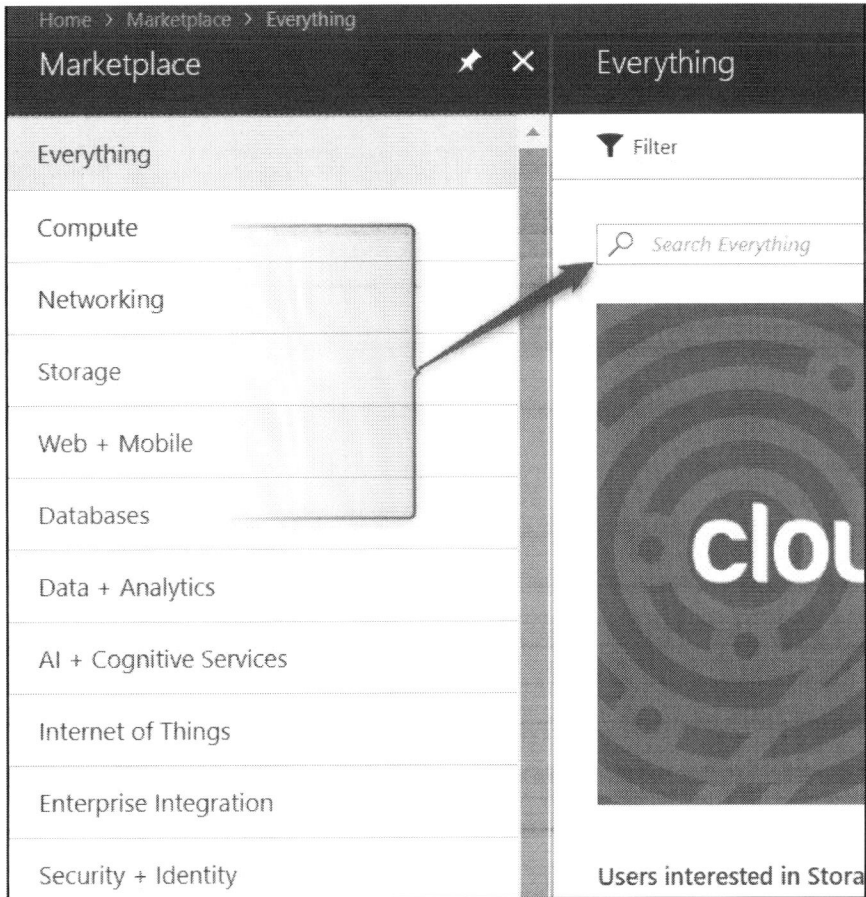

Marketplace

Everything

Everything

Compute

Networking

Storage

Web + Mobile

Databases

Data + Analytics

AI + Cognitive Services

Internet of Things

Enterprise Integration

Security + Identity

Filter

Search Everything

clou

Users interested in Stora

3. For example, to use the OpenVPN Access Server, select the **Security + Identity** category and then search for the OpenVPN Access Server as shown in the following figure.

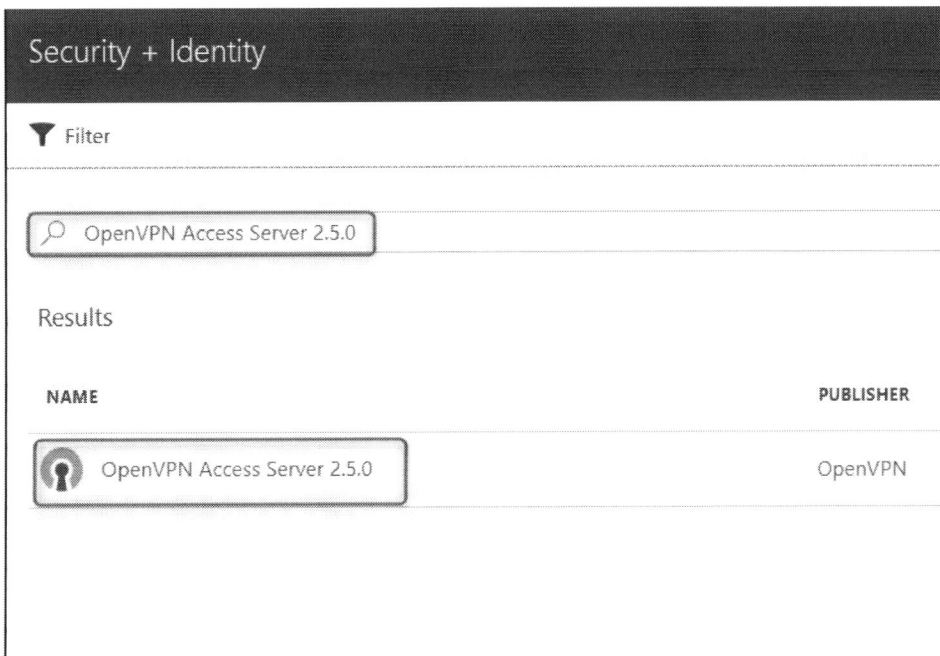

Security + Identity

Filter

OpenVPN Access Server 2.5.0

Results

NAME	PUBLISHER
OpenVPN Access Server 2.5.0	OpenVPN

Almost all the marketplace resources have the documentation link to their respective platform and services support. You need to visit their support center and documentation link for the further reading and deployment guide.

Similarly, you can search, select and use hundreds of preconfigured software, tool, applications, and solutions from Azure Marketplace.

Lab 33: Working with Azure VPN Gateways

An Azure VPN gateway is a virtual network gateway that securely sends traffic to and from an on-premise location to Azure virtual networks over a public network. Only one VPN gateway can be created for each virtual network in the Azure cloud. However, multiple connections are allowed to the same VPN gateway.

For VPN gateway, we use Virtual network gateway. A virtual network gateway consists of two or more virtual machines that are deployed to a specific subnet called the **GatewaySubnet**. When you create a virtual network gateway, in the backend, Azure deploys few VMs in the GatewaySubnet. These VMs are configured with appropriate routing tables and gateway services specific to the gateway. Ideally, you should not deploy any additional resources to the GatewaySubnet.

Depending on the number of connections you want to have for VPN, performance and network bandwidth you may wish to use - You choose the appropriate SKU for the VPN gateway. The Gateway SKU determines how powerful the VMs are being deployed in the backend.

In Azure Cloud, you can configure the following types of VPN gateways:

1. **Point-to-site:**
    Allows multiple clients to connect azure virtual network. Supports up to 100 Mbps speed. Does not require an on-premises public-facing IP address or a VPN device.
2. **Site-to-site:**
    Allows your on-premise VPN server to connect and communicate to Azure virtual networks. Supports up-to 1 Gbps speed. Require on premise public facing IP address or VPN device.
3. **ExpressRoute:**
    A dedicated private network connection from your on-premise datacenter to Azure cloud virtual network. Available in various bandwidth speeds depending on the need of customer.

Point-to-Site VPN Connection

A Point-to-Site (P2S) VPN gateway connection allows you to create a secure connection from individual client computers to your Azure virtual network. P2S VPN uses either SSTP or IKEv2 VPN protocol for secure connection. P2S authentication can be established either using the native Azure certificate authentication or using Active Directory Domain server. With Azure certificate authentication, a client certificate installation is required to authenticate the connecting user. Along with the Azure certificate, a VPN client configuration zip file, provided by Azure cloud, is also needed. It contains settings required by these Windows or Mac clients to connect to Azure.

P2S native Azure certificate authentication connections require the following components:

1. A RouteBased VPN gateway.
2. The public key (.cer file) for the root certificate.
3. A client certificate generated from the root certificate.
4. A VPN client configuration

In order to show demo how to create, configure, and connect Azure P2S VPN connection, we will be using the following configuration settings:

Creating Virtual Network

First, we need to create a Virtual network with the following configuration settings:

- Virtual Network Name: **MyTestVPNVnet1**
- IP Address space: **192.168.0.0/16**
- Resource Group: **MyTestRG**
- Location: **South India**
- Subnet Name: **MytestVPNSubnet1**
- Subnet Address Range: **192.168.1.0/24**

To create a virtual network using Azure Portal, you need to perform the following steps:

1. In Azure Portal, navigate to the **Virtual Networks** blade, click **Add** and specify the above configuration values as shown in the following figure.

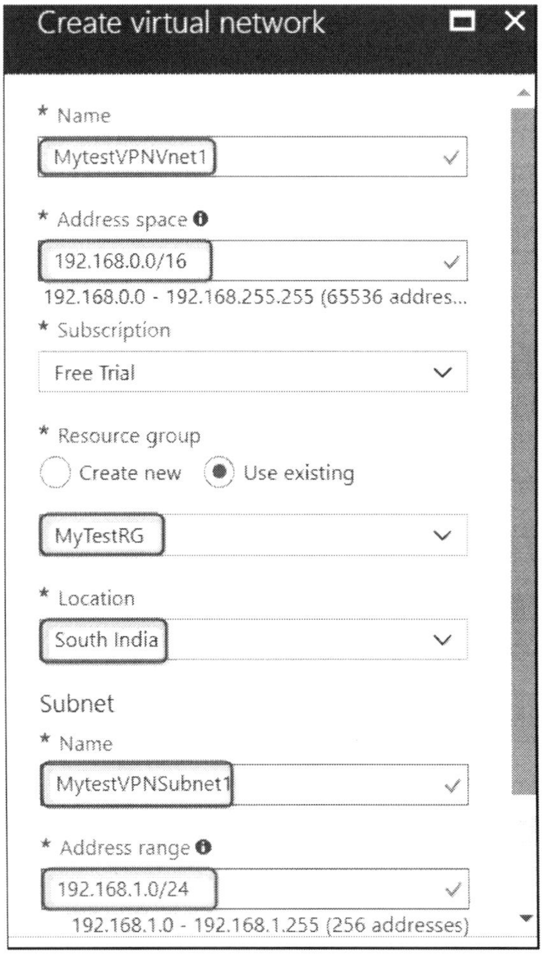

2. Now, select the created virtual network (MyTestVPNVnet1) and navigate to the **Subnets** options.
3. Click **+Gateway subnet** to create a new gateway subnet as shown in the following figure.

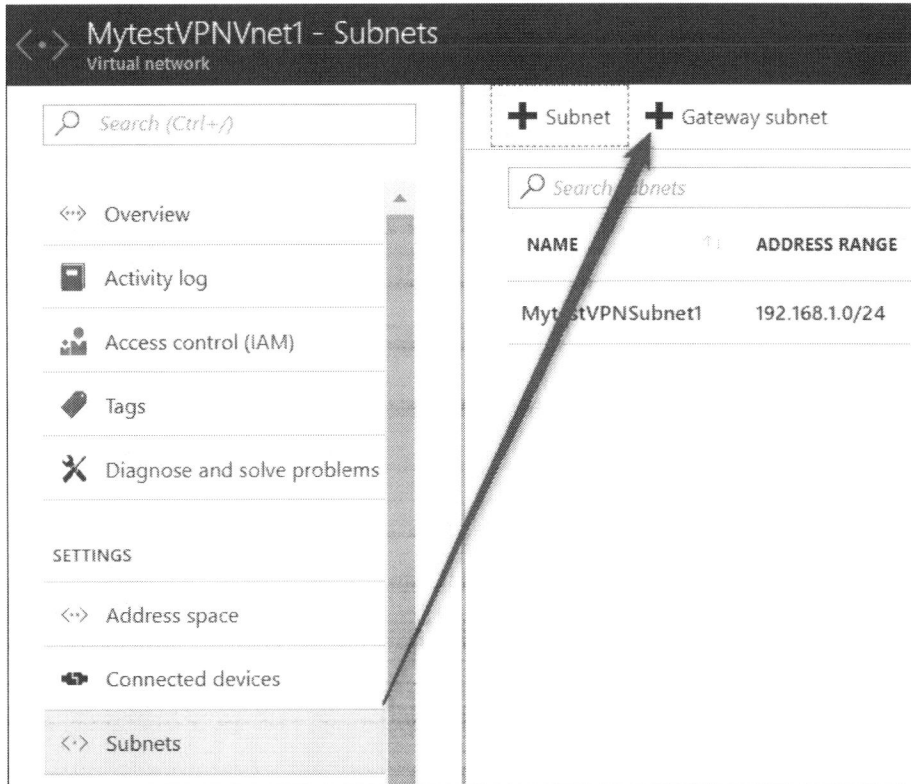

MytestVPNVnet1 - Subnets
Virtual network

Search (Ctrl+/)

➕ Subnet   ➕ Gateway subnet

Search subnets

NAME	ADDRESS RANGE
MytestVPNSubnet1	192.168.1.0/24

- Overview
- Activity log
- Access control (IAM)
- Tags
- Diagnose and solve problems

SETTINGS

- Address space
- Connected devices
- Subnets

4. On the **Add gateway subnet** blade, create the **Gateway subnet** with **192.168.100.0/24** subnet range as shown in the following figure.

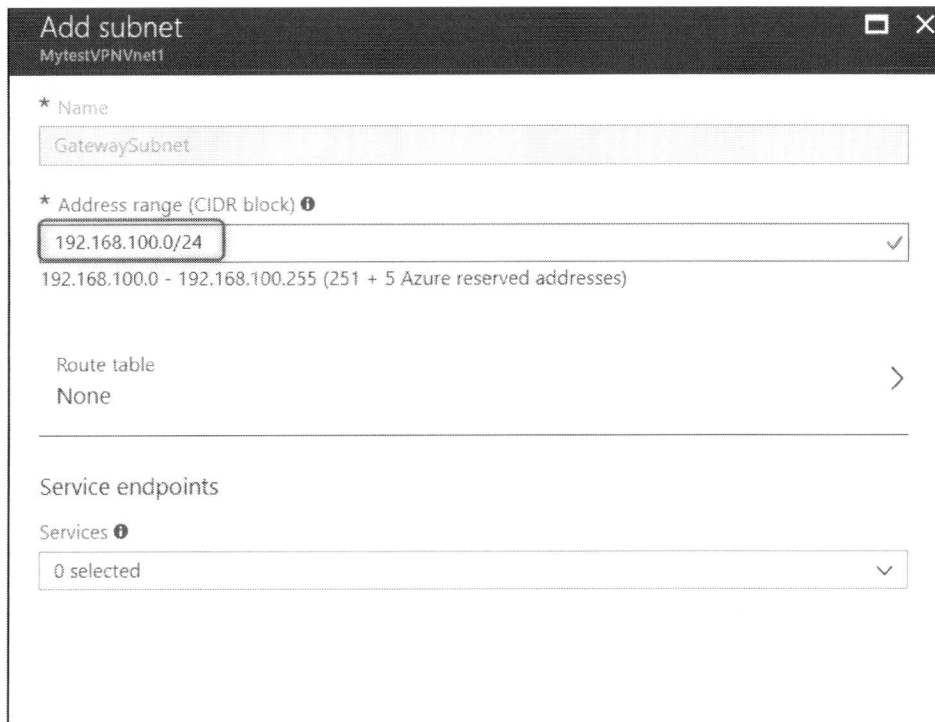

Add subnet
MytestVPNVnet1

* Name

GatewaySubnet

* Address range (CIDR block) ❶

192.168.100.0/24   ✓

192.168.100.0 - 192.168.100.255 (251 + 5 Azure reserved addresses)

Route table
None   >

Service endpoints

Services ❶

0 selected   ⌄

5. Now you have a virtual network with GatewaySubnet.

Creating VPN Gateway

To create a VPN gateway in Azure cloud, you need to perform the following steps:

1. Navigate to the **Create resource** blade, type virtual network gateway in the search box and then click **Create** as shown in the following figure.

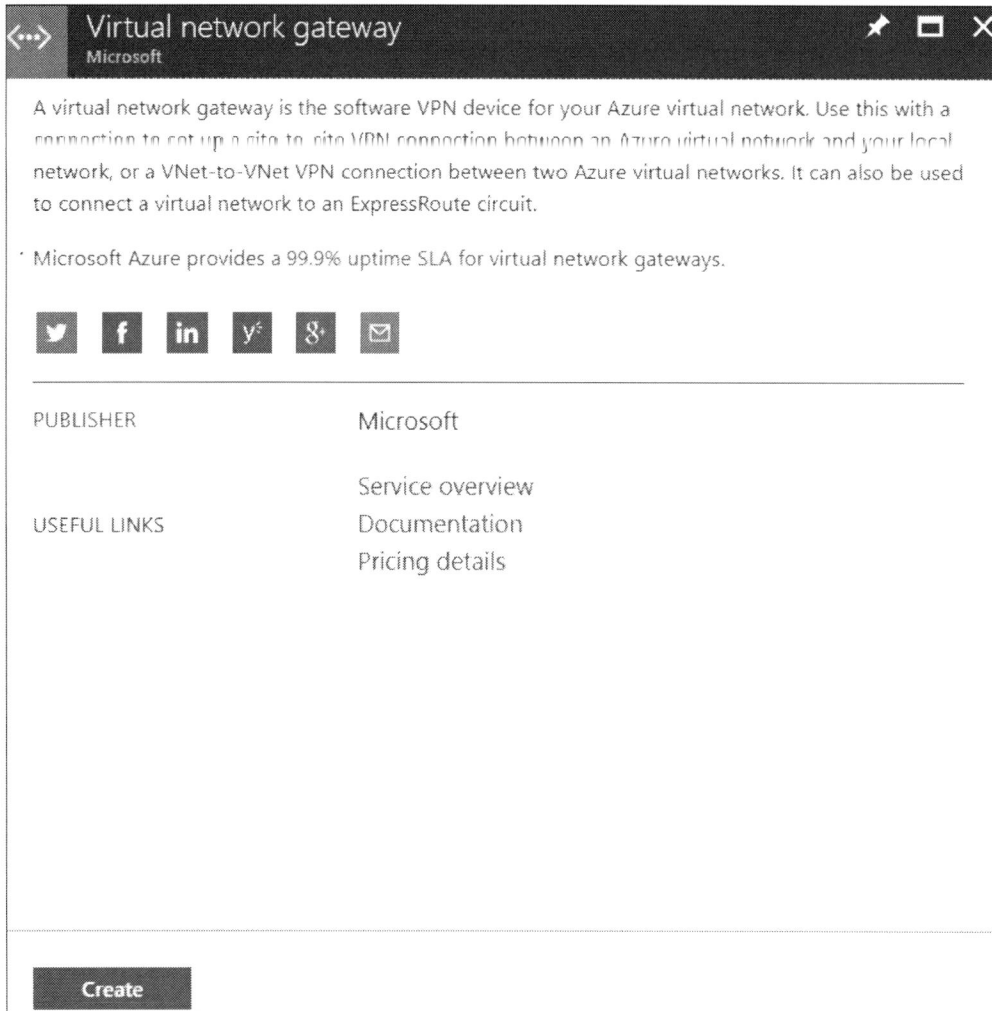

2. On the **Create virtual network gateway** blade, specify the following settings:
   - Virtual Network Gateway Name: **MyTestVPNGW1**
   - Gateway Type: **VPN**
   - VPN Type: **Route-based**
   - SKU: **VpnGW1**
   - Virtual network gateway: **MytestVPNVnet1**
   - Public IP Address Name: **MyTestVPNGW1-pip** (Create new)
   - Resource group: **MyTestRG**
   - Location: **South India**

3. Once the appropriate settings are defined as shown in the following figure, click **Create** to proceed.

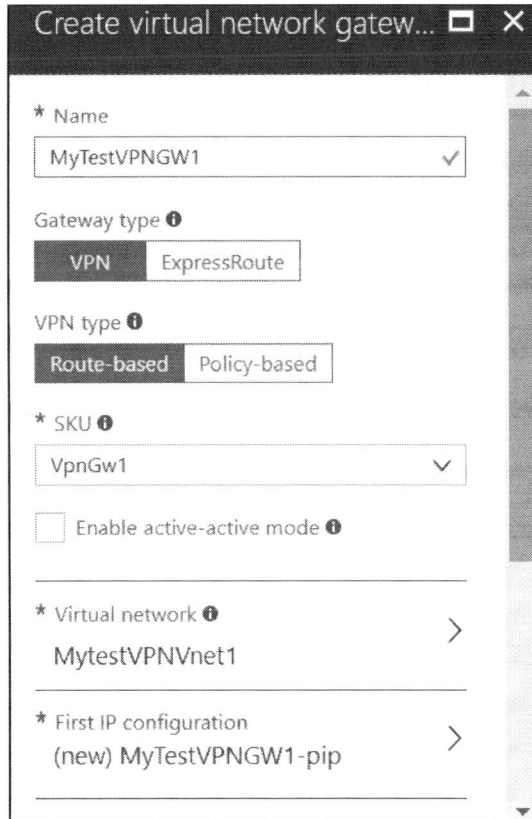

Create virtual network gatew... □ ✕

* Name

MyTestVPNGW1 ✓

Gateway type ❶

VPN | ExpressRoute

VPN type ❶

Route-based | Policy-based

* SKU ❶

VpnGw1 ⌄

☐ Enable active-active mode ❶

* Virtual network ❶ ＞

MytestVPNVnet1

* First IP configuration ＞
(new) MyTestVPNGW1-pip

4. The **Deploying Virtual Network Gateway** process may take half-an-hour. You can proceed to the next step and let the deployment process running. We will come back later in the Azure Portal.

Obtain The .cer File for The Root Certificate

You need to generate and upload a root certificate for VPN gateway. You can either use an enterprise root certificate or you can generate your own self-signed certificate. For this, you need a Windows 10 or Windows Server 2016 server with elevated PowerShell prompt.

To generate a self-signed root certificate for Azure VPN gateway, you need to perform the following steps:

1. Execute the following **PowerShell** cmdlet. Replace your certificate name appropriately, in our case, it is MyTestRootCert.

   $cert = New-SelfSignedCertificate -Type Custom -KeySpec Signature `
   -Subject "CN=MyTestRootCert" -KeyExportPolicy Exportable `
   -HashAlgorithm sha256 -KeyLength 2048 `
   -CertStoreLocation "Cert:\CurrentUser\My" -KeyUsageProperty Sign -KeyUsage CertSign

2. Please refer the following figure to generate a self-signed root certificate using Windows PowerShell.

3. The certificate will be created and installed automatically under the user's personal certificates store (Certificates – Current User\Personal\Certificates).
4. Open the **Certificate Manager** console (certmgr.msc) and verify that the certificate is created and available as shown in the following figure.

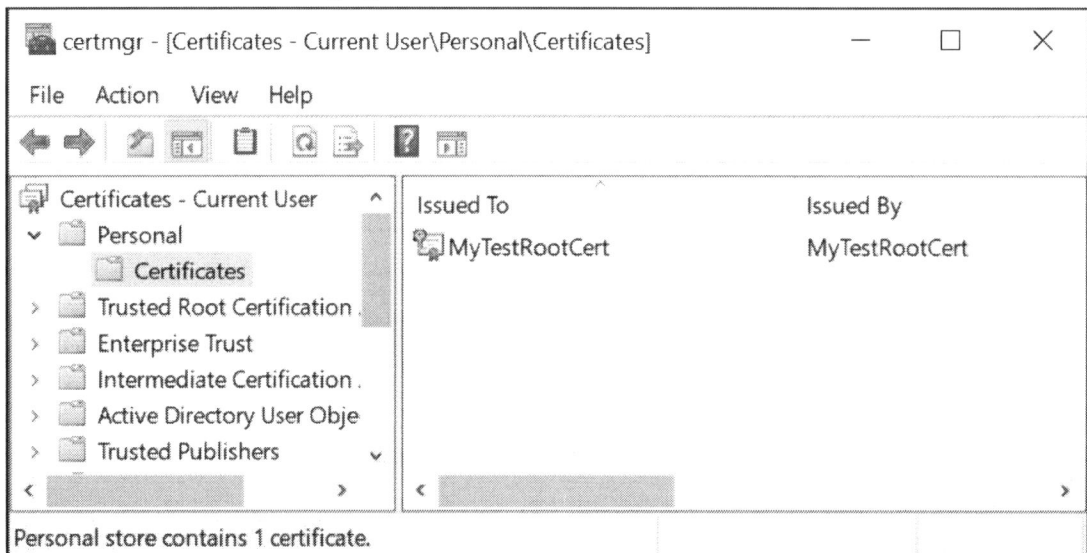

Creating Client Certificate Using Self-Signed Root Certificate

Each user's machine that would like to connect to the Azure virtual network using Point-to-Site VPN needs to generate and install client certificate. This can be done by using the self-signed root certificate. After that, you need to export and install the client certificate on the user's machine before the client can authenticate to the Azure VPN gateway.

On the machine, where you generate the client certificate, this certificate will automatically be installed. You can export this client certificate, and import and install on another machine from which you may wish to connect Azure virtual network.

Since we have just created the self-signed root certificate, we can create a child certificate for clients. For this, you need to perform the following steps:

1. We assume that you have the active PowerShell session with administrative privileges. Now, execute the following command to view the installed root certificate.
   ```
   Get-ChildItem -Path "Cert:\CurrentUser\My"
   ```
2. Copy the **thumbprint text** (of your root certificate) displayed by executing the above command. Please refer the following figure.

3. In case, if there are more than one root certificates on your system, make sure you copy the thumbprint value of your root certificate that you generated in the previous step. In our case, MyTestRootCert.

4. Now, specify the variable for your root certificate using the thumbprint text copied from the previous step. Replace your THUMBPRINT text in the following command.

```
$cert = Get-ChildItem -Path
"Cert:\CurrentUser\My\854517900DA1EFF6FB2F86BD3AB1D5A6865AC5E5"
```

5. Now, execute the following command to generate the client certificate using the self-signed certificate you created earlier. Replace the client certificate **DnsName** and **CN** name values appropriately. In this case, it is MyTestClientCert.

```
New-SelfSignedCertificate -Type Custom -DnsName MyTestClientCert -
KeySpec Signature `
-Subject "CN=MyTestClientCert" -KeyExportPolicy Exportable `
-HashAlgorithm sha256 -KeyLength 2048 `
-CertStoreLocation "Cert:\CurrentUser\My" `
-Signer $cert -TextExtension @("2.5.29.37={text}1.3.6.1.5.5.7.3.2")
```

6. The client certificate will be created and automatically installed under the "**Current User\Personal\Certificates**" location in the **Certificate Manager** as shown in the following figure.

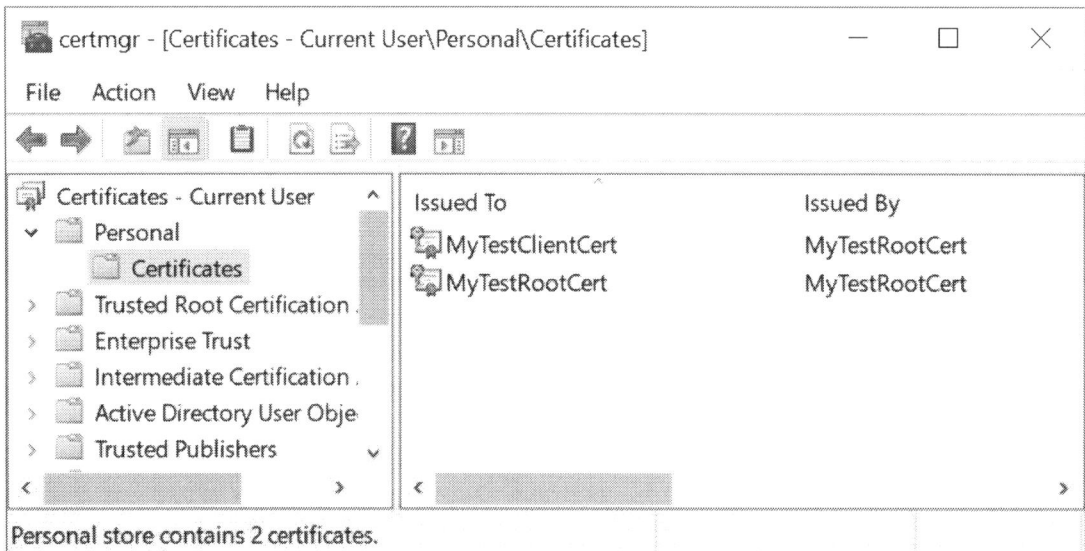

7. Now, you have created VPN root and client certificates for Azure certificate-based P2S authentication.

Exporting Root Certificate's Public File

To export your self-signed root certificate's public file, you need to perform the following steps:

1. Select and right-click your root certificate in the **Certificate Manager** window (MyTestRootCert).
2. Select **All Tasks** and then select **Export** as shown in the following figure.

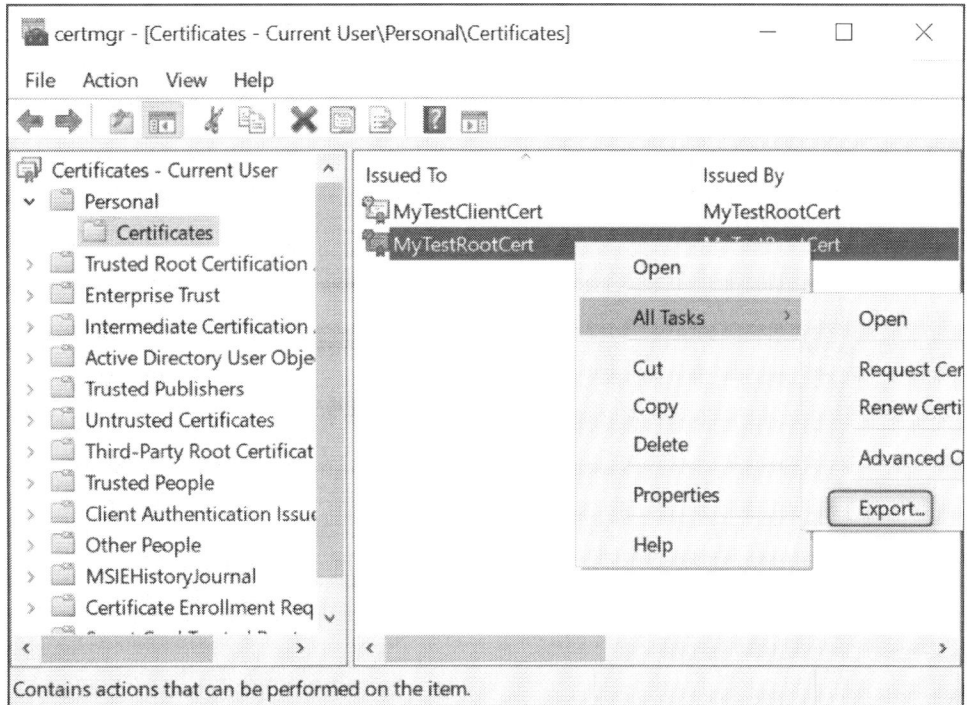

3. On the **Welcome** page of the **Certificate Export** wizard, click **Next**.
4. On the **Export private key** page, make sure **Do not export private key** option is selected as shown in the following figure and then click **Next**.

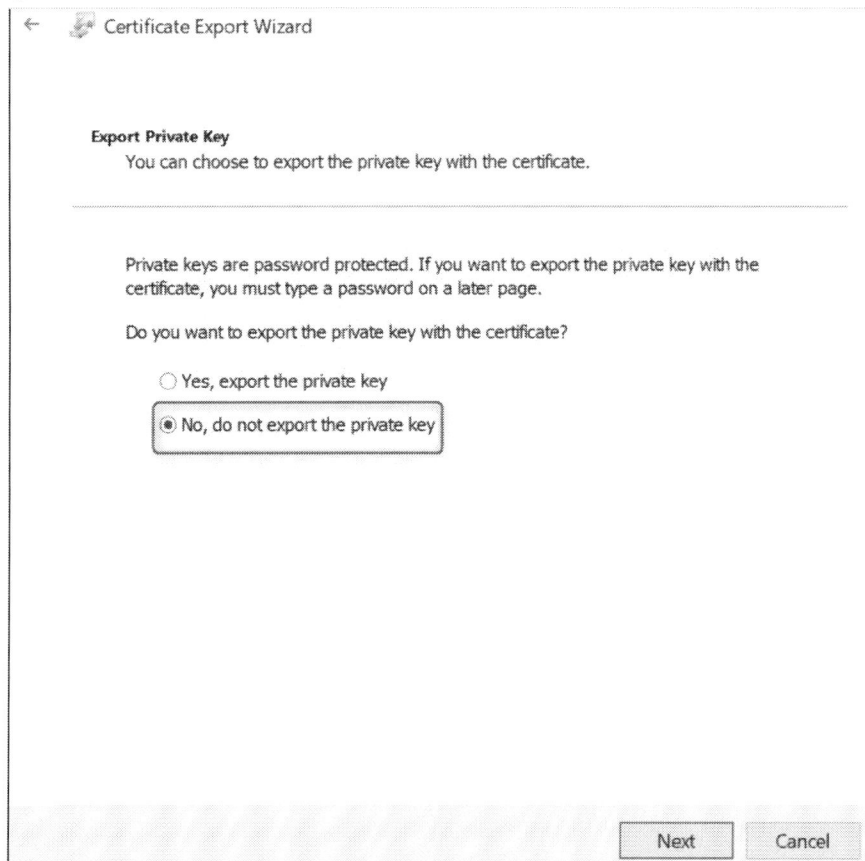

5. On the **Export file format** page, select the **Base-64 encoded X.509 (.CER)** option as shown in the following figure and then click **Next**.

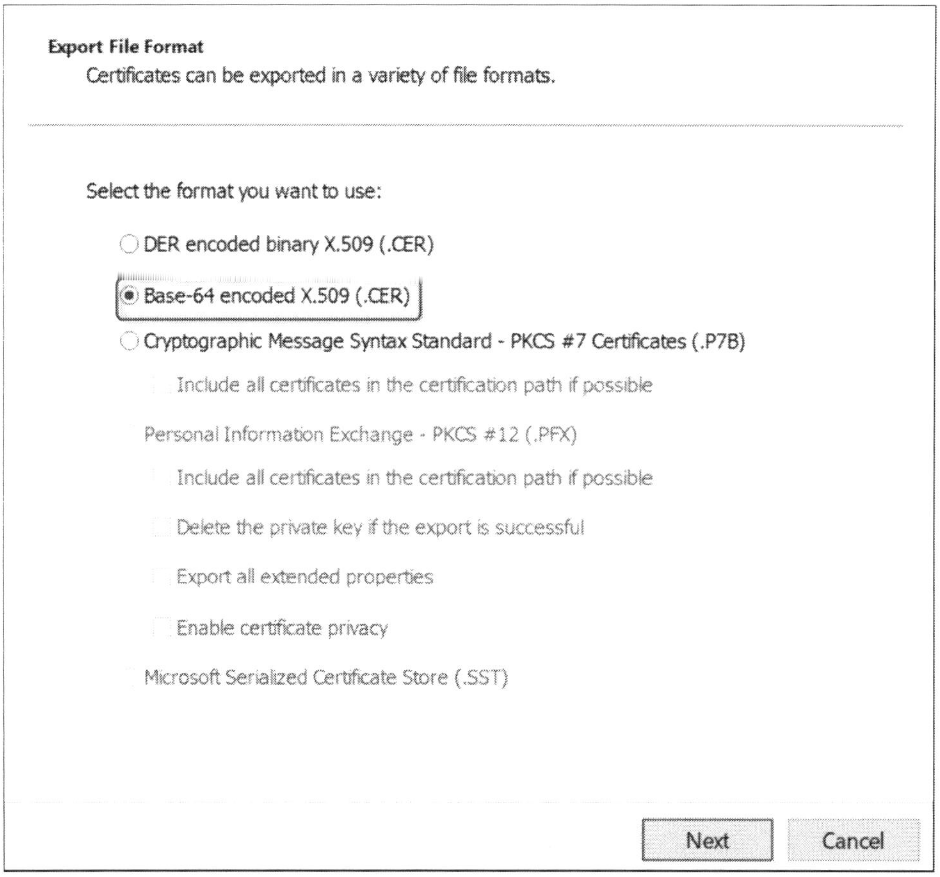

Export File Format
Certificates can be exported in a variety of file formats.

Select the format you want to use:

○ DER encoded binary X.509 (.CER)

◉ Base-64 encoded X.509 (.CER)

○ Cryptographic Message Syntax Standard - PKCS #7 Certificates (.P7B)

　　Include all certificates in the certification path if possible

Personal Information Exchange - PKCS #12 (.PFX)

　　Include all certificates in the certification path if possible

　　Delete the private key if the export is successful

　　Export all extended properties

　　Enable certificate privacy

Microsoft Serialized Certificate Store (.SST)

| Next | Cancel |

6. On the **File to export** page, click **Browse**, select **Desktop** as location and specify **MyTestRoot.cer** as a file name as shown in the following figure.

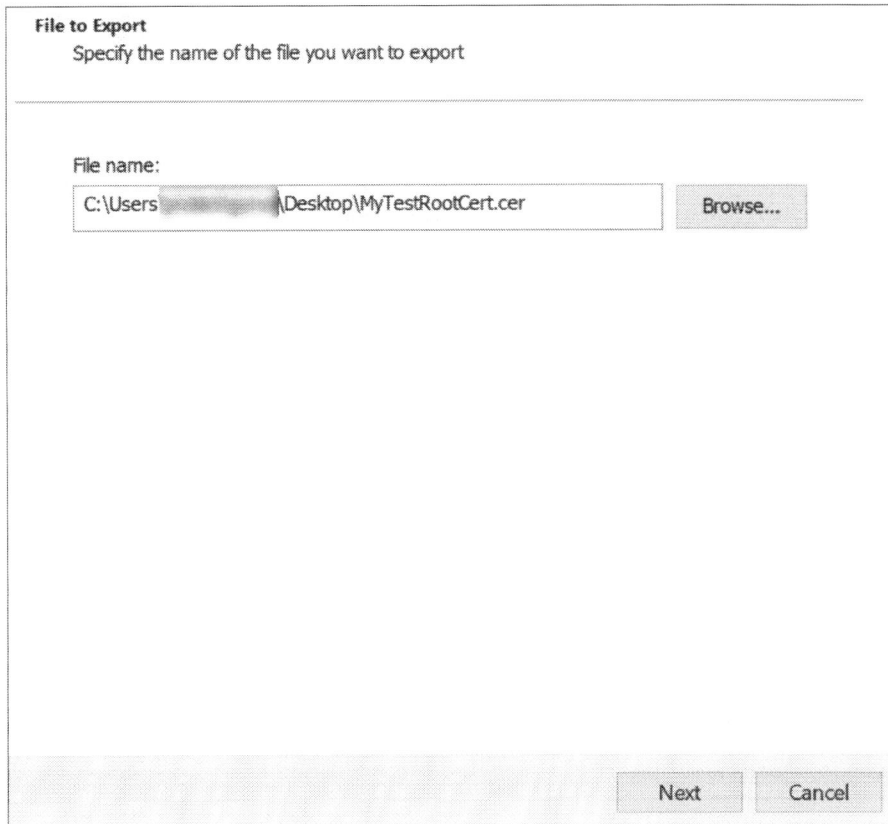

File to Export
Specify the name of the file you want to export

File name:

C:\Users [redacted] \Desktop\MyTestRootCert.cer   Browse...

Next   Cancel

7. Click **Next**, click **Finish**, and then click **OK** to finish the wizard. The certificate's public file (MyTestRootCert.cer) will be exported to the selected location.

8. Now, select the exported public file and open it with notepad. You will see the text something like as shown in the following figure.

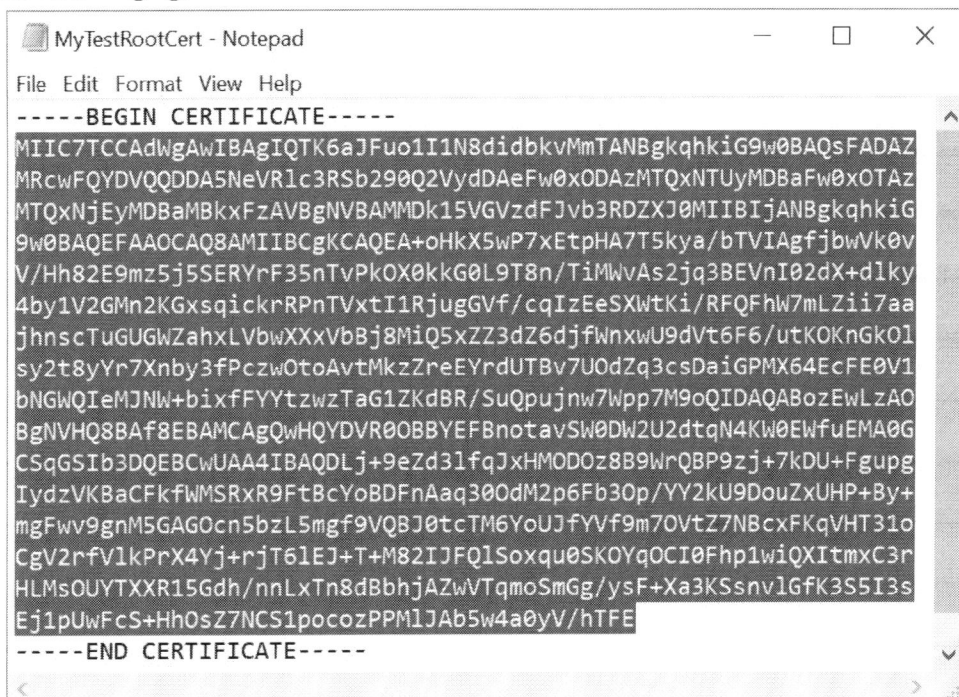

MyTestRootCert - Notepad

File   Edit   Format   View   Help

```
-----BEGIN CERTIFICATE-----
MIIC7TCCAdWgAwIBAgIQTK6aJFuo1I1N8didbkvMmTANBgkqhkiG9w0BAQsFADAZ
MRcwFQYDVQQDDA5eVR1c3RSb290Q2VydDAeFw0x0DAzMTQxNTUyMDBaFw0x0TAz
MTQxNjEyMDBaMBkxFzAVBgNVBAMMDk15VGVzdFJvb3RDZXJ0MIIBIjANBgkqhkiG
9w0BAQEFAAOCAQ8AMIIBCgKCAQEA+oHkX5wP7xEtpHA7T5kya/bTVIAgfjbwVk0v
V/Hh82E9mz5j5SERYrF35nTvPkOX0kkG0L9T8n/TiMWvAs2jq3BEVnI02dX+dlky
4by1V2GMn2KGxsqickrRPnTVxtI1RjugGVf/cqIzEeSXWtKi/RFQFhW7mLZii7aa
jhnscTuGUGWZahxLVbwXXxVbBj8MiQ5xZZ3dZ6djfWnxwU9dVt6F6/utKOKnGkOl
sy2t8yYr7Xnby3fPczwOtoAvtMkzZreEYrdUTBv7UOdZq3csDaiGPMX64EcFE0V1
bNGWQIeMJNW+bixfFYYtzwzTaG1ZKdBR/SuQpujnw7Wpp7M9oQIDAQABozEwLzAO
BgNVHQ8BAf8EBAMCAgQwHQYDVR0OBBYEFBnotavSW0DW2U2dtqN4KW0EWfuEMA0G
CSqGSIb3DQEBCwUAA4IBAQDLj+9eZd3lfqJxHMODOz8B9WrQBP9zj+7kDU+Fgupg
IydzVKBaCFkfWMSRxR9FtBcYoBDFnAaq30OdM2p6Fb3Op/YY2kU9DouZxUHP+By+
mgFwv9gnM5GAGOcn5bzL5mgf9VQBJ0tcTM6YoUJfYVf9m7OVtZ7NBcxFKqVHT31o
CgV2rfVlkPrX4Yj+rjT6lEJ+T+M82IJFQlSoxqu0SKOYqOCI0Fhp1wiQXItmxC3r
HLMsOUYTXXR15Gdh/nnLxTn8dBbhjAZwVTqmoSmGg/ysF+Xa3KSsnvlGfK3S5I3s
Ej1pUwFcS+HhOsZ7NCS1pocozPPMlJAb5w4a0yV/hTFE
-----END CERTIFICATE-----
```

9. We will upload this certificate public key text later in Azure Cloud for P2S certificate-based authentication.

Exporting Client Certificates and Private Key

Now, export the client certificate along with its private key. For this, you need to perform the following steps:

1. In the **Certificate Manager** window, select **MyTestClient** certificate, select **All Tasks**, and then select **Export**.
2. On the **Welcome** page, click **Next**.
3. On the **Export private key** page, select **Yes, export the private key** option and then click **Next**.
4. On the **Export file format** page, make sure that the default options are selected as shown in the following figure and then click **Next**.

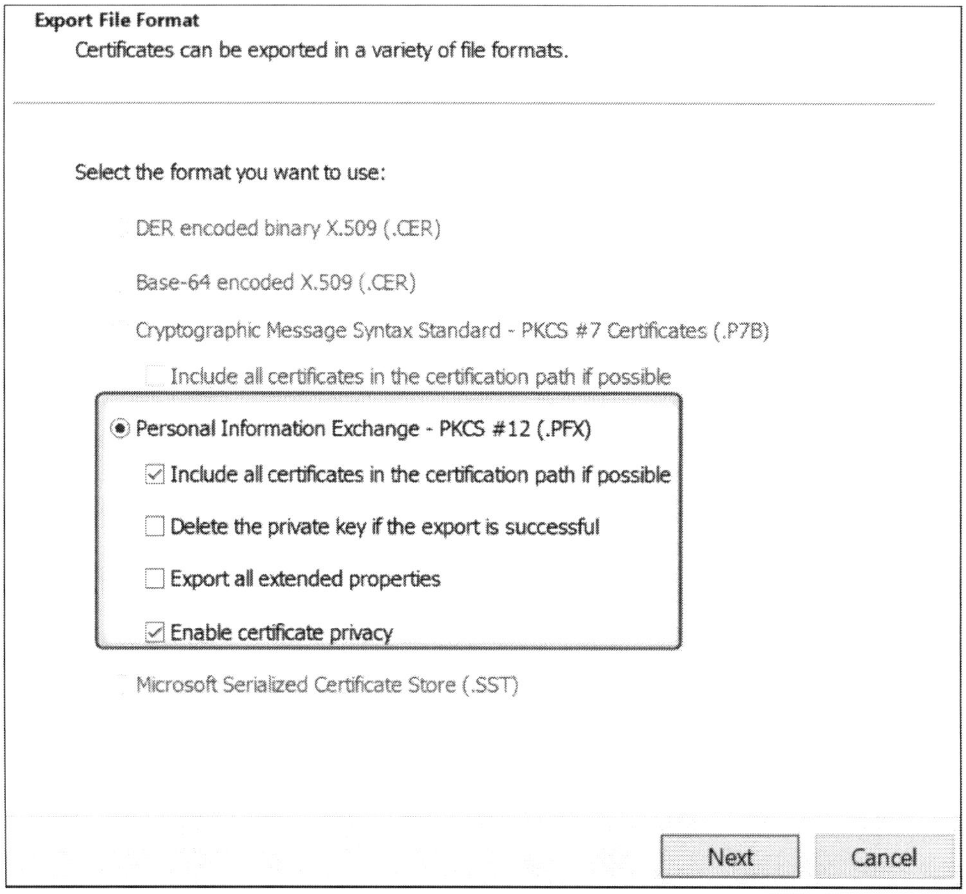

10. On the **Security** page, specify a password to secure the private key as shown in the following figure and then click **Next**.

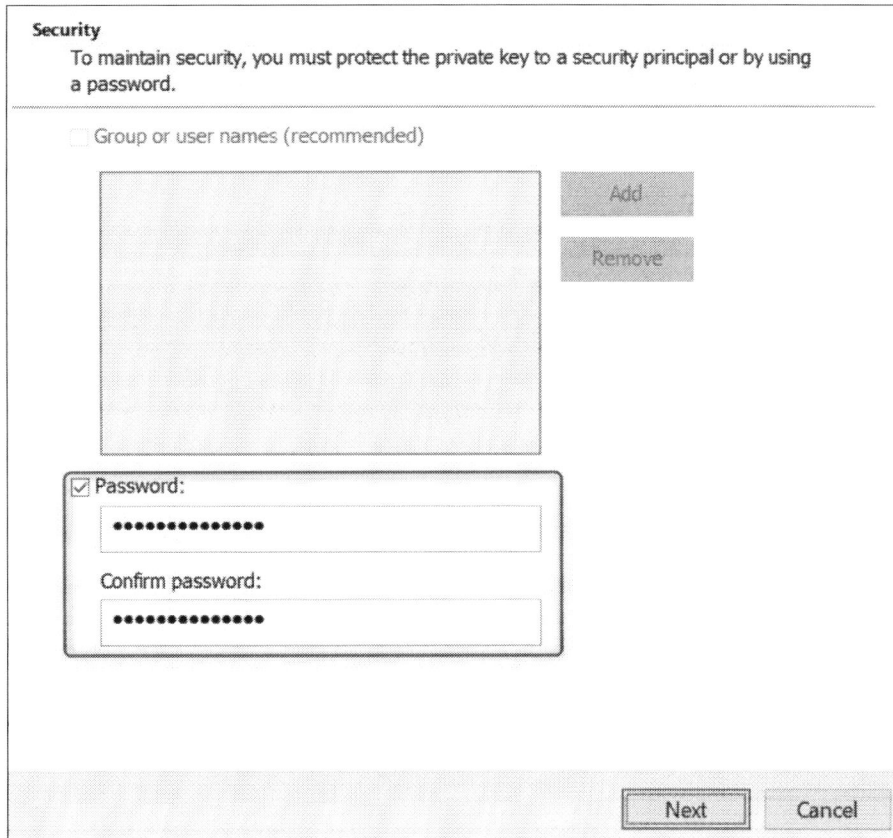

Security

To maintain security, you must protect the private key to a security principal or by using a password.

Group or user names (recommended)

Add

Remove

☑ Password:

••••••••••••••

Confirm password:

••••••••••••••

Next   Cancel

11. On the **File to export** page, click **Browse**, select the location where you want to save this certificate.
12. Specify a certificate name such as **MyTestClientCert** and then click **Next**.
13. Click **Finish** and then click **OK** to finish the wizard. Your client certificate will be exported and saved in the given location.

Installing Azure VPN Certificates on Clients

Now, you can copy and install this certificate on the client machine which supposed to connect Azure virtual network using the Azure VPN gateway. Depending on the client platform (Windows or Mac), you need to follow appropriate steps to install the certificate. However, the installation process is pretty simple. For more information how to install the certificate, please refer the following link:

- https://docs.microsoft.com/en-us/azure/vpn-gateway/point-to-site-how-to-vpn-client-install-azure-cert

Upload Self-Signed Root Certificate in Azure Cloud for VPN Gateway

For this, you need to perform the following steps:

1. Login to Azure Portal, navigate to the **Virtual Network Gateway** section.
2. Select the Virtual network gateway we have created earlier – **MyTestVPNGW1**.
3. On the **virtual network gateway** settings blade, select **Point-to-site configuration** and the click **Configure now** as shown in the following figure.

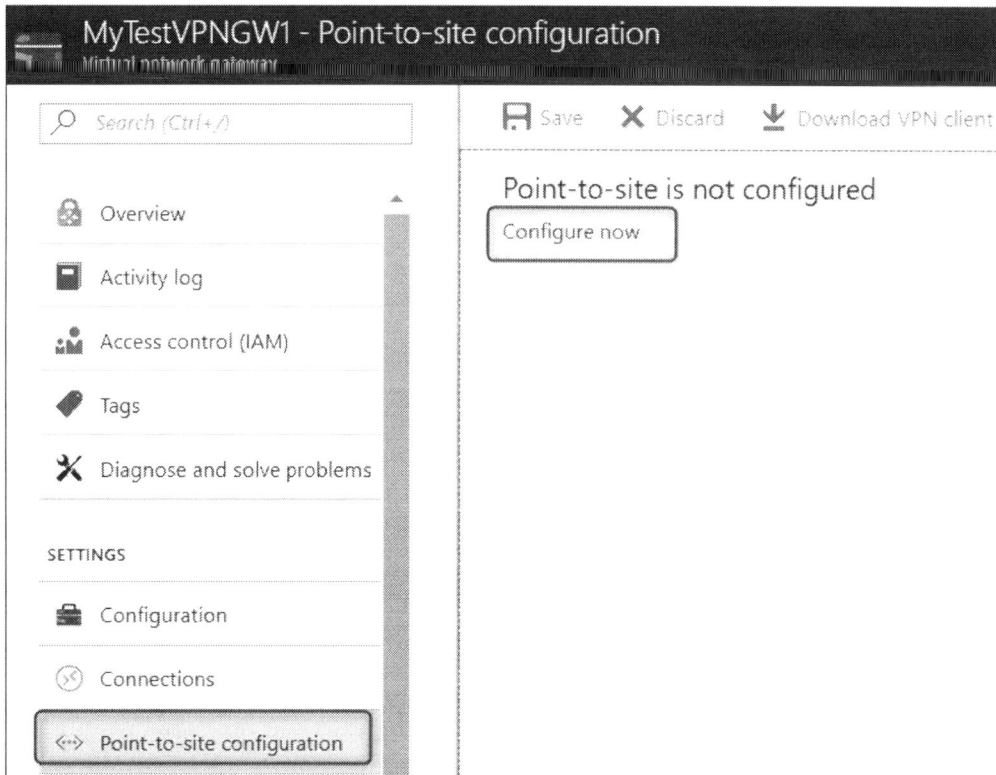

4. On the **Address pool** box, specify the IP address subnet range from which VPN clients will get IP addresses. For this lab exercise, let us use **172.16.100.0/24**.
5. Accept the default tunnel types. (SSTP and IKEv2)
6. Under the **Authentication type**, make sure that **Azure certificate** option is selected.
7. In the **Name** text box, type a descriptive certificate name such as **MyTestRootCert**.
8. In the **Public Certificate Data** text box, paste the content of your self-signed root certificate's public (.cer) file you exported earlier. But, make sure that only the highlighted text is copied before pasting here.

```
MyTestRootCert - Notepad                    —    □    ✕
File  Edit  Format  View  Help
-----BEGIN CERTIFICATE-----
MIIC7TCCAdWgAwIBAgIQTK6aJFuo1I1N8didbkvMmTANBgkqhkiG9w0BAQsFADAZ
MRcwFQYDVQQDDA5eVRlc3RSb290Q2VydDAeFw0xODAzMTQxNTUyMDBaFw0xOTAz
MTQxNjEyMDBaMBkxFzAVBgNVBAMMDk15VGVzdFJvb3RDZXJ0MIIBIjANBgkqhkiG
9w0BAQEFAAOCAQ8AMIIBCgKCAQEA+oHkX5wP7xEtpHA7T5kya/bTVIAgfjbwVk0v
V/Hh82E9mz5j5SERYrF35nTvPkOX0kkG0L9T8n/TiMWvAs2jq3BEVnI02dX+dlky
4by1V2GMn2KGxsqickrRPnTVxtI1RjugGVf/cqIzEeSXWtKi/RFQFhW7mLZii7aa
jhnscTuGUGWZahxLVbwXXxVbBj8MiQ5xZZ3dZ6djfWnxwU9dVt6F6/utKOKnGkOl
sy2t8yYr7Xnby3fPczwOtoAvtMkzZreEYrdUTBv7UOdZq3csDaiGPMX64EcFE0V1
bNGWQIeMJNW+bixfFYYtzwzTaG1ZKdBR/SuQpujnw7Wpp7M9oQIDAQABozEwLzAO
BgNVHQ8BAf8EBAMCAgQwHQYDVR0OBBYEFBnotavSW0DW2U2dtqN4KW0EWfuEMA0G
CSqGSIb3DQEBCwUAA4IBAQDLj+9eZd3lfqJxHMODOz8B9WrQBP9zj+7kDU+Fgupg
IydzVKBaCFkfWMSRxR9FtBcYoBDFnAaq30OdM2p6Fb3Op/YY2kU9DouZxUHP+By+
mgFwv9gnM5GAGOcn5bzL5mgf9VQBJ0tcTM6YoUJfYVf9m7OVtZ7NBcxFKqVHT31o
CgV2rfVlkPrX4Yj+rjT6lEJ+T+M82IJFQlSoxqu0SKOYqOCI0Fhp1wiQXItmxC3r
HLMsOUYTXXR15Gdh/nnLxTn8dBbhjAZwVTqmoSmGg/ysF+Xa3KSsnvlGfK3S5I3s
Ej1pUwFcS+HhOsZ7NCS1pocozPPM1JAb5w4a0yV/hTFE
-----END CERTIFICATE-----
```

9. The final selection of your point-to-site configuration blade should look like as follows.

10. Click **Save** once your settings are defined appropriately.

Generating VPN Client Configuration Files

Now you need to generate VPN client package configuration file that clients will use to authenticate and connect to Azure virtual networks. For this, you need to perform the following steps:

1. In the **Point-to-site configuration** blade, click **Download VPN client** link as shown in the following figure.

2. It will take a few minutes to generate client configuration package files. A zip file will be downloaded on your system that will contain Generic, WindowsAmd64, and WindowsX86 architecture-based client packages files.
3. Copy and move the VPN client zip file to the destination client form where you would like to connect Azure virtual network.
4. Extract the zip file and execute the appropriate client package file depending on your system architecture (32-bit or 64-bit). For Windows 10 system, you will see something like the following warning.

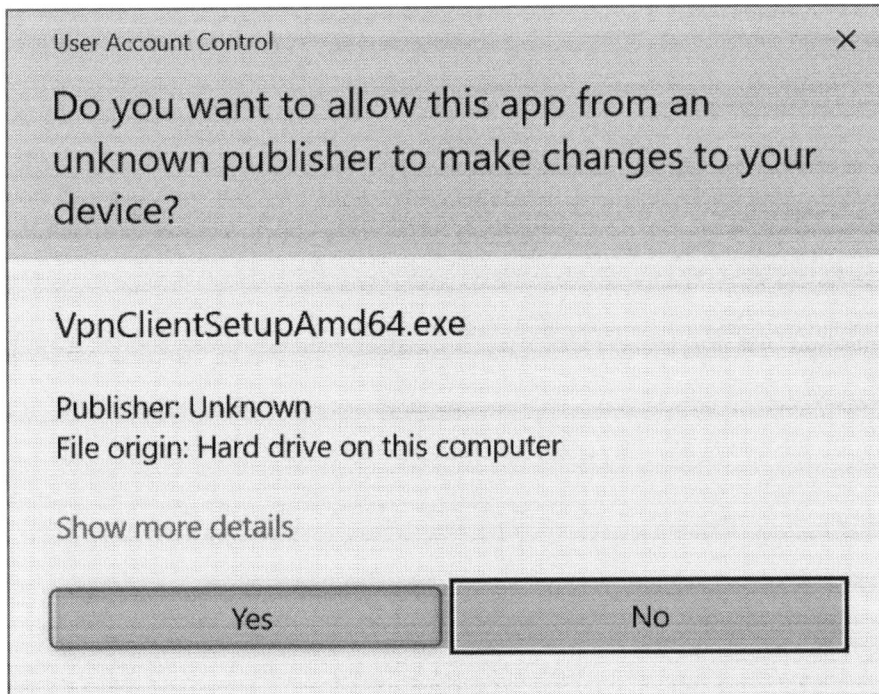

User Account Control

Do you want to allow this app from an unknown publisher to make changes to your device?

VpnClientSetupAmd64.exe

Publisher: Unknown
File origin: Hard drive on this computer

Show more details

Yes   No

5. Click **Yes** to proceed and then again click **Yes** to install VPN client package file. You may need to allow your **Antivirus** to run the VPN client package file.
6. Once installed, a VPN connection will be created on the client machine. Open the **network settings** and select **VPN**.
7. Select the created VPN connection (in our case – MyTestVPNVnet1) and then click **Connect** as shown in the following figure

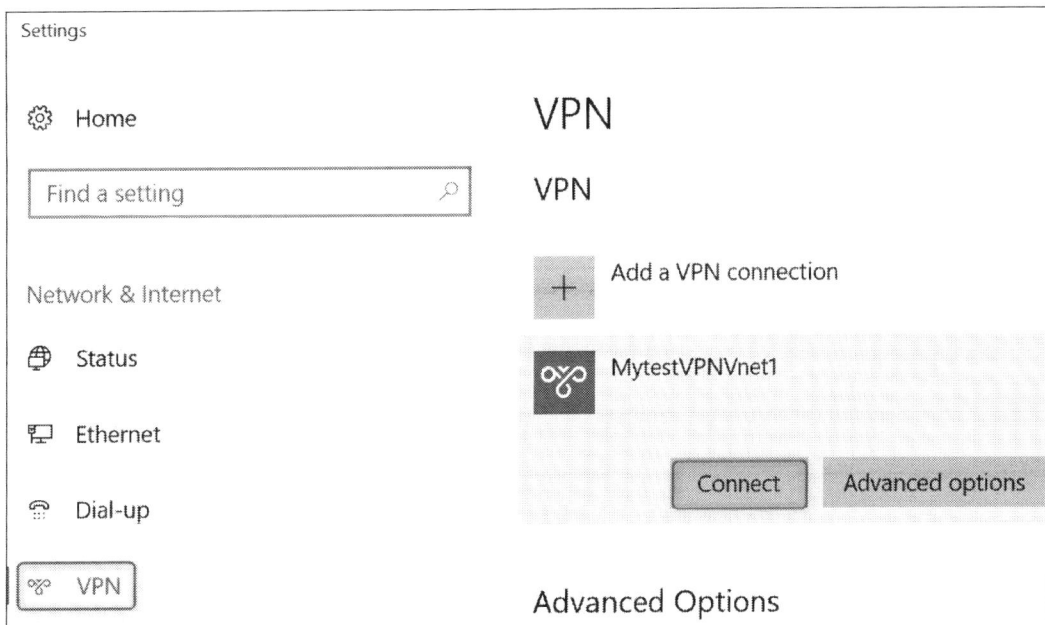

Settings

Home

Find a setting

Network & Internet

Status

Ethernet

Dial-up

VPN

VPN

VPN

+   Add a VPN connection

&&& MytestVPNVnet1

Connect   Advanced options

Advanced Options

8. On the VPN connection pop-up window, click **Connect** as shown in the following figure.

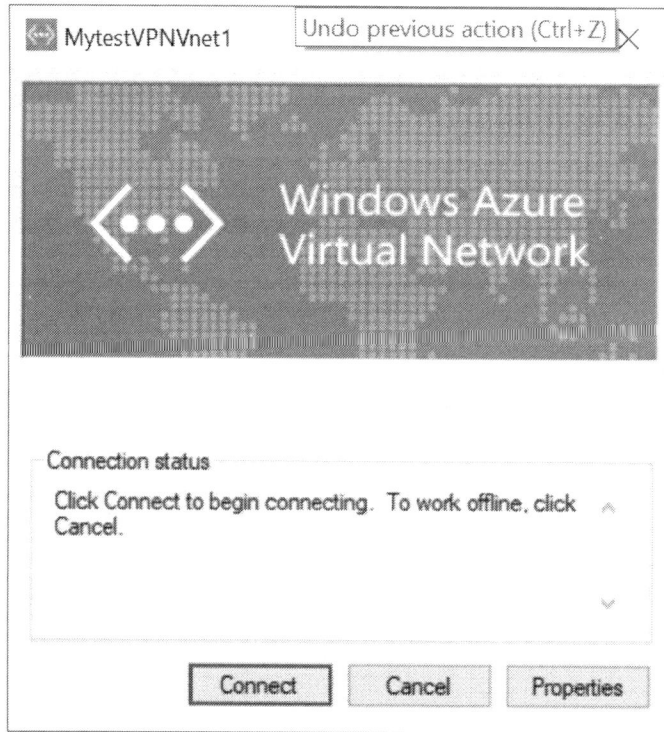

9. If everything followed correctly, you will be connected to the Azure virtual network using the P2S VPN connection. You will also get an IP address from the given address pool under the P2S connection configuration options as shown in the following figure.

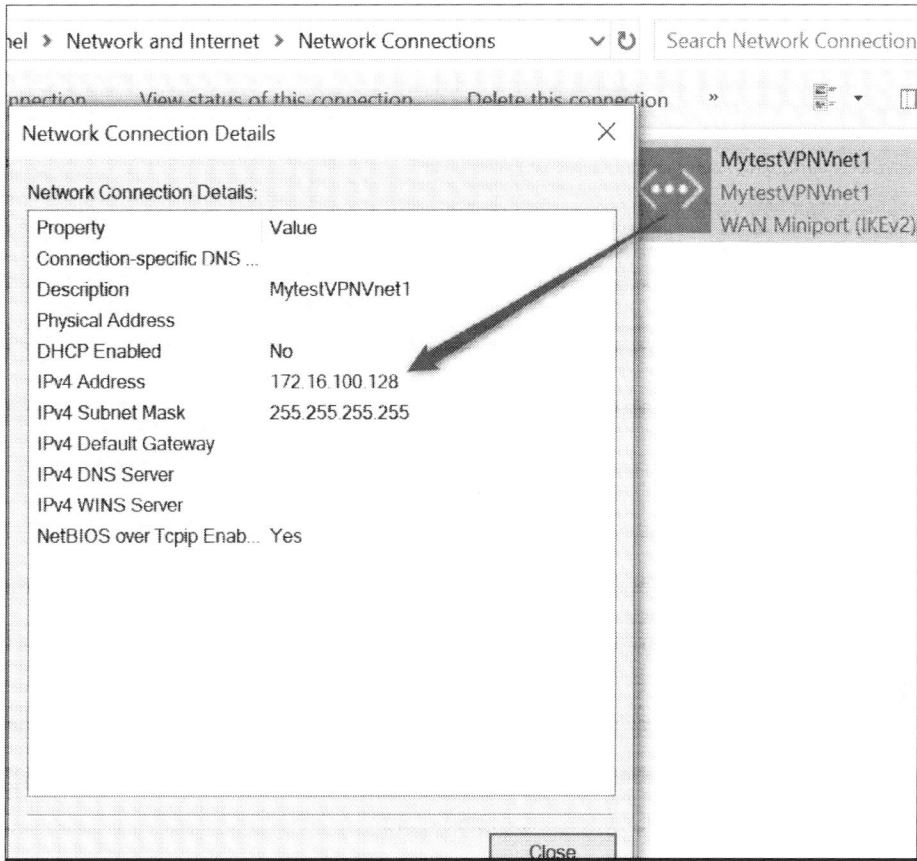

Network Connection Details

Property	Value
Connection-specific DNS ...	
Description	MytestVPNVnet1
Physical Address	
DHCP Enabled	No
IPv4 Address	172.16.100.128
IPv4 Subnet Mask	255.255.255.255
IPv4 Default Gateway	
IPv4 DNS Server	
IPv4 WINS Server	
NetBIOS over Tcpip Enab...	Yes

10. Now, you can securely connect Azure cloud resources and services using P2S VPN connection. However, you still need to adjust your network security group (NSG) rules to allow connections and protocols to VPN Virtual network. We have explored it in the next section.

That's all you need to know about how to create, configure, and connect using an Azure Virtual Private Gateway with Point-to-Site VPN connection in Azure Cloud. In the next section, we will create a Windows Server 2016 Azure VM and will connect RDP using the P2S VPN connection with the VM's private IP address securely from your local machine.

Lab 34: Creating a Windows Server Virtual Machine

In this quick hands-on lab, we will explain how to create a Windows virtual machine such as Windows Server 2016 Datacenter. However, the process is simple but just have a look the settings we are going to select. We will use this virtual machine for next few lab exercises. The virtual machine configuration settings should be as follows:

- Operating System: **Windows Server 2016 Datacenter**
- VM size: **DS1_V2**
- VM Name: **MyTestServer2** (You can also give its name as MyTestServer1)
- Virtual network: **MyTestVPNvNet1**
- Subnet: **MyTestVPNSubnet1**
- Public IP: **None**
- Resource Group: **MyTestRG**
- Region: **South India**

To create a virtual machine with the above-mentioned settings, you need to perform the following steps:

1. Navigate to the **Add virtual machine** blade in the Azure Portal.
2. In the **Compute** gallery, select **Windows Server 2016 Datacenter** as shown in the following figure.

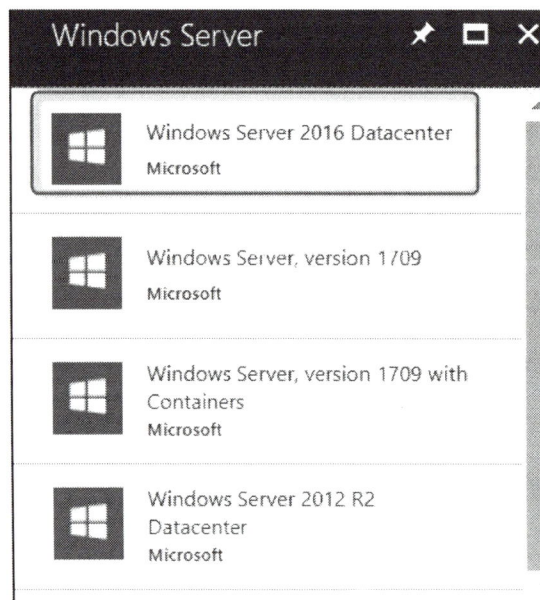

3. Click **Create** to proceed.
4. On the **Basics** blade, specify the following values.
    - Name: **MyTestServer2**
    - VM Disk Type: **SSD**
    - User: **winadmin**
    - Password: as you wish
    - Resource Group: **MyTestRG**
    - Location **South India**
5. Click **OK** to proceed on the next blade.

6. On the **Size** blade, select **DS1_V2** as shown in the following figure.

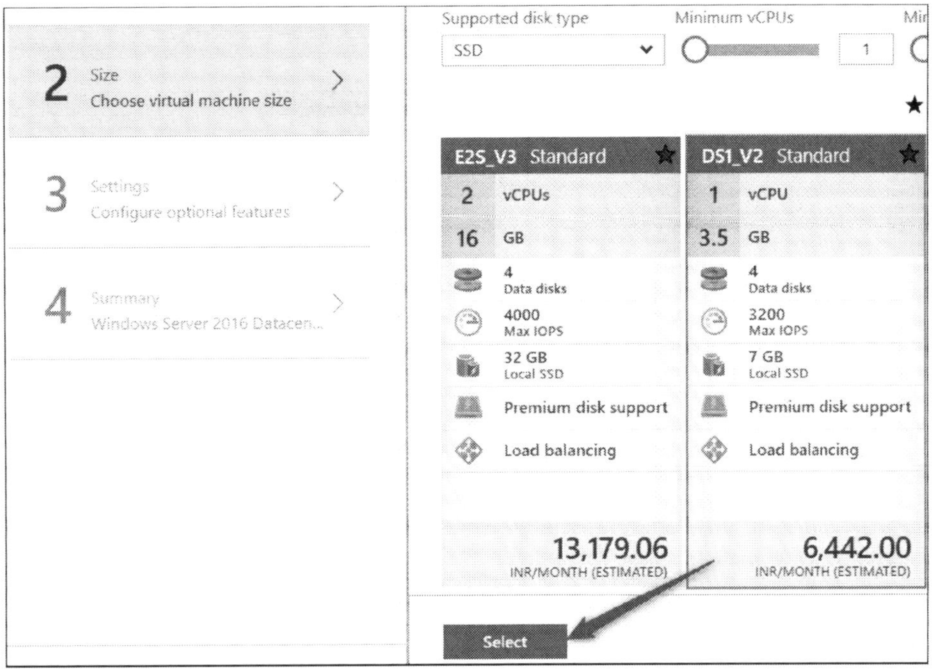

7. On the **Settings** blade, adjust your virtual machine's settings as follow.
   - Availability set: **None**
   - Virtual Network: **MyTestVPNVnet1**
   - Subnet: **MyTestVPNSubnet1**
   - Public IP address: **None**
   - Network Security Group: **MyTestServer2-nsg**
8. Accept the rest of the options with the default settings as shown in the following figure.

			No	Yes	
1	Basics Done	✓			

Network

* Virtual network ❶
>
MytestVPNVnet1

* Subnet ❶
>
MytestVPNSubnet1 (192.168.1...

* Public IP address ❶
>
None

* Network security group (firewall) ❶
>
(new) MyTestServer2-nsg

2 Size
Choose virtual machine size >

3 Settings
~~Configure optional features~~

4 Summary
Windows Server 2016 Datacen...

Extensions

Extensions ❶
>
No extensions

Auto-shutdown

Enable auto-shutdown ❶

Off	On

OK

9. On the **Summary** page, review your selected settings and modify them if something was selected incorrectly.
10. Click **Create** to complete the wizard. The virtual machine will be deployed and ready in few minutes. We will use this VM to connect using Azure P2S VPN connection.

Lab 35: Connecting Your Windows VM Using P2S VPN Gateway Securely

In the previous lab exercise, we have created a P2S VPN gateway and installed the client certificate on Windows 10 client. Now, let's connect our Windows Server VM using the P2S VPN connection. For this, you need to perform the following steps:

Allow your MyTestServer2-nsg to communicate with the VPN gateway network to access RDP. For this, you need to perform the following steps:

1. Select **MyTestServer2** VM and navigate to the **Networking** section.
2. In the right blade, select the default created RDP allow inbound rule.
3. Change the **Source IP Address/CIDR ranges** from * to **172.16.100.0/24**. So the only VPN connection established clients can access RDP of this server as shown in the following figure.

4. Click **Save** to save the changes.
5. Now switch on to Windows 10 client where you have installed the VPN client certificate.
6. Under **Network and Internet Settings**, connect to your Azure VPN Gateway network using the VPN connection as shown in the following figure.

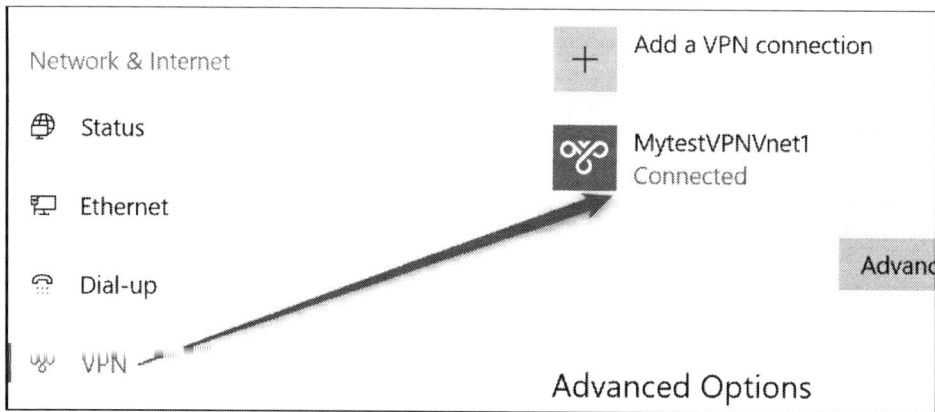

Network & Internet

Add a VPN connection

Status

MytestVPNVnet1
Connected

Ethernet

Dial-up

Advanced Options

7. Open the **MSTSC** dialog box and type the Private IP Address of your server. In our case, **192.168.1.4**.
8. Click **Connect** to access RDP, you will be asked to provide the username and password you set during the VM creation.
9. Specify the credentials and click **OK** to connect as shown in the following figure.

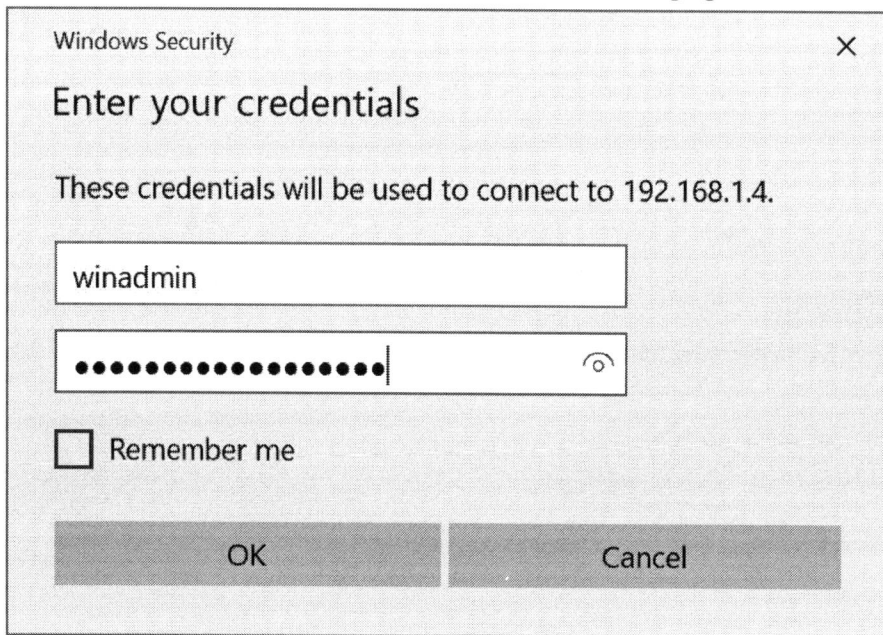

Windows Security ✕

Enter your credentials

These credentials will be used to connect to 192.168.1.4.

```
winadmin
```

```
••••••••••••••••••••
```

☐ Remember me

OK   Cancel

10. Accept the certificate warning and click **Yes** to proceed.
11. You will be connected to **MyTestServer2** VM securely using Azure P2S VPN connection. That's all you need to create and configure Azure VPN network connection, and connect from a Windows client using the P2S VPN connection.

Lab 36: Configuring vNet Peering Between Azure Virtual Networks

By default, subnets inside an Azure virtual network are allowed to communicate to each other. However, one subnet of one virtual network cannot communicate with another subnet of another virtual network by default. To allow communication between different subnets of different azure virtual networks, you must create and configure **vNet Peering** at the both source and destination virtual networks ends. In AWS cloud, it is called VPC (Virtual Private Cloud) Peering. VPC of AWS is equal to vNet of Azure Cloud.

The following are few of the major features and benefits of Azure vNet Peering

1. The network traffic between peered virtual networks is private.
2. As of now, vNet peering between virtual networks in the same region is available. vNet peering between virtual networks in different regions is currently in preview.
3. The IP address ranges between peered virtual networks must not be overlapped.
4. IP address ranges cannot be added to or deleted from the address space of a virtual network once a virtual network is peered with another virtual network.
5. The traffic between resources in peered virtual networks is routed directly through the Microsoft backbone infrastructure, not through Internet.

Azure vNet Peering Diagram

Let's assume that we have the following azure virtual network diagram and want to configure vNet peering between these virtual networks.

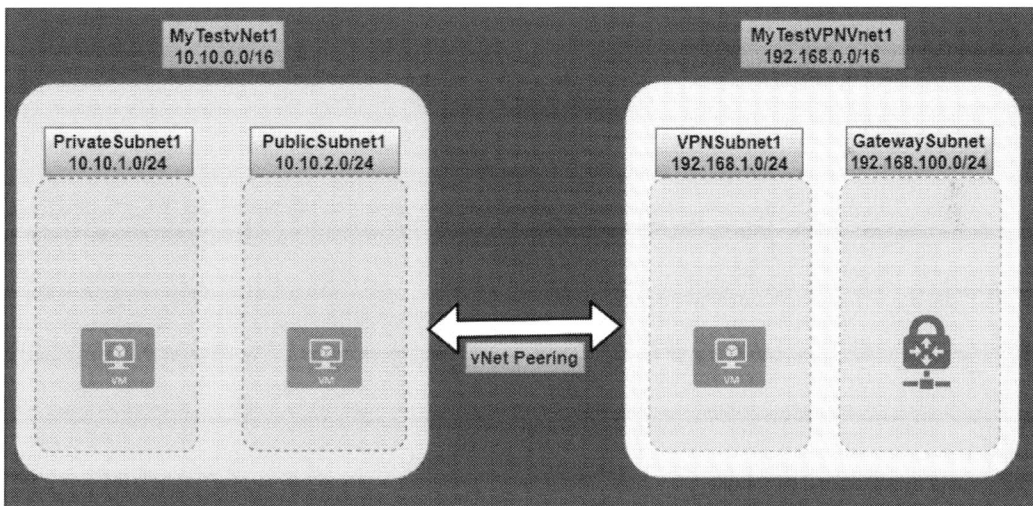

Creating vNet Peering at Source Virtual Network

For this, first you need to create a vNet peering at source virtual network end. In order to do so, you need to perform the following steps:

1. Select the source virtual network such as **MyTestVPNVnet1**. Let's assume this is our source virtual network.
2. Navigate to the P**eering** section and click **Add** to add a vNet peering connection as shown in the following figure.

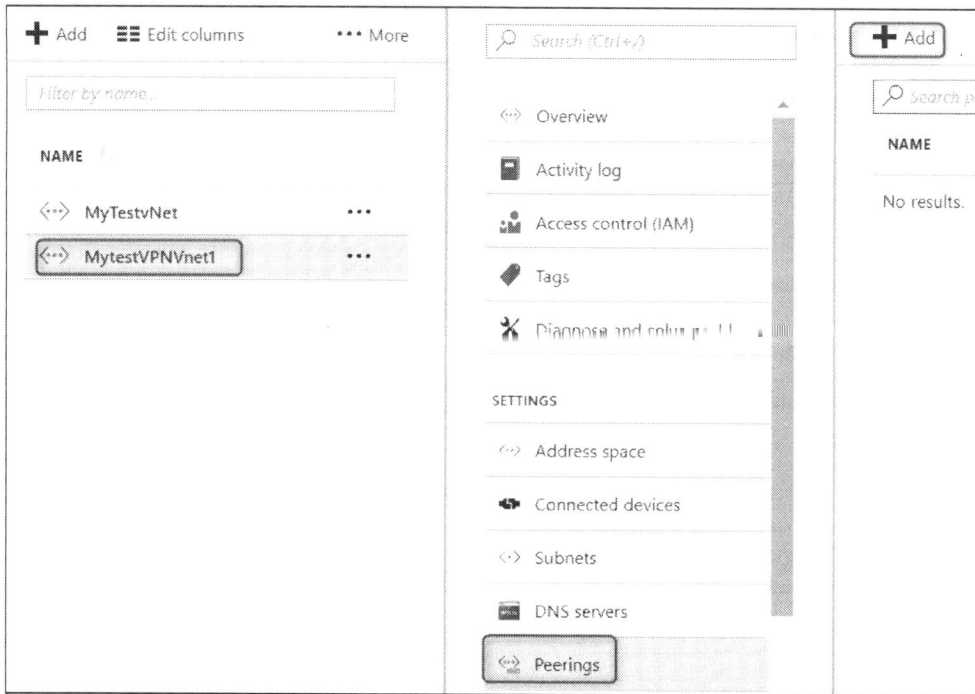

Add	Edit columns	⋯ More	🔍 Search (Ctrl+/)	➕ Add

Filter by name..

NAME

‹··› MyTestvNet ⋯

‹··› MytestVPNVnet1 ⋯

‹··› Overview

▪ Activity log

👤 Access control (IAM)

🏷 Tags

✖ Diagnose and solve pr... ⬅

SETTINGS

‹··› Address space

🔌 Connected devices

‹··› Subnets

▦ DNS servers

‹··› Peerings

🔍 Search pe

NAME

No results.

3. On the **Add peering** blade, specify the vNet peering name such as **MyTestvNetPeer1**.
4. Select the destination virtual network to which you want to create vNet peering, in our case **MyTestvNet**.
5. Select **Allow gateway transit** if your source vNet has also been configured with Azure Gateway connection, in our case, VPN Gateway Connection.
6. Once the settings are defined appropriately as shown in the following figure, click **OK** to proceed.

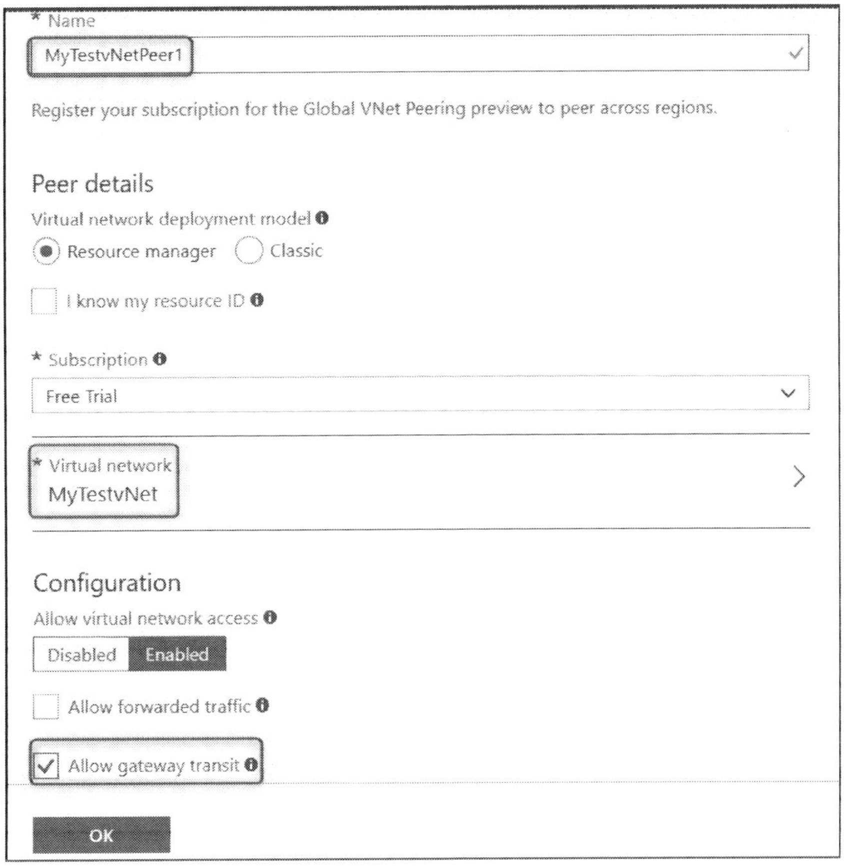

7. The vNet peering connection will be created at source virtual network end. However, it will remain in the **Initiated state** as shown in the following figure until you create vNet Peering at the destination virtual network end.

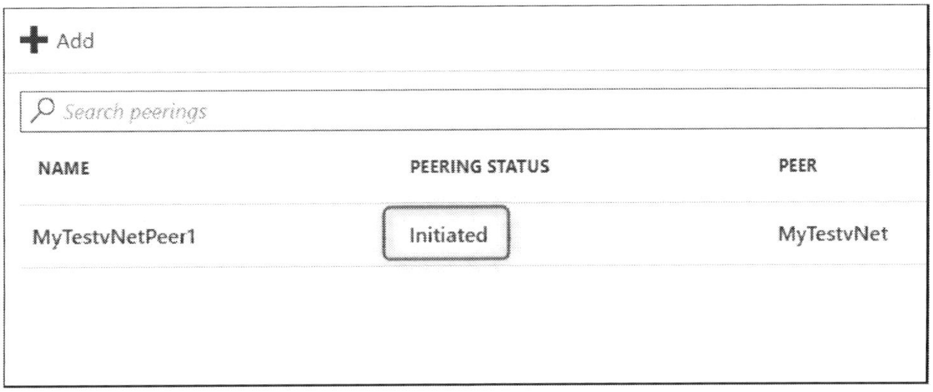

Creating vNet Peering at Destination Virtual Network

Now, create an another vNet peering connection at the destination virtual network end (in our case – MyTestvNet1) with the following settings:

- Name: **MyTestvNetPeer2**
- Virtual network: **MyTestVPNVnet1** (Virtual network to which you want to create peer).

- Configuration: **Use remote gateway**. (select this option if you want to use peer's virtual network gateway such as VPN connection).

Once created, the peering state will change from initiated to connected at both virtual network ends as shown in the following figure.

Verifying vNet Peering Between Azure Virtual Networks

If the **vNet Peering** was successful, you will be able to access resources from the peered source virtual network to the peered destination virtual network. However, your NSG rules at the both virtual network sides must allow the connection for the protocol such as (RDP, ICMP) you want to test. The good thing is that - by default, connections between subnets within azure virtual network and with the peered virtual networks is allowed.

In a previous lab exercise (Create VM from captured Image), we have created **MyTestVM2** in 10.10.1.0/24 subnet of the MyTestvNet virtual network. Start **MyTestVM2**, connect to Azure VPN connection on your Windows 10 client. Take RDP of **MyTestServer2** (192.168.1.4).

From MyTestServer2 VM, try to take RDP of MyTestVM2 (10.10.1.6), you will be able to take RDP of MyTestVM2 if everything followed correctly. Otherwise, you may need to check the NSG rules applied at MyTestVM2 & MyTestServer2 virtual machines, and **MyTestvNet** & **MyTestVPNvNet1** virtual networks.

Deleting vNet Peering

Deleting vNet peering is a very simple task. Just go to the peering section of the virtual network, select the vNet peering you want to delete and then click **Delete** as shown in the following figure.

That's all you need to create, configure, and delete vNet peering in Azure Cloud.

Lab 37: Working with Load Balancers in Azure Cloud

Like other load balancers, an Azure Load Balancer also provides high availability and network performance to your applications. Azure Load Balancer comes with Basic and Standard tiers.

You can configure an Azure Load Balancer for the following purposes:

1. To load balance incoming Internet traffic to virtual machines hosted in the Azure cloud (Internet facing load balancer).
2. To load balance traffic between virtual machines in a virtual network (Internal load balancer)
3. To forward external traffic to a specific virtual machine.

Azure Load Balancer Features

Azure load balancer has many great features, few of them are mentioned following:

1. **Hash-based distribution**: Azure load balancer uses a 5-tuple hash: source IP, source port, destination IP, destination port, and protocol type.
2. **Port forwarding**: Azure Load Balancer allows you to define custom ports for inbound communication.
3. **Automatic reconfiguration**: Azure Load Balancer can reconfigure itself whenever scaling of instances goes up or down.
4. **Service monitoring**: Azure Load Balancer can check and validate the health of the various server instances.
5. **Source NAT**: With Azure load balancer, all outbound traffic to the Internet that initiates from your internal VMs (service) goes through source NAT (SNAT).

Azure Load Balancer Techniques

There are various methods available in the Azure cloud to distribute the traffic:

1. **Azure Load Balancer**: Since it works at the transport layer of the OSI model, hence it provides network-level distribution of traffic across instances of an application.
2. **Application Gateway**: It works at the application layer of the OSI model. It acts as a reverse-proxy service. It terminates the client connection and forwards requests to the back-end endpoints.
3. **Traffic Manager**: It works at the Domain name service (DNS) level. It uses DNS responses to direct end-user traffic to globally distributed endpoints.
   The following table shows the quick comparison of all these three load balancer techniques.

Service	Azure Load Balancer	Application Gateway	Traffic Manager
Layer	Transport layer	Application layer	DNS level
Supported protocols	Any	HTTP, HTTPS, WebSockets	Any
Supported Endpoints	Azure VMs, Cloud Services role	Internal IP, Public IP, Azure VMs, Cloud Services	Azure VMs, Cloud Services, Azure Web Apps, External Endpoints
Supported vNet	Internal-facing and Internet-facing IPs	Internal-facing and Internet-facing IPs	Only Internet-facing IPs

Note: Basic tier VMs do not support Azure load balancer feature.

Lab 38: Configuring Azure Load Balancer

In this lab exercise, we will configure and test an Azure load balancer as per the following topology.

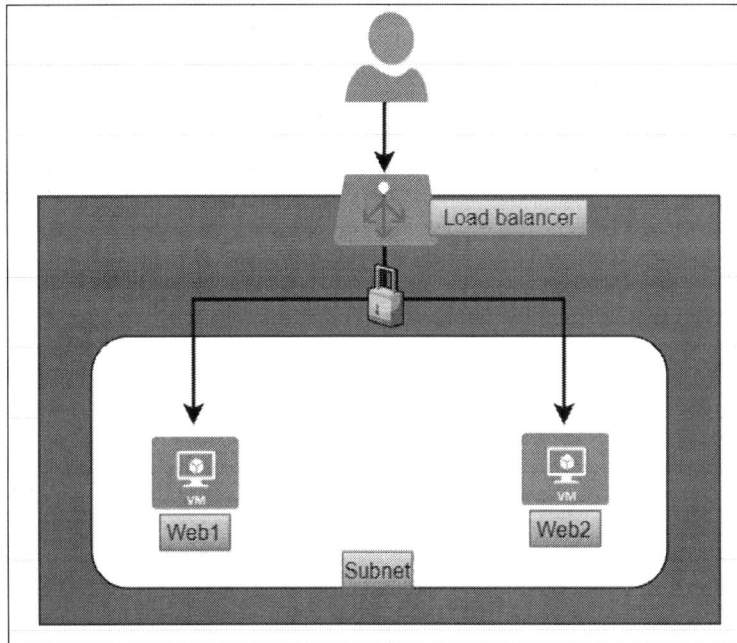

In this topology, we have two Windows Server 2016 VMs behind a load balancer. Both VMs will have IIS installed with the default pages. To add VMs in Azure load balancer, you also need to create a VM with availability set. Make sure you create an availability set while creating VM as shown in the following figure.

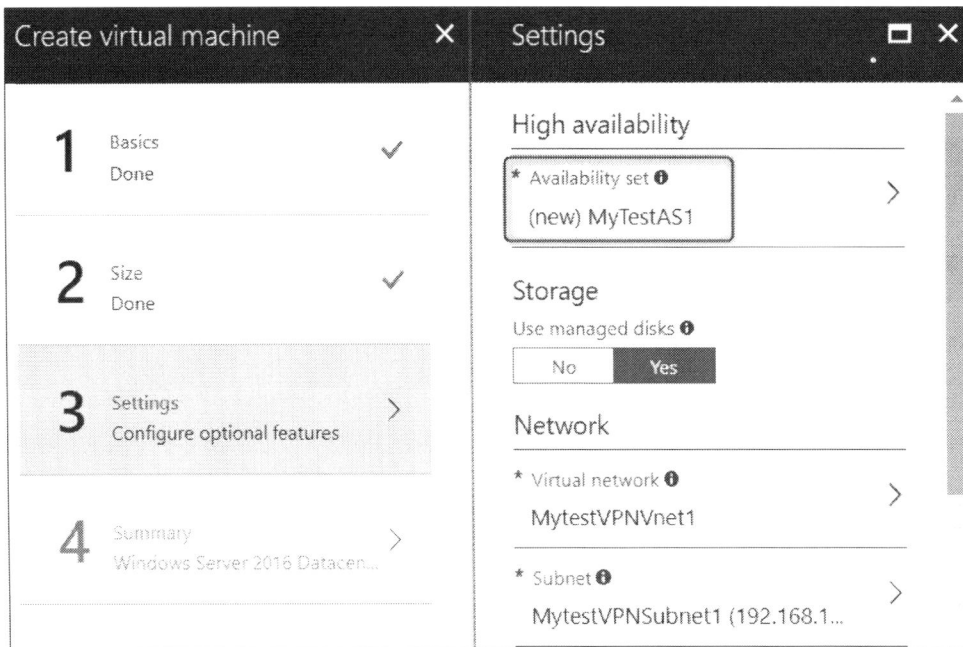

To configure Azure load balancer as per the above-mentioned topology, the following tasks need to be performed.

Create a new VM named as MyTestWeb1 with the following settings:

- VM Name: **MyTestWeb1**
- Operating System: **Windows Server 2016 Datacenter**
- VM size: **DS1_V2**
- Availability set: **MyTestAS1**
- Virtual network: **MyTestVPNVnet1**
- Subnet: **MyTestVPNSubnet1**
- Public IP: **None**
- NSG: **MyTestWeb1-nsg**

Note: If you are working with free trial subscription, we recommend to delete any unused VMs first. Otherwise, you may get the capacity filled issue as you are limited to use only few VMs with free subscription.

Create one more VM with the following settings:

- VM Name: **MyTestWeb2**
- Operating System: **Windows Server 2016 Datacenter**
- VM size: **DS1_V2**

- Availability set: **MyTestAS1**
- Virtual network: **MyTestVPNVnet1**
- Subnet: **MyTestVPNSubnet1**
- Public IP: **None**
- NSG: **MyTestWeb2-nsg**

Please refer the following figure for the MyTestWeb2 VM deployment.

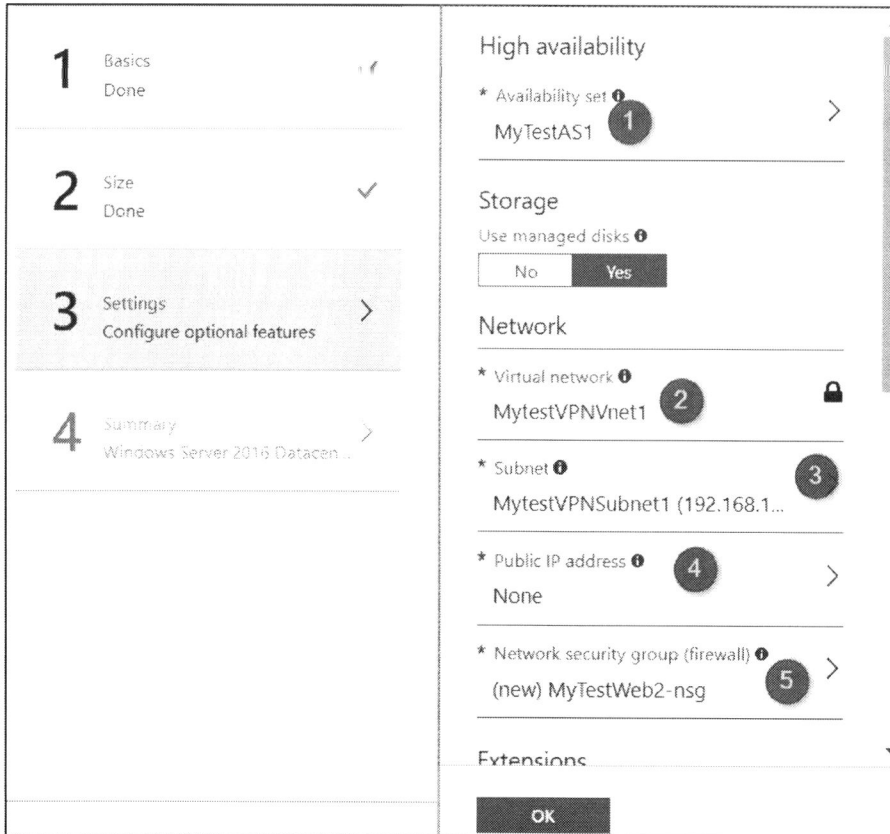

Installing IIS in Windows Server VMs

Connect to your VPN connection and take RDP of MyTestWeb1 VM. Install the **IIS Service** with the default selections on MyTestWeb1 and MyTestWeb2 VMs using the **Server Manager** tool. Alternatively, you can just type the following command to install IIS using Windows PowerShell.

```
Install-WindowsFeature -name Web-Server -IncludeManagementTools
```

After installing IIS Service role, browse the default website on both Web servers locally (use local private IP address) and make sure the default pages on both VMs are accessible as shown in the following figure.

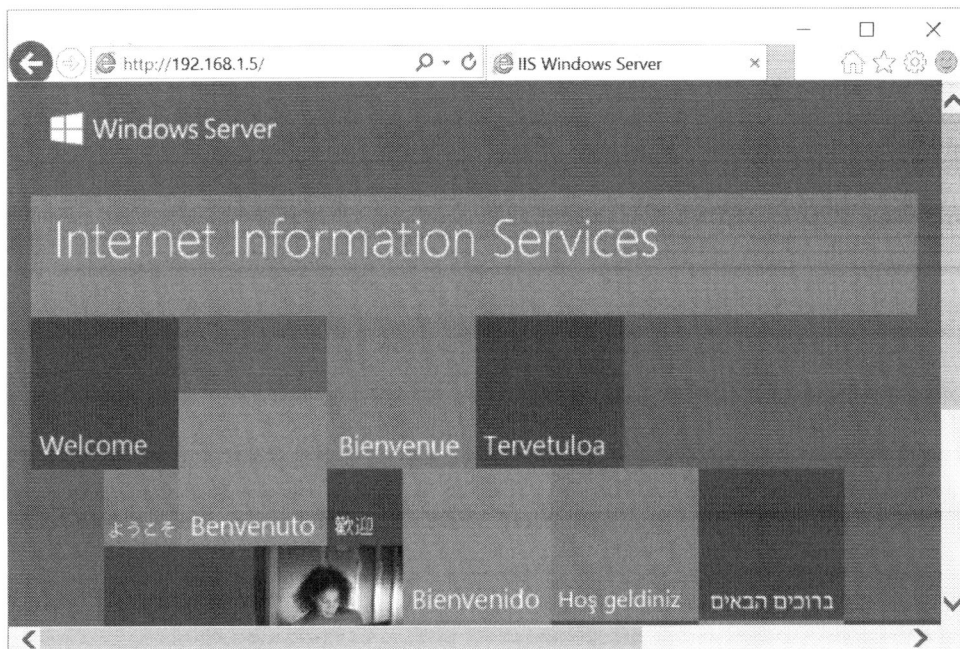

Now you have MyTestWeb1 and MyTestWeb2 VMs in an availability set with the default web pages configured.

Creating Azure Load Balancer

Before creating an Azure load balancer, let's have a look what configurations are required by the Azure load balancer:

- **Front-end IP configuration** - contains public IP addresses for incoming network traffic.
- **Back-end address pool** - contains Network Interfaces Cards (NICs) for the virtual machines to receive network traffic from the load balancer.
- **Load balancing rules** - contains rules mapping a public port on the load balancer to port in the back-end address pool.

- **Inbound NAT rules** - contains rules mapping a public port on the load balancer to a port for a specific virtual machine in the back-end address pool.
- **Probes** - contains health probes used to check availability of virtual machine instances in the back-end address pool.

To create and configure Azure load balancer, you need to perform the following steps:

1. In Azure Portal, click **Create Resource > Networking> Load Balancer** as shown in the following figure.

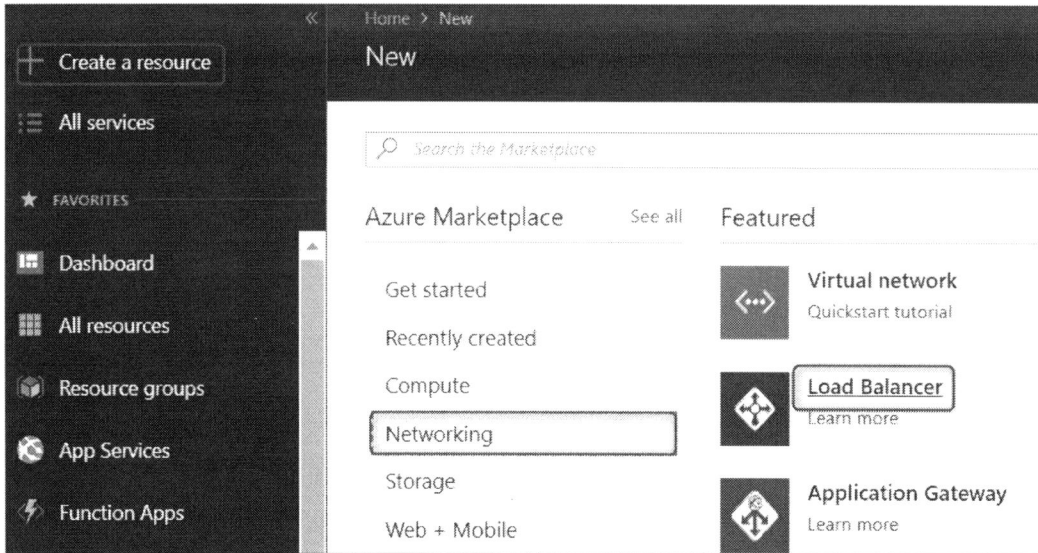

2. On the **Create load balancer** blade, specify the load balancer configuration values as shown in the following figure.

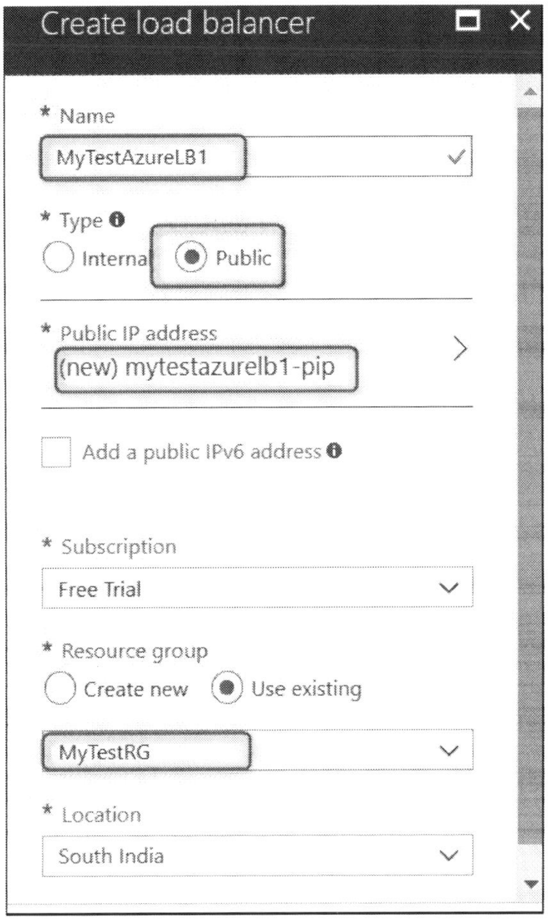

Create load balancer

* Name

MyTestAzureLB1 ✓

* Type ℹ
   ○ Internal   ⦿ Public

* Public IP address
   (new) mytestazurelb1-pip   >

☐ Add a public IPv6 address ℹ

* Subscription
   Free Trial ∨

* Resource group
   ○ Create new   ⦿ Use existing

   MyTestRG ∨

* Location
   South India ∨

Note: You also need to create a public IP address for your load balancer such as mytestazurelb1-pip as shown in the above figure.

---

3. Click **Create** to create Azure load balancer. The load balancer will be created within a few minutes.

Creating a Backend Address Pool

After creating the Azure load balancer, next, you need to define the backend address pool. The backend address pool allows you to add virtual machines that will participate in this azure load balancer. For this, you need to perform the following steps:

1. Select **MyTestAzureLB1** in the **Load balancers** section.
2. In the **Backend pools** blade, select the **Backend pools** option and then click **Add** to add virtual machines as shown in the following figure.

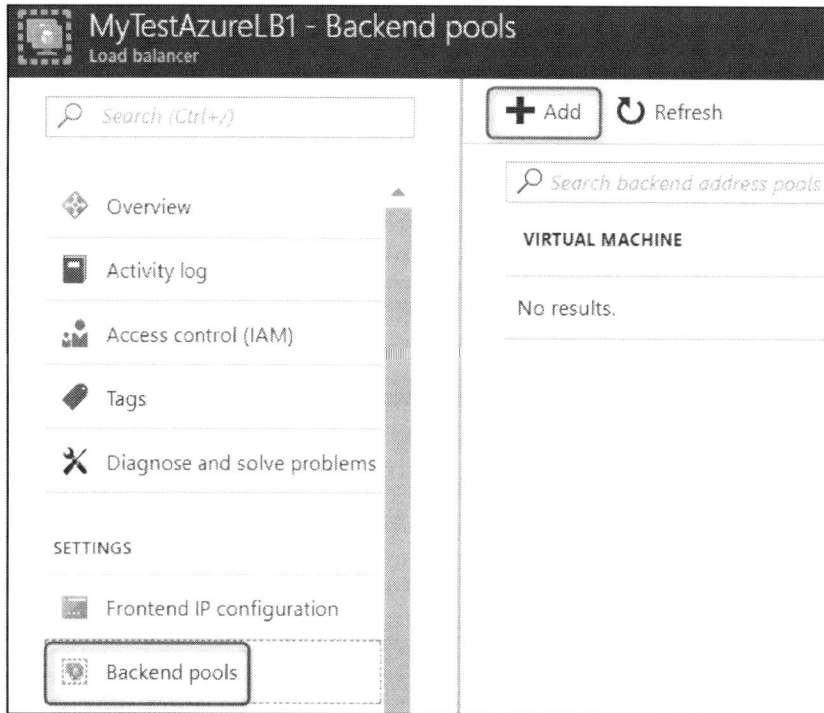

MyTestAzureLB1 - Backend pools
Load balancer

Search (Ctrl+/)

+ Add   ↻ Refresh

Overview

Activity log

Access control (IAM)

Tags

Diagnose and solve problems

SETTINGS

Frontend IP configuration

Backend pools

Search backend address pools

VIRTUAL MACHINE

No results.

3. On the **Add backend pool** blade, specify the backend pool name as **MyTestLBPool1**.
4. Under the **Associated to** drop-down list, click **Availability set** and select your availability set created earlier "**MyTestAS1**".
5. Select your first VM as **MyTestWeb1** and its associated network interface.
6. Select your second VM as **MyTestWeb2** and its associated network interface as shown in the following figure.

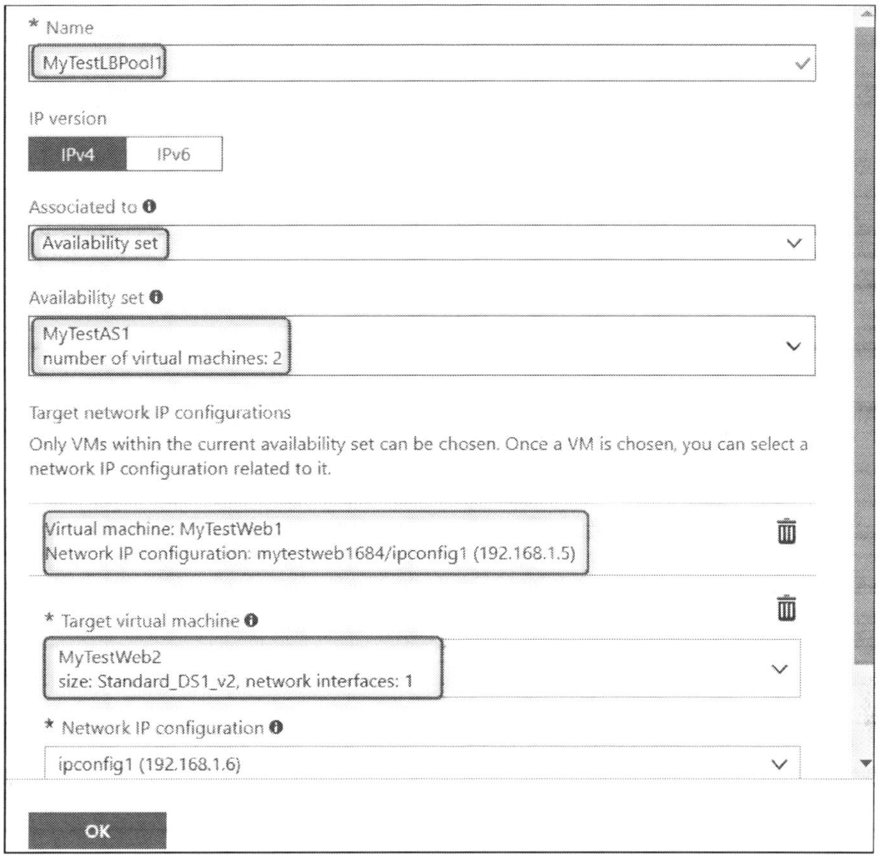

7. Click **OK** to proceed. The **MyTestLBPool1** backend pool will be created soon. Verify that both the VMs are added and are running as shown in the following figure.

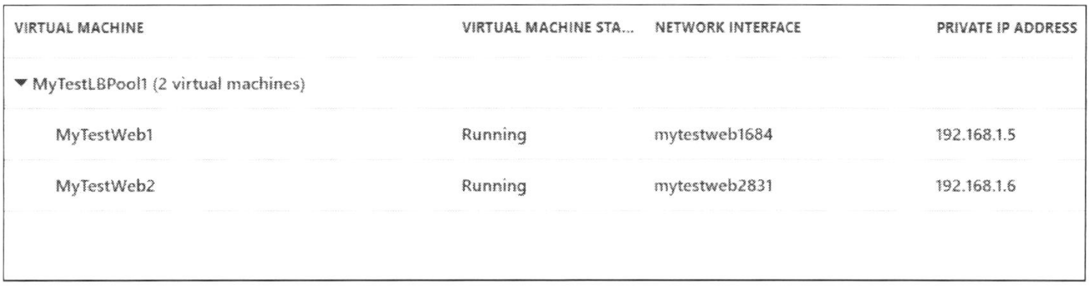

VIRTUAL MACHINE	VIRTUAL MACHINE STA...	NETWORK INTERFACE	PRIVATE IP ADDRESS
▼ MyTestLBPool1 (2 virtual machines)			
MyTestWeb1	Running	mytestweb1684	192.168.1.5
MyTestWeb2	Running	mytestweb2831	192.168.1.6

Creating Health Probe Check

Azure load balancer uses health probe to check whether the backend virtual machines are accessible and able to serve the requests. For this, the backend port and the default home path need to be defined so the load balancer can keep checking the backend VMs' status periodically. When any VM from the backend pool goes down, the health probe fails. The Azure load balancer will detect it and will redirect the traffic to other healthy virtual machines in the backend pool.

To configure health probe, you need to perform the following steps:

1. In the **Load Balancers** blade, select **Health Probes** and then click **Add** as shown in the following figure.

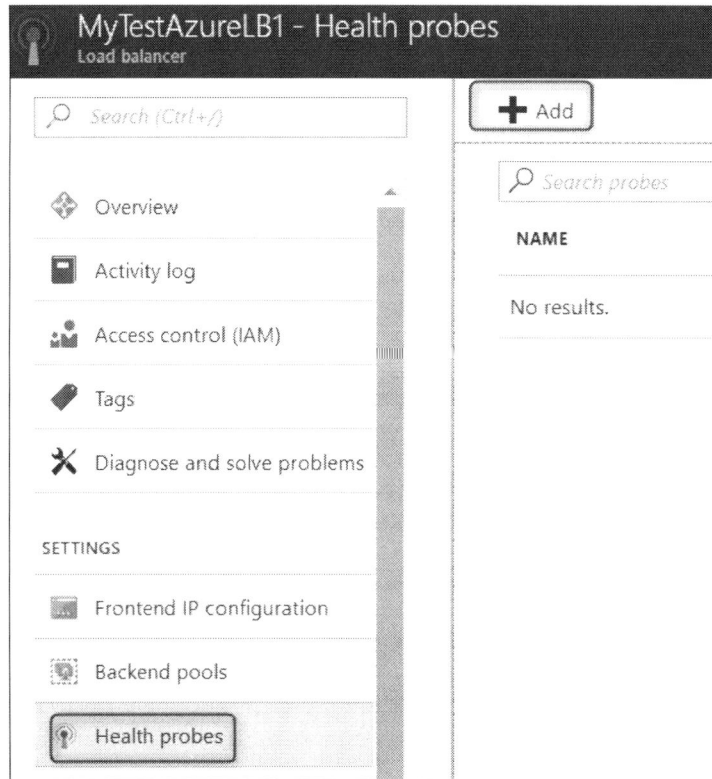

2. On the **Health Probe** blade, specify the following settings:

- **Name**: Name of the health probe such as MytestHealthProbe1
- **Protocol**: HTTP or TCP
- **Port**: Specify the backend port of your service such as 80.
- **Path**: Specify the default home path that should accessible by Azure Load Balancer.
- **Interval**: Specify the time in seconds, after which Azure load balancer will keep trying to check health probes.
- **Unhealthy threshold**: Number of retry attempts after which load balancer considers the service/VM as down.

3. Specify the settings as per the following figure and click **OK** for this lab exercise.

```
  ┌──────────────────────────────────────────────────────────┐
  │  🖫 Save    ✕ Discard    🗑 Delete                        │
  ├──────────────────────────────────────────────────────────┤
  │  * Name                                                    │
  │  ┌───────────────────────────────────────────────────┐    │
  │  │ MyTestHealthProbe1                                 │    │
  │  └───────────────────────────────────────────────────┘    │
  │                                                            │
  │  IP version                                                │
  │  IPv4                                                      │
  │                                                            │
  │  Protocol                                                  │
  │  ┌──────────┬──────────┐                                  │
  │  │  HTTP    │   TCP    │                                  │
  │  └──────────┴──────────┘                                  │
  │                                                            │
  │  * Port                                                    │
  │  ┌───────────────────────────────────────────────────┐    │
  │  │ 80                                                 │    │
  │  └───────────────────────────────────────────────────┘    │
  │                                                            │
  │  * Path ❶                                                 │
  │  ┌───────────────────────────────────────────────────┐    │
  │  │ iisstart.htm                                       │    │
  │  └───────────────────────────────────────────────────┘    │
  │                                                            │
  │  * Interval ❶                                             │
  │  ┌───────────────────────────────────────────────────┐    │
  │  │ 5                                                  │    │
  │  └───────────────────────────────────────────────────┘    │
  │                                             seconds        │
  │  * Unhealthy threshold ❶                                  │
  │  ┌───────────────────────────────────────────────────┐    │
  │  │ 2                                                  │    │
  │  └───────────────────────────────────────────────────┘    │
  │                                   consecutive failures     │
  └──────────────────────────────────────────────────────────┘
```

Configuring Load Balancer Rule

A Load balancer rule defines the frontend and backend ports, backend pool, and health probe related settings. To create a load balancer rule, you need to perform the following steps:

1. Select **Load balancing rules** in the **Load Balancers** blade and then click **Add**.
2. Specify the load balancer rule settings as shown in the following figure.

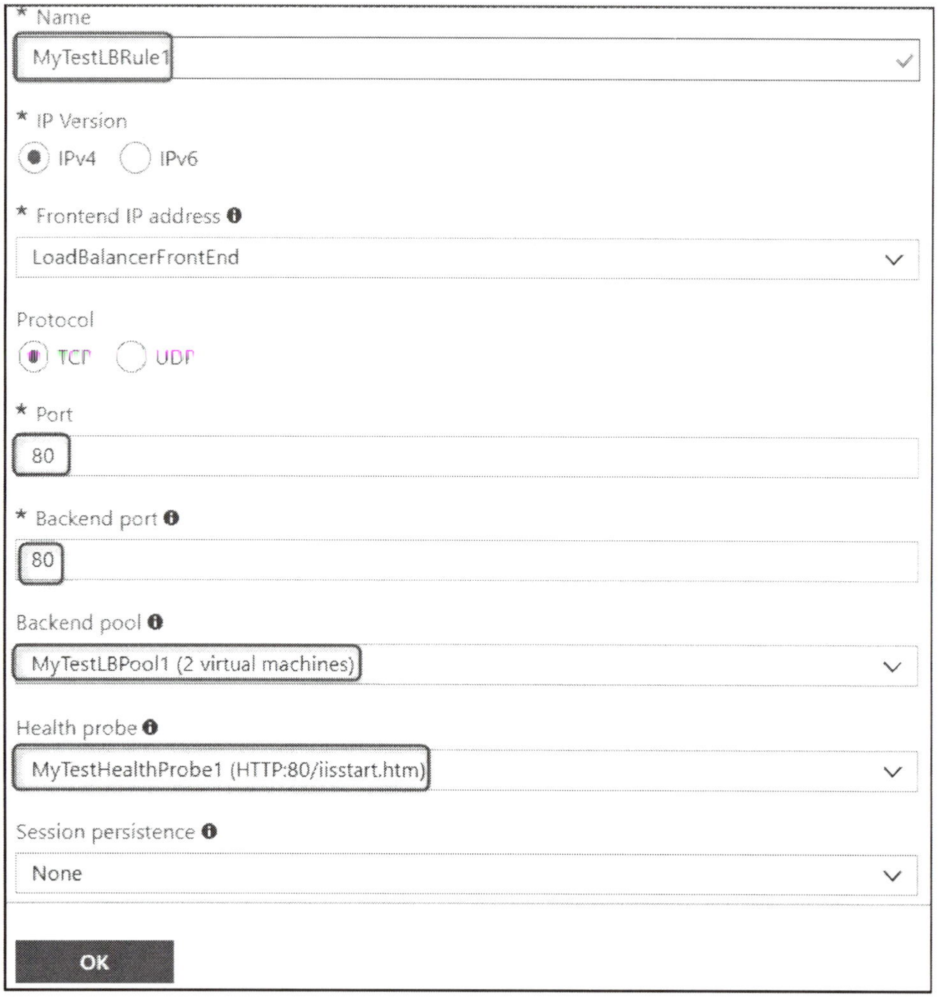

* Name

MyTestLBRule1 ✓

* IP Version

◉ IPv4   ○ IPv6

* Frontend IP address ❶

LoadBalancerFrontEnd ⌄

Protocol

◉ TCP   ○ UDP

* Port

80

* Backend port ❶

80

Backend pool ❶

MyTestLBPool1 (2 virtual machines) ⌄

Health probe ❶

MyTestHealthProbe1 (HTTP:80/iisstart.htm) ⌄

Session persistence ❶

None ⌄

OK

3. Click **OK** to finish the configuration.

Updating Network Security Groups

Now, your load balancer is ready to be used. However, you need to allow HTTP port in both the NSGs attached to each VM. Add the following NSG inbound rule in both **MyTestWeb1-nsg** and **MyTestWeb2-nsg** security groups.

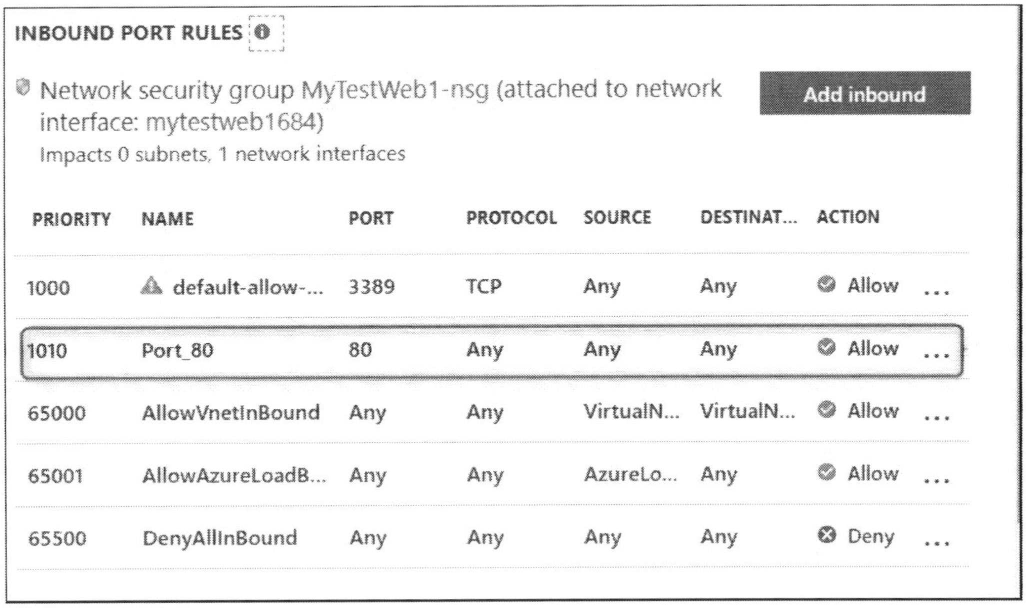

INBOUND PORT RULES ⓘ

Network security group MyTestWeb1-nsg (attached to network interface: mytestweb1684)
Impacts 0 subnets, 1 network interfaces

[Add inbound]

PRIORITY	NAME	PORT	PROTOCOL	SOURCE	DESTINAT...	ACTION
1000	⚠ default-allow-...	3389	TCP	Any	Any	✅ Allow ...
1010	Port_80	80	Any	Any	Any	✅ Allow ...
65000	AllowVnetInBound	Any	Any	VirtualN...	VirtualN...	✅ Allow ...
65001	AllowAzureLoadB...	Any	Any	AzureLo...	Any	✅ Allow ...
65500	DenyAllInBound	Any	Any	Any	Any	❌ Deny ...

Verifying Azure Load Balancer Configuration

Now, navigate to the **Overview** section of **MyTestAzureLB1** load balancer and copy its public IP address as shown in the following figure.

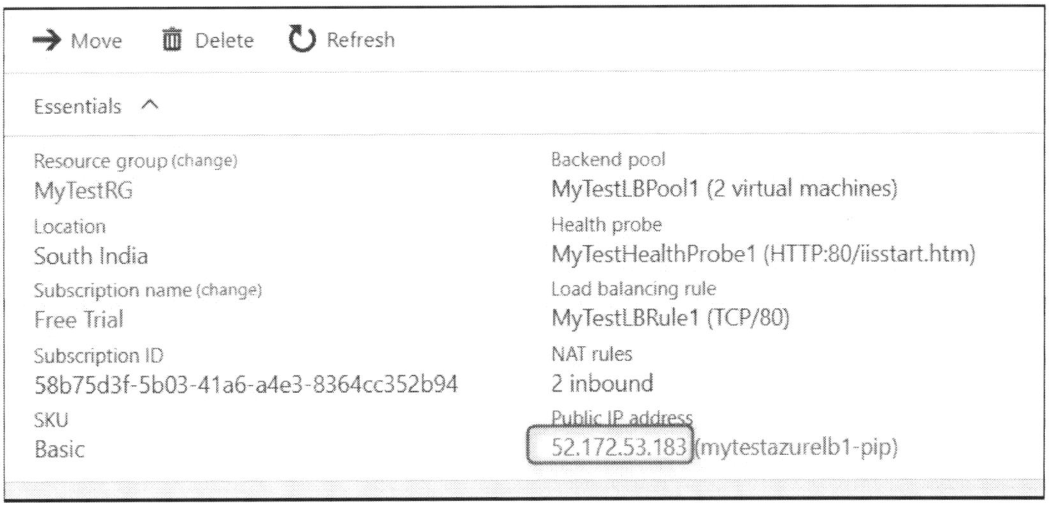

→ Move   🗑 Delete   ↻ Refresh

Essentials ∧

Resource group (change)	Backend pool
MyTestRG	MyTestLBPool1 (2 virtual machines)
Location	Health probe
South India	MyTestHealthProbe1 (HTTP:80/iisstart.htm)
Subscription name (change)	Load balancing rule
Free Trial	MyTestLBRule1 (TCP/80)
Subscription ID	NAT rules
58b75d3f-5b03-41a6-a4e3-8364cc352b94	2 inbound
SKU	Public IP address
Basic	52.172.53.183 (mytestazurelb1-pip)

Paste the load balancer's public IP on your local system's browser. You should be able to browse the default page of your web servers running behind the Azure load balancer. To verify that both VMs are working fine and participating in the Azure load balancer, stop **MytestWeb1** VM and refresh the browser. You should still be able to browse the default page from **MyTestWeb2** VM.

Now, stop the **MyTestWeb2** VM also and check that you are not able to browse the default page because both the virtual machines are stopped and load balancer does not have any healthy backend node. To further verify, start **MyTestWeb1** VM, but keep **MyTestWeb2** VM in the stopped state. Once MyTestWeb1 VM started, refresh the browser and make sure that the default web page starts opening from the **MyTestWeb1** backend node.

Deleting Azure Load Balancer

1. To delete an Azure load balancer, just select the created load balancer in Azure Portal.
2. In the **Load Balancer** blade, select **Overview**, and then click **Delete** to delete the selected load balancer as shown in the following figure

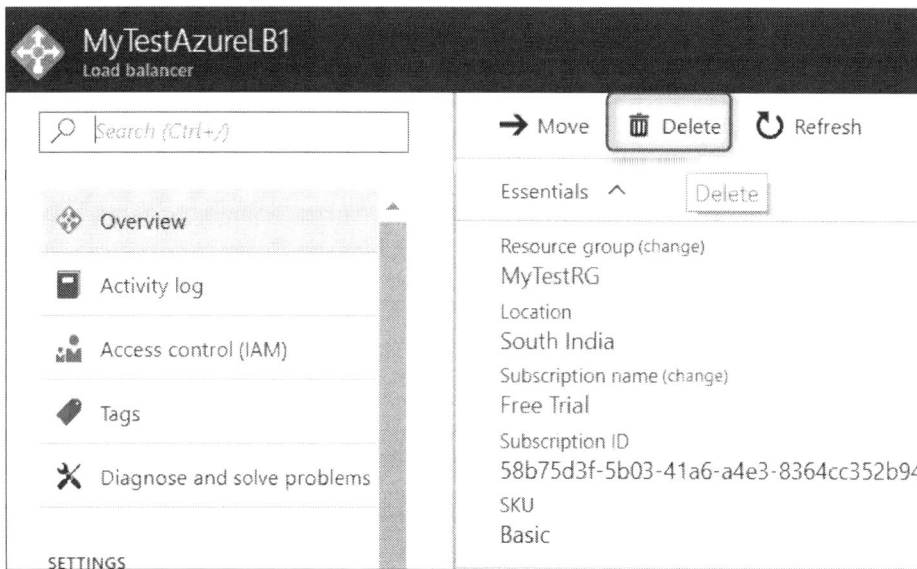

3. Click **Yes** to confirm the deletion and the load balancer will be deleted.

That's all you need to understand, create, configure, and verify Azure load balancers.

Lab 39: Configuring VM Scale Set in Azure Cloud

Virtual machine scale set (VM scale set) is a feature of Azure cloud which allows you to deploy and manage a set of identical VMs. The VM Scale Set is really helpful for those kinds of applications which support multi-servers' architecture such as a web server. Web server configured with the VM scale set can automatically IN and OUT the number of virtual machines based on the traffic and load hitting the site. For this, you define the policy and threshold values. When the threshold value triggers, the VMs increase and decrease accordingly and automatically. This is extremely helpful for those organizations whose traffic is unexpected and cannot be predicted. Let's have a look at the following use case.

ABC company is a large online sailing company hosted their infrastructure in the Azure cloud. The management of the company decides to have a big mega sale world-wide for the new year occasion. However, how much traffic will come and how far the sale will go up is completely unpredictable. There might be 1000 users coming every minute or might be one million users accessing the site due to the sudden popularity of the big mega sale. As a solutions architect, how will you handle the traffic without any hassle and quickly. The answer is **Using VM scale set**.

With VM scale set, you configure a master image that has everything preconfigured with all system and application configuration. If the application also requires a database such as MongoDB, you can have MongoDB server in the database tier and application VMs in web tier behind a load balancer with. The VM scale set can increase and decrease the number of virtual machines either manually or automatically with the help of rules and policies.

To know more technical details, features, and limitation of VM scale set, please visit the following link.

- Azure VM Scale Set FAQs
  https://docs.microsoft.com/en-us/azure/virtual-machine-scale-sets/virtual-machine-scale-sets-overview#frequently-asked-questions-for-scale-sets

We have not covered how to configure VM scale set in the Azure cloud. However, if you are interested, please visit the following link for creating and using the Azure VM Scale Set.

- Creating Azure VM Scale Set
  https://docs.microsoft.com/en-us/azure/virtual-machine-scale-sets/virtual-machine-scale-sets-create-portal

Lab 40: Configuring Application Gateway in Azure Cloud

We discussed the basic features of Application Gateway in Working with Load Balancers section. Please review this section to know how Application Gateway is different from Azure Load Balancer.

Azure Application Gateway is a dedicated virtual appliance which offers various layer 7 load balancing capabilities for your backend running application. It helps customers to optimize web farm productivity, because Application Gateway offloads CPU intensive SSL termination to the application gateway. It also provides various other layer 7 routing capabilities such as round robin distribution of incoming traffic, cookie-based session affinity, URL path-based routing, and hosting multiple websites behind a single Application Gateway.

Application Gateway can also be configured along with Web Application Firewall (WAF) to enhance the security on web servers. WAF provides protection to the web applications from various common web vulnerabilities and exploits.

Benefits of Application Gateway

An **Application Gateway** provides various rich security and high availability features, few of them are as follows:

- Application Gateways are helpful for the applications which require requests from the same user/client session to be always reached to the same back-end virtual machine.
- Application Gateways help in removing SSL termination overhead for web server farms.
- Application Gateways are helpful for the applications that require multiple HTTP requests on the same long-running TCP connection to be routed to different back-end servers.
- Application Gateways help to protect web applications from common web-based attacks such as SQL injection, cross-site scripting attacks, and session hijacks.
- Application Gateways are also helpful in logical distribution of traffic based on different routing criteria such as, URL, Path or Domain headers.

Application Gateway FAQs

If you are interested to know the common FAQs about the Application gateway, please visit the following link.

- Azure Application Gateway FAQs
  https://docs.microsoft.com/en-us/azure/application-gateway/application-gateway-faq

Creating Azure Application Gateway

In this exercise, we will configure the Application Gateway as per the following network topology.

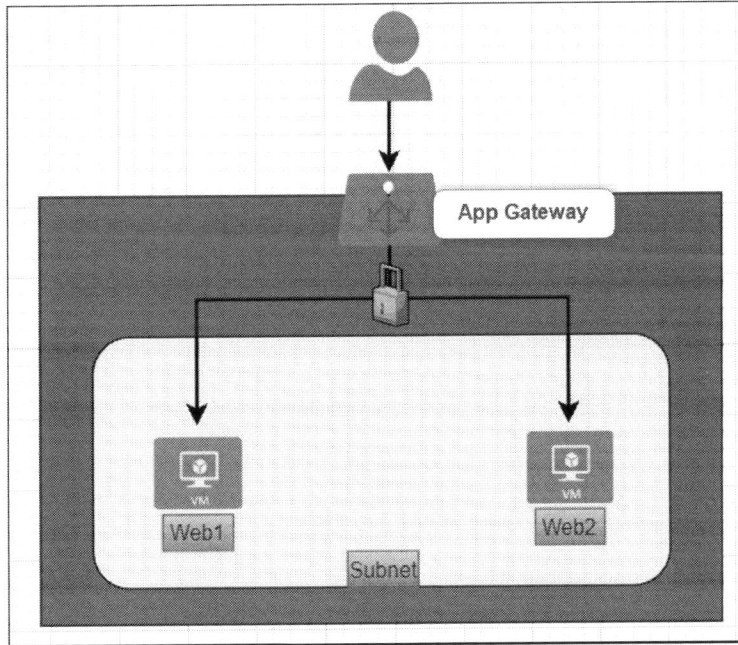

We will use the same virtual machines that we used in the previous lab exercise "Azure Load Balancer". Make sure you have deleted Azure Load Balancer in the previous lab exercise so the VMs could be free to use with Application gateway.

Creating Subnet for Application Gateway

Application gateway should use a separate subnet. In this subnet, it is recommended to not deploy any other resources. Keep reserve this subnet for the Application Gateway use only. Let's create a subnet called MyAppWGSubnet with the Following settings:

- Virtual Network: **MyTestVPNVnet1**
- Subnet name: **MyAppGWSubnet**
- Range: **192.168.2.0/24**
- Network Security Group: **None**

To create the subnet with above-mentioned settings, you need to perform the following steps:

1. Select **Virtual networks** in Azure Portal.
2. Select **MyTestVPNVnet1** virtual network in Azure Portal.
3. Select **Subnets** and then click **Add** to add a new subnet.
4. On **Add a subnet** blade, specify the **Name** and **Address range** of subnet as shown in the following figure.

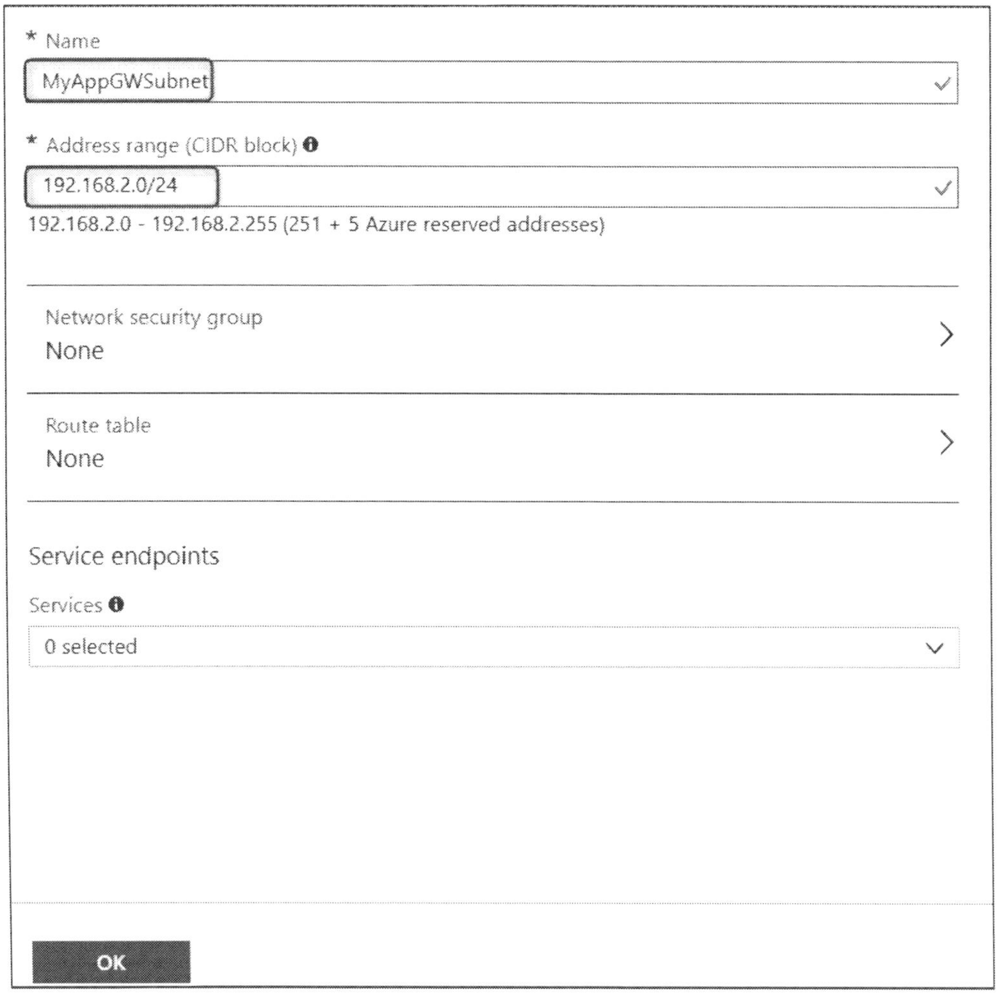

5. Click **OK** to finish. Your MyAppGWSubnet will be created soon.

Creating Application Gateway

To create an Application Gateway, you need to perform the following steps:

1. In Azure Portal, click **Create a resource**, select **Networking**, and then select **Application Gateway** as shown in the following figure.

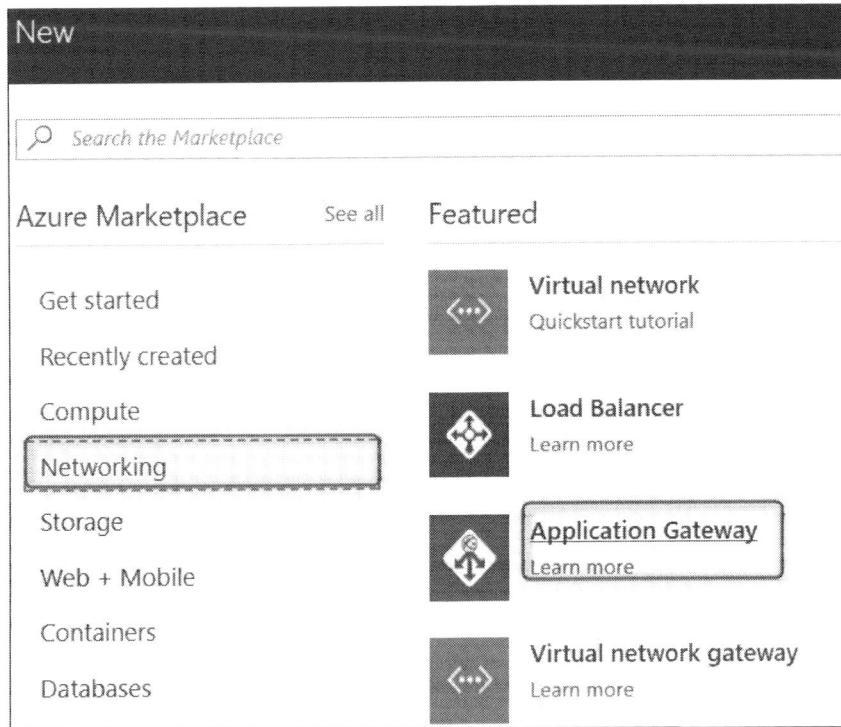

2. On the **Basics** blade of **Create application gateway** blade, specify the following settings:
   - **Name**: Name of the application gateway such as **MyTestAppGW1**
   - **Tier**: **Standard** for without WAF, and **WAF** for Application Gateway with WAF security
   - **SKU Size**: Select the size of application gateway depending on the load you expect to be served by the application gateway. The available SKU sizes are: **Small**, **Medium**, and **Large**
   - **Instance count**: The number of instances that Azure cloud will create for you. Minimum two instances are required and can go up to 10 instances
   - **Resource Group**: Select the desired resource group such as MyTestRG
   - **Location**: Select the desired region
3. Specify the Application Gateway settings as shown in the following figure.

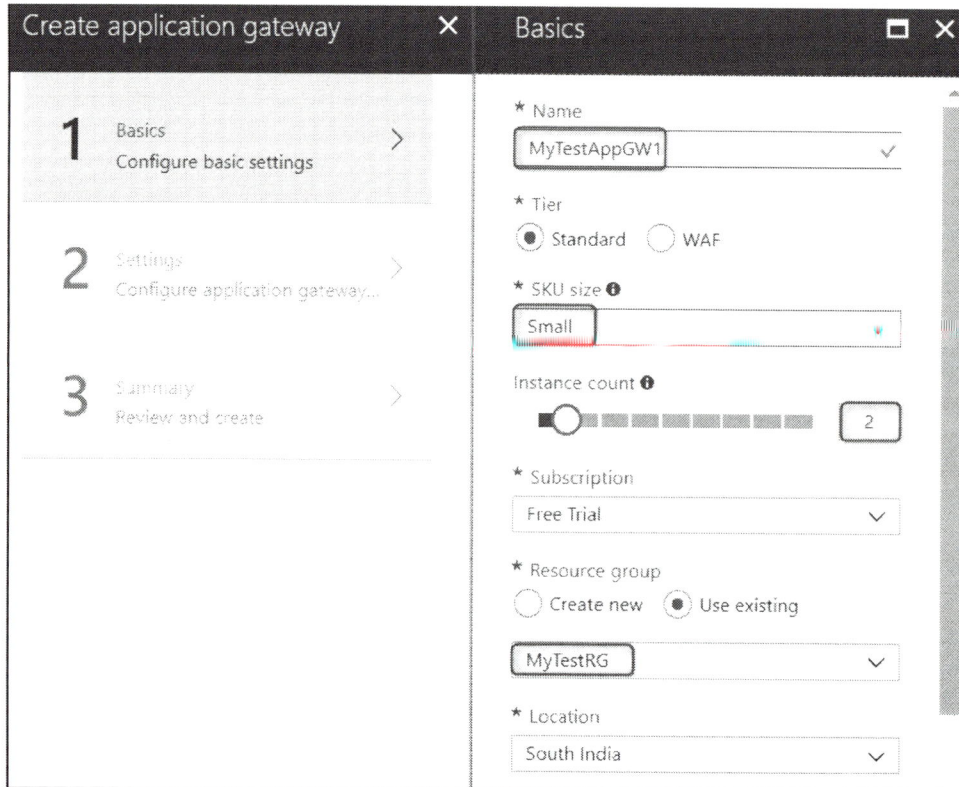

Note: In this lab exercise, we will configure Application Gateway without WAF. In the next lab exercise, we have covered Application Gateway with WAF.

---

4. Click **OK** to proceed on the next blade.
5. On the **Settings** blade, select **MyVPNTestVnet1** virtual network.
6. Under the **Subnets** section, make sure that **MyAppGWSubnet** is selected.
7. In the **IP address type** section, select **Public**.
8. In the **Public IP address** section, select **Create new**.
9. In the **Listener configuration** section, select **HTTP** as protocol.
10. In the **Port** section, make sure that port **80** is selected and then click **OK** as shown in the following figure.

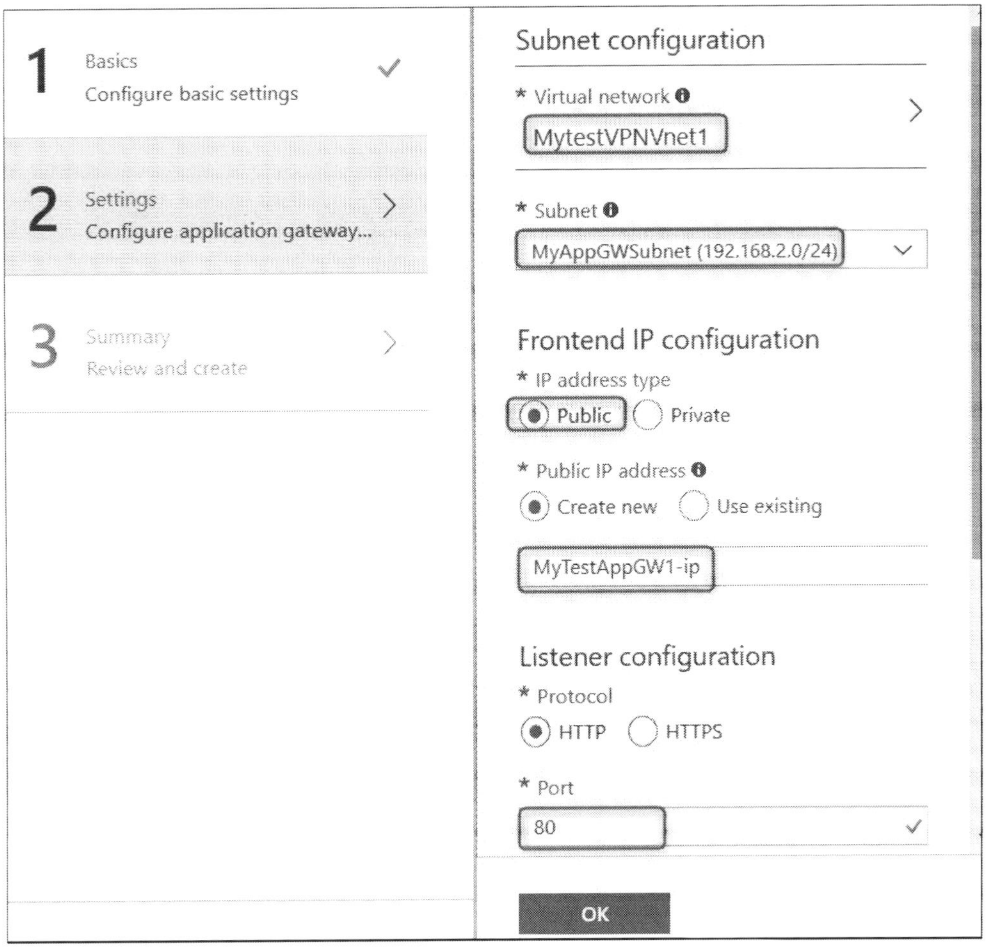

Subnet configuration

* Virtual network ❶
MytestVPNVnet1

* Subnet ❶
MyAppGWSubnet (192.168.2.0/24)

Frontend IP configuration
* IP address type
(●) Public   ( ) Private

* Public IP address ❶
(●) Create new   ( ) Use existing

MyTestAppGW1-ip

Listener configuration
* Protocol
(●) HTTP   ( ) HTTPS

* Port
80

OK

11. On the **Summary** blade, review your selections and click **OK** to create the Application Gateway. The application gateway deployment may take a few minutes. Please wait until the application gateway deployment process finishes.

Adding Backend Servers

Now, you have created the application gateway for your web farm. We assume that your MyTestWeb1 and MyTestWeb2 virtual machines are still exist and running. If you have deleted them, you need to create two virtual machines and install IIS service role inside them in a different subnet. Different than MyAppGWSubnet but in the same vNet (MyTestVPNVnet1) that you have selected for your Application Gateway.

To add backend servers with your Application Gateway, you need to perform the following steps.

1. In Azure Portal, navigate to **All resources** > **MyTestAppGW1** > **Backend pools** as shown in the following figure.

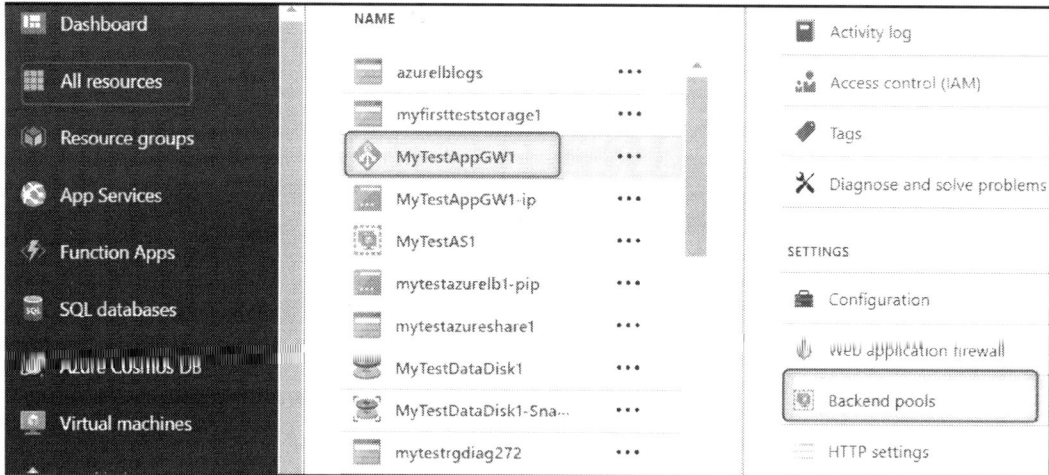

2. In the right blade, select the default created backend pool **appGatewayBacknedPool**.
3. On the **appGatewayBackendPool** blade, click **Add target**, select Virtual machine in the **Type** section.
4. Select **MyTestWeb1** virtual machine and its IP address.
5. Similarly, add **MyTestWeb2** virtual machine also and then click **Save** as shown in the following figure.

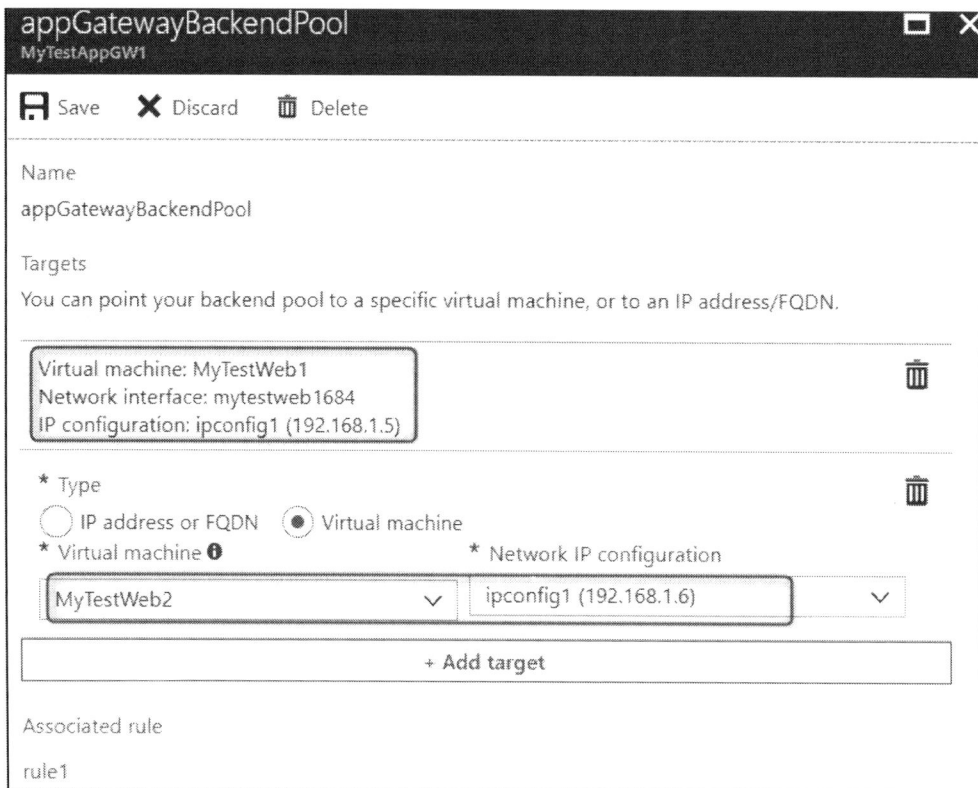

6. MyTestWeb1 and MytestWeb2 virtual machines will be added into your application gateway backend pool. The adding target process may take a few minutes.

Verifying Application Gateway Configuration

We assume the you have MyTestWeb1 and MyTestWeb2 virtual machines running with the IIS web service. We also assume that you have allowed HTTP port in the both VM's inbound NSG security rules. We already have done this in previous lab exercise with Azure Load Balancer.

To verify Azure Application Gateway functionalities, navigate to the **Overview** section of **MyTestAppGW1** and copy its **public IP address** as shown in the following figure.

Paste the copied public IP address in your local system's browser and verify that you are able to browse the default web page. To further verify the Application Gateway functionalities, you can stop and start one-by-one web virtual machines and check the functionalities as we checked in the **Configuring Azure Load Balancer** exercise.

> *Note: Do not delete the Application Gateway or running virtual machines, as these will be used in the next lab exercise "Configure WAF with Application Gateway"*

Lab 41: Configuring WAF in Azure Cloud

Web Application Firewall (WAF) provides additional security with the Application gateways from common vulnerabilities. Some of the common among these exploits are SQL injection attacks, cross-site scripting attacks. A Web application firewall is based on rules from the OWASP core rules set 3.0 or 2.2.9. These core rules set are collections of rules that help you to protect your web applications for malicious activities. If you are interested, you can explore more about the OWASP core rule sets using the following link.

- OWASP Code Rule Set
  https://www.owasp.org/index.php/Category:OWASP_ModSecurity_Core_Rule_Set_Project

WAF protects multiple web applications at the same time behind running an application gateway. As discussed earlier, an application gateway supports hosting up to 20 websites behind a single gateway. These all websites could all be protected against web attacks with WAF. With WAF, you can monitor your web application against attacks using the real-time WAF logs.

WAF also provides detailed reporting on each threat it detects. Logging is integrated with Azure Diagnostics logs and the alerts are recorded in the JSON format.

Web Application Firewall Modes

A WAF can be configured to run in the following two modes:

1. **Detection mode:** In this mode, WAF monitors and logs all threat alerts into a log file.
2. **Prevention mode:** In this mode, the WAF aggressively blocks intrusions and attacks detected based on the configured rules.

WAF Prerequisites

Before you could configure WAF with application gateway, the following requirements must meet.

1. Application gateway should be configured with the minimum medium SKU size.
2. A storage account is required to store the WAF logs.
3. Diagnostic must be configured to use WAF.

Creating a Storage Account

To create a storage account for a WAF, you need to perform the following steps:

1. In Azure Portal, navigate to **Create a resource** > **Storage** > **Storage account – blob, file, table queue** as shown in the following figure.

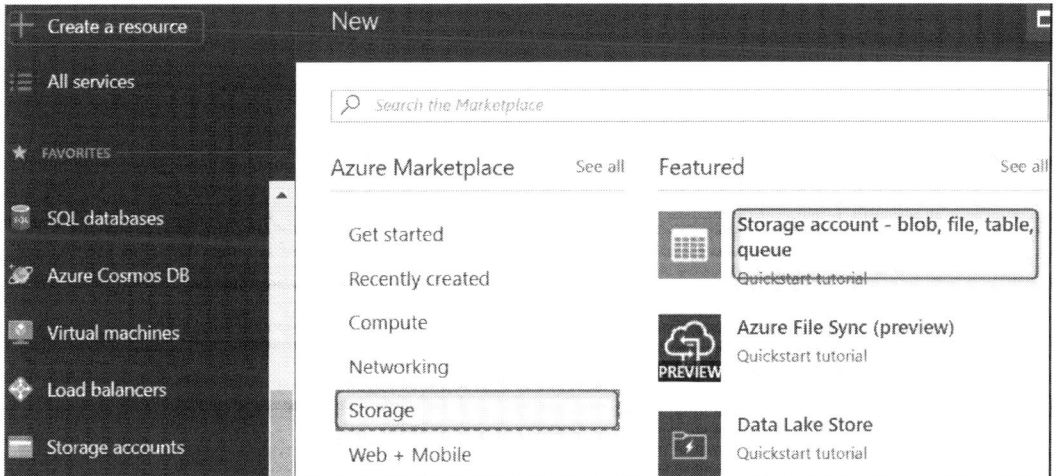

2. On the **Create a storage account** blade, specify the following settings:
   - **Name**: mytestwaflog1 (must be globally unique)
   - **Account kind**: Storage (general purpose version1)
   - **Replication**: Locally-redundant storage (LRS)
   - **Resource group**: MyTestRG
   - **Location:** Your desired region
3. Once the above settings are defined as shown in the following figure, click **Create**.

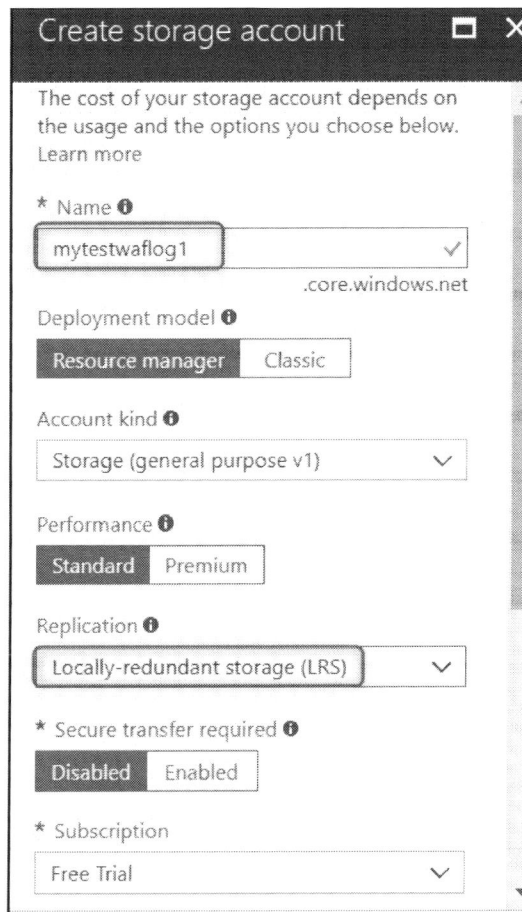

4. Mytestwaflog1 storage account will be created where the WAF logs will be saved.

Registering Subscription for Diagnostics Logs

By default, your free azure subscription may not be registered with **Microsoft.Insights** service. Microsoft.Insights registration is required to enable and configure Diagnostics logs. To register for Diagnostics log, you need to perform the following steps.

1. In Azure Portal, navigate to **All services** > **Subscriptions** > **Select your subscription**.
2. In the **Subscriptions** blade, scroll-down and select **Resource providers**.
3. In the **Search** box of the right blade, type **microsoft.insights** and click the **Register** link as shown in the following figure.

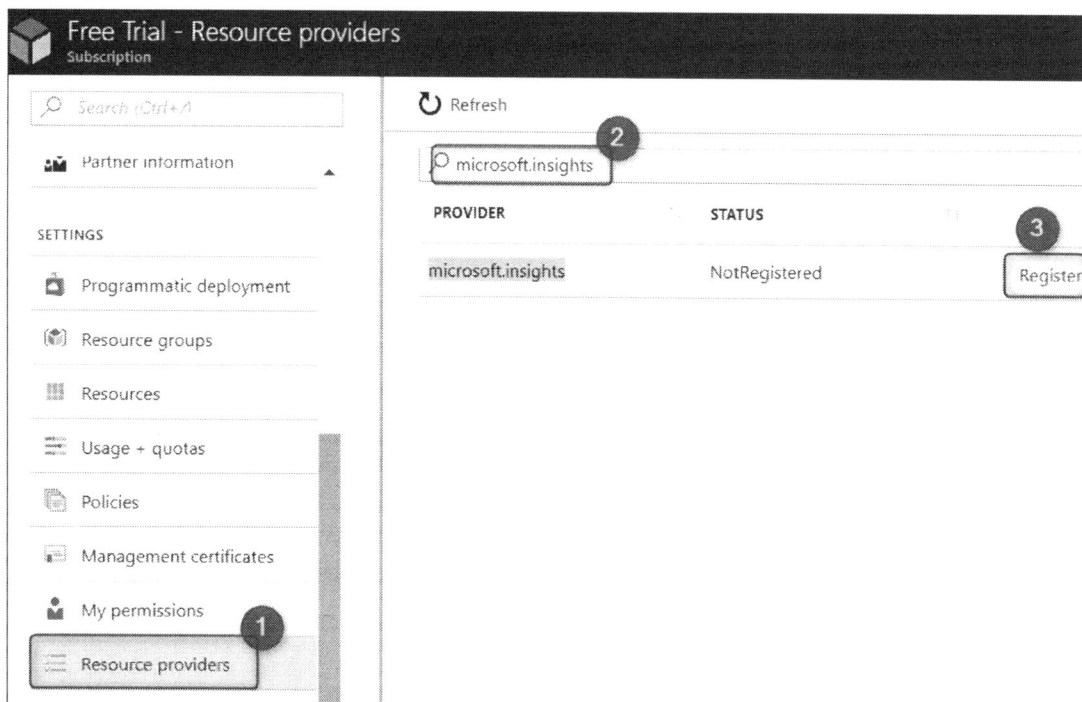

4. Wait until the state changes from **Registering** to **Registered**. You may need to refresh the blade.

Configuring WAF Diagnostics

Remember, we have already created the MyTestAppGW1 application gateway in the previous lab exercise. But we have not enabled WAF with this application gateway. We will continue to use the same application gateway for the WAF configuration.

To configure WAF diagnostics, you need to perform the following steps.

1. In Azure Portal, click **All resources**, select your Application Gateway **MyTestAppGW1**.
2. In the **Application Gateway settings** blade, under the **Monitoring** section, select **Diagnostics logs** and then click **Turn on diagnostics** as shown in the following figure.

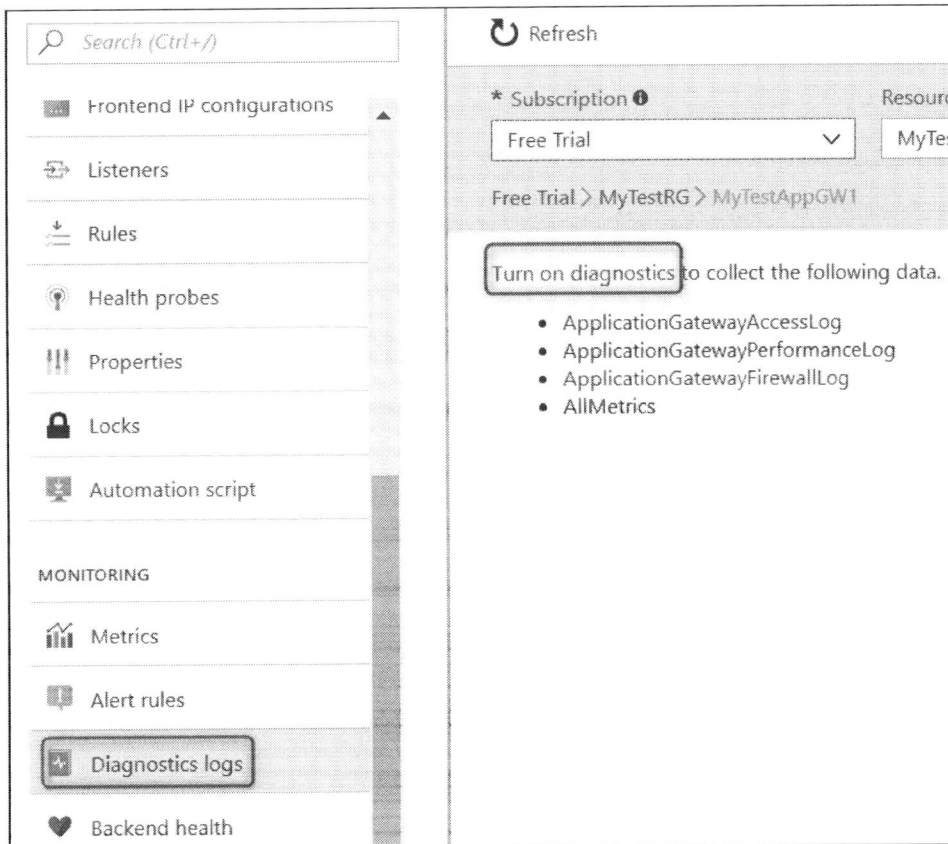

3. On the Diagnostics settings blade specify the following settings.
   - Name: **MyTestWAFDiagLog1**
   - Select the **Archive to a storage account** checkbox.
   - Select **mytestwaflog1** storage account created recently.
   - Select all three log check boxes under the **Log** section.
   - Select **All Metrics** check box.
4. Finally, click **Save,** as shown in the following figure.

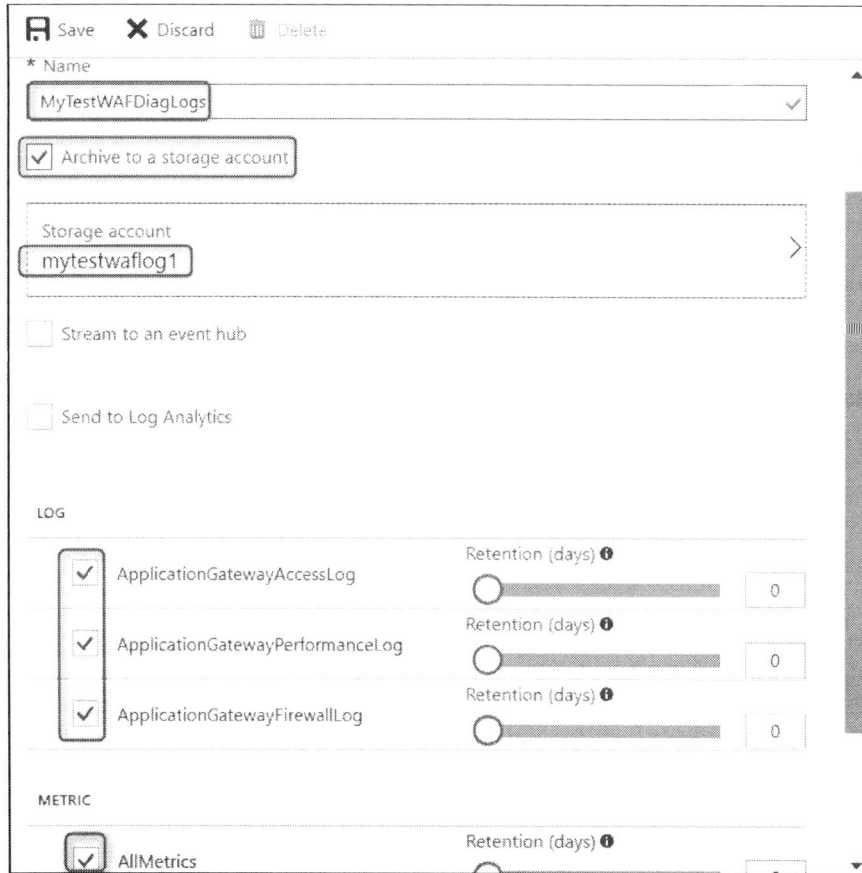

```
H Save    X Discard    🗑 Delete

* Name

┌──────────────────────────────────────────────────────────┐
│ MyTestWAFDiagLogs                                      ✓  │
└──────────────────────────────────────────────────────────┘

┌─┐
│✓│ Archive to a storage account
└─┘

  ┌ ─ ─ ─ ─ ─ ─ ─ ─ ─ ─ ─ ─ ─ ─ ─ ─ ─ ─ ─ ─ ─ ─ ─ ─ ─ ─ ─ ┐
    Storage account
  │ ┌─────────────────────────┐                          │
    │ mytestwaflog1           │                        ›
  │ └─────────────────────────┘                          │
  └ ─ ─ ─ ─ ─ ─ ─ ─ ─ ─ ─ ─ ─ ─ ─ ─ ─ ─ ─ ─ ─ ─ ─ ─ ─ ─ ─ ┘

┌─┐
│ │ Stream to an event hub
└─┘

┌─┐
│ │ Send to Log Analytics
└─┘

LOG

  ┌─┐                                    Retention (days) ❶
  │✓│  ApplicationGatewayAccessLog       ○────────────────  [ 0 ]

  ┌─┐                                    Retention (days) ❶
  │✓│  ApplicationGatewayPerformanceLog  ○────────────────  [ 0 ]

  ┌─┐                                    Retention (days) ❶
  │✓│  ApplicationGatewayFirewallLog     ○────────────────  [ 0 ]

METRIC

  ┌─┐                                    Retention (days) ❶
  │✓│  AllMetrics                        ○────────────────
```

5. Close the **Diagnostics settings** blade.

Enabling WAF with Application Gateway

Now we all set to enable WAF with our Application Gateway "MyTestAppGW1". For this, you need to perform the following steps.

1. In Azure Portal, navigate to **All resources** > **MytestAppGW1**.
2. On the **Web Application Firewall settings** blade, select upgrade to WAF tier (small to medium).
3. Make sure that the **Firewall status** is **Enabled**.
4. Select the **Firewall mode**: **Detection** or **Prevention**.
5. Select the **OWASP rule set**: either **OWASP 3.0** or **OWASP 2.2.9**
6. Finally, click **Save,** as shown in the following figure.

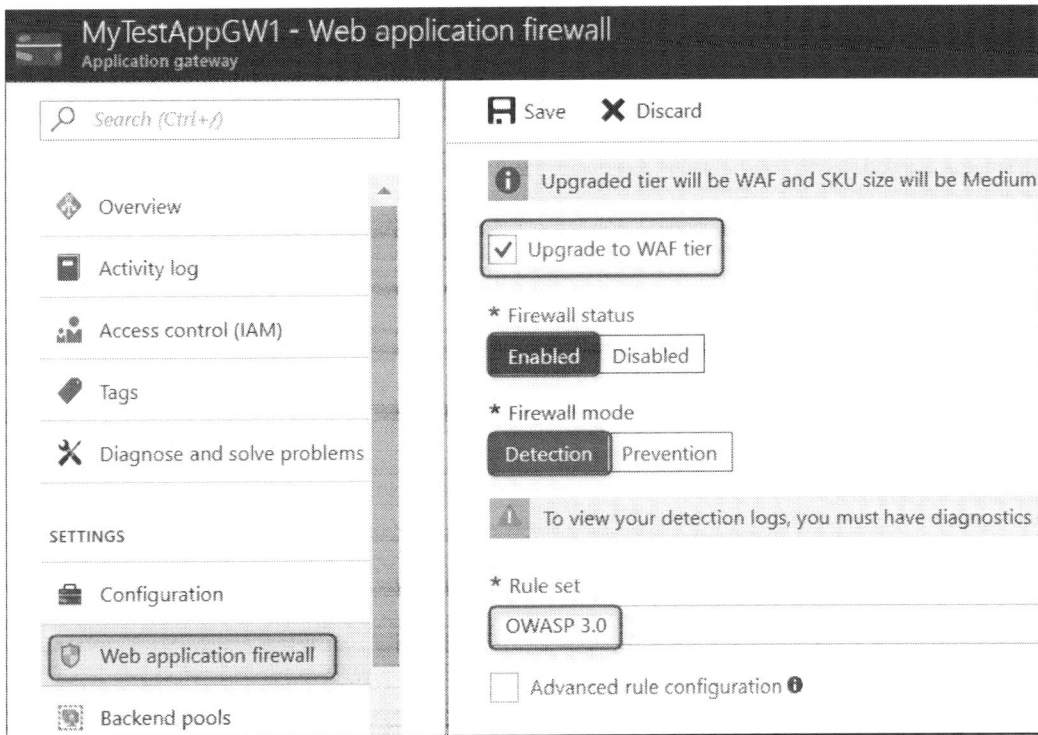

Verifying App Gateway WAF

Now, your web application is protected by the WAF. However, we have chosen detection mode, so all the logs and malicious activity will be recorded, but WAF will not prevent from the malicious attacks. For the prevention, you need to change the WAF mode from Detection to Prevention.

To view the logs recorded by WAF, you need to navigate to the following location.

Storage accounts > **mytestwaflog1** > **Blobs** > Select WAF log container and browse to the application gateway logs.

Lab 42: Working with Azure Cloud Management Tools

There are various GUI and CLI tools that you can use to manage Azure cloud resources. Depending on the users' choice, users can use the following tools to manage Azure cloud services and resources.

- Azure SDK
- Azure PowerShell
- Azure CLI
- Azure Cross-platform CLI (xplat-cli)
- AzCopy

Managing Azure Cloud Services Using Azure SDK

Software Development Kits (SDKs) are the most favorite methods for developers to work and interact with the application. Microsoft offers various Azure SDKs for different platforms such as Azure SDK for.Net Azure SDK for Java and so on. Here, we will explain how to manage Azure cloud resources using Azure SDK for .Net. For this, you need to perform the following steps:

Download and Install Visual Studio

1. To download Visual Studio, visit the Microsoft download center and download preferred Visual Studio such as Visual Studio 2015 shown in the following figure.
   - https://azure.microsoft.com/en-in/downloads

2. It will download the **Microsoft Web Platform Installer (Web PI)** file. Just execute the Web PI file.
3. On the **Web Platform Install** page, click **Install**.
4. On the **Prerequisites** page, accept the license agreement.
5. The installation process will begin as shown in the following figure.

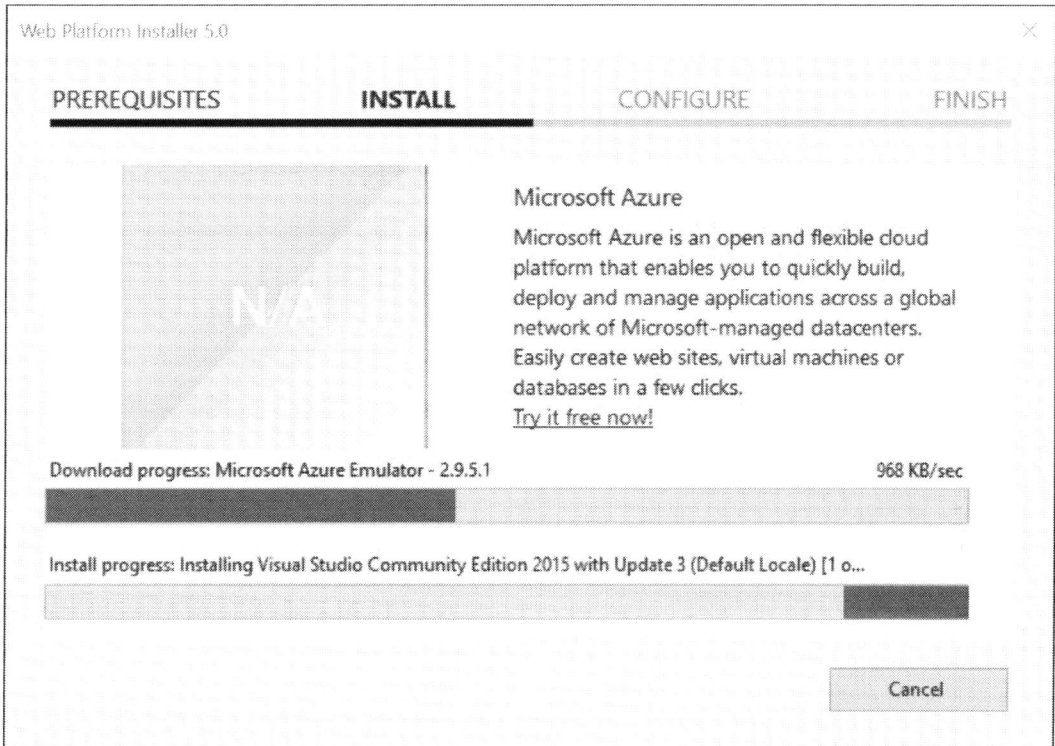

6. Depending on the Internet speed, downloading time may vary. Let it finish.
7. Once downloaded and installed, you can manage Azure Cloud resources using Azure SDK.

Since this guide is basically focused for Azure Solutions Architects, hence we will not cover developer tools in details. If you are interested, please visit the following link for more details about managing Azure Cloud resources using Azure SDK.

* Getting Started with Azure SDK for .Net
  https://docs.microsoft.com/en-us/azure/cloud-services/cloud-services-dotnet-get-started

Lab 43: Managing Azure Account Using PowerShell

Visual Studio is basically preferred by Azure developers, but the SysOps administrators need more dedicated tools for administrative purpose specially for the Windows-based environment. For this, they prefer Azure CLI and Azure PowerShell. Here, we are going to explain how to use Azure PowerShell to manage Azure Cloud Resources.

Downloading and Installing Azure PowerShell

You can install Azure PowerShell as Web PI either from Microsoft download center or from the GitHub repository as a standalone installer.

1. To download Azure PowerShell standalone installer, please visit the following link.
   - Download Microsoft Azure PowerShell
     https://github.com/Azure/azure-powershell/releases
2. On the **GitHub Releases** page, click the **MSI installer package** option, as shown in the following figure link to download it.

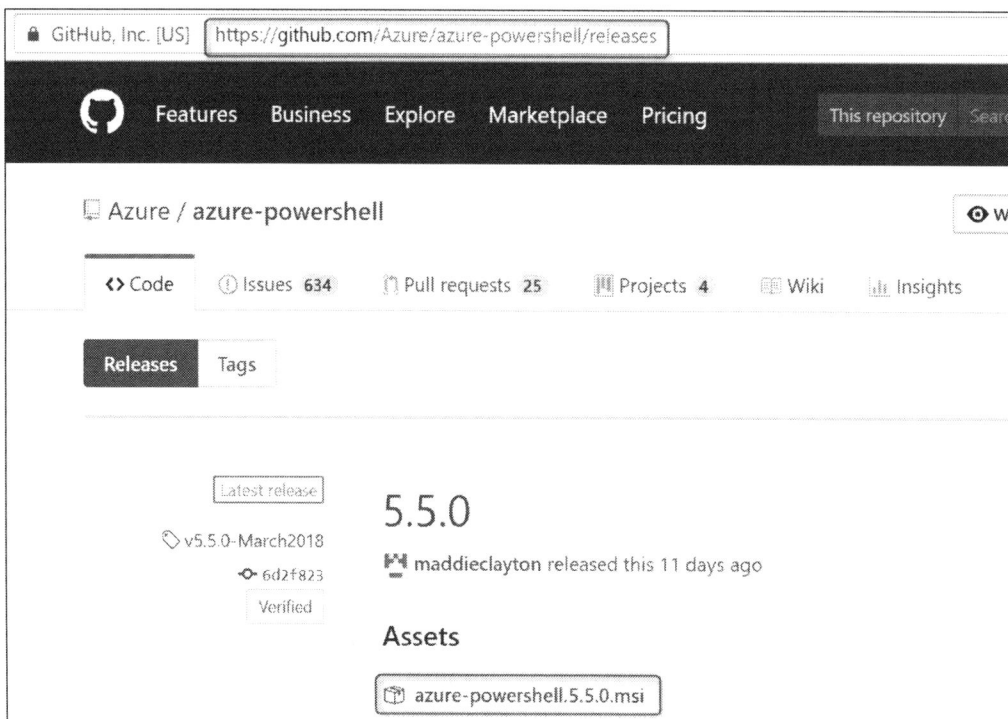

3. Once downloaded, execute the installer **MSI file** and finish the installation.
4. The installation method is simple and should not be any challenge there.

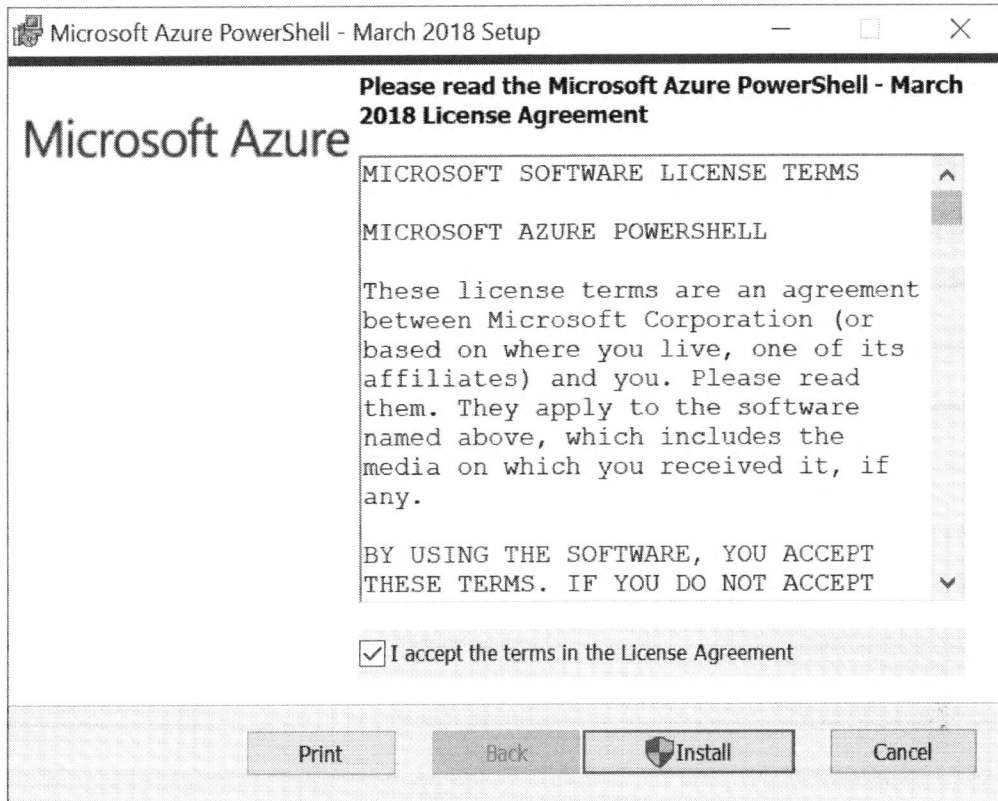

Connecting Azure Account Using Windows PowerShell

You can connect PowerShell to your Microsoft Azure cloud either using a Microsoft account or using a management certificate.

To connect to your Microsoft Azure cloud using a Microsoft account, you need to follow the following steps:

1. Open the **Windows PowerShell** with admin privileges on your system and type the following command.

```
Add-AzureAccount
```

2. A credentials window will be displayed as shown in the following figure. Specify your Azure username and password.

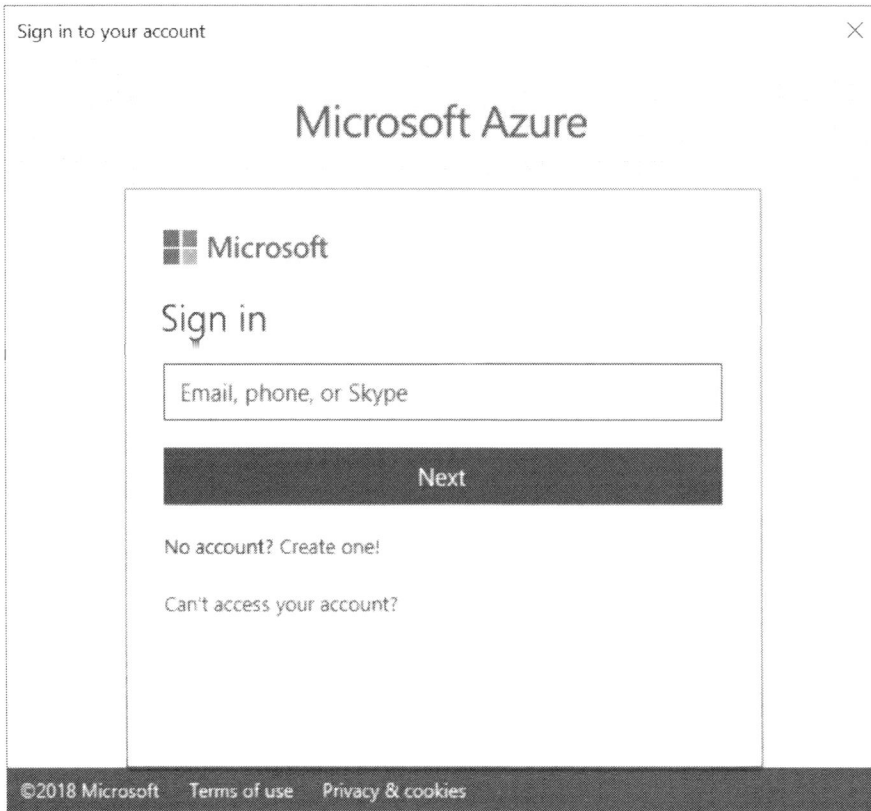

3. After the successful authentication, you will be connected to your Azure Cloud account as shown in the following figure.

4. Once connected successfully, you can perform most of the Azure cloud tasks that you perform using the Azure Portal. We will not cover the Azure PowerShell cmdlets here because there are hundreds of cmdlets to manage the Azure cloud. In fact, you can do anything using the Azure PowerShell what you do using Azure Portal.

Connecting Azure Cloud Subscription Using Management Certificate

The second method to connect your Azure subscription from Windows PowerShell is using Management Certificate. The Management certificate contains all the necessary information to login to the Azure Cloud subscription. For this, you need to perform the following steps.

1. Open the **Windows PowerShell** with admin privileges and execute the following command:

    ```
    Get-AzurePublishSettingsFile
    ```

2. It will redirect you to **Azure Portal** login web page. Login to your Azure Portal.
3. On the **Generate Publish Settings** blade, select your subscription, click **Validate** and then click **Download Publish Settings,** as shown in the following figure.

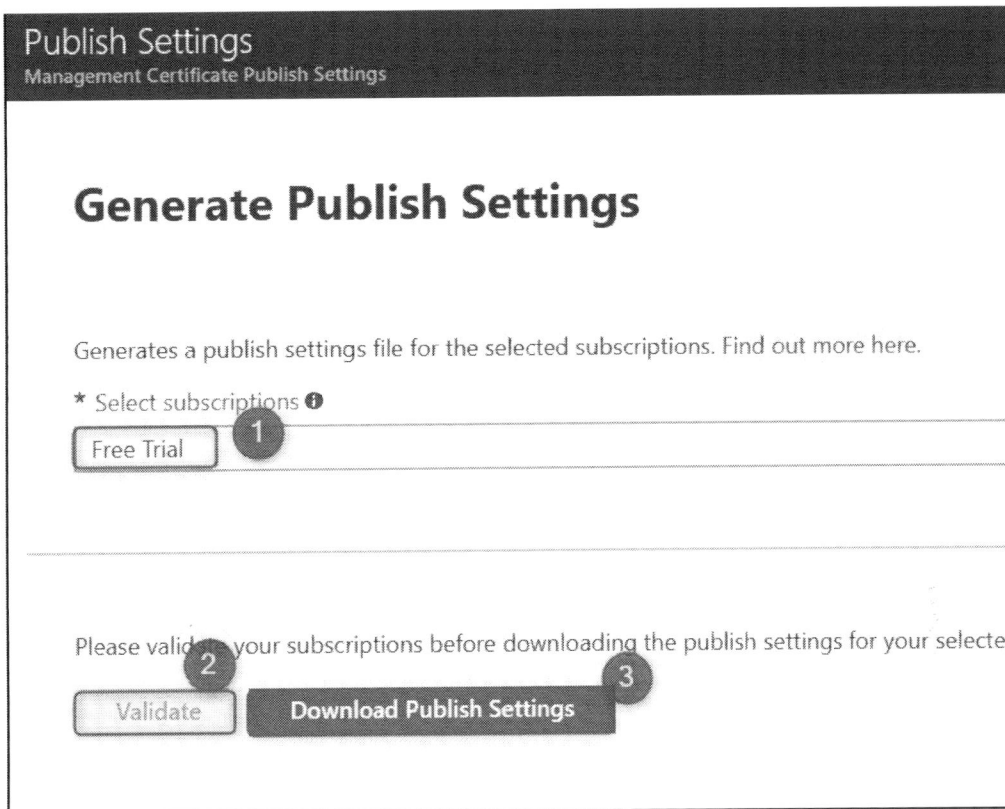

4. Save the .publishsettings file in a safe location on your local system. Rename it something a simple file name.
5. Now import your .publishsettings file using the following command.

    ```
    Import-AzurePublishSettingsFile "C:\MyAzureAccount.publishsettings"
    ```

6. To verify that you are able to execute Azure PowerShell cmdlets without credentials, execute the following commands as shown in the following figure.

    ```
    Get-AzureSubscription
    ```

```
Administrator: Windows PowerShell                                    —    □    ✕

Windows PowerShell
Copyright (C) Microsoft Corporation. All rights reserved.

PS C:\Windows\system32> Get-AzurePublishSettingsFile
PS C:\Windows\system32> Get-AzurePublishSettingsFile
PS C:\Windows\system32> Import-AzurePublishSettingsFile "C:\MyAzureAccount.publishsettings"

Id                              Name          State ExtendedProperties
--                              ----          ----- ------------------
                                Free Trial          {[Account,                        ...


PS C:\Windows\system32> Get-AzureSubscription


SubscriptionId             :
SubscriptionName           : Free Trial
Environment                : AzureCloud
DefaultAccount             :
IsDefault                  : True
IsCurrent                  : True
TenantId                   :
CurrentStorageAccountName  :
```

Now, you can execute the desired Azure PowerShell cmdlets to manage your Azure account. For more
details about using the Azure PowerShell to manage Azure Cloud resources, please visit the following
link.

- Using Azure PowerShell
  https://docs.microsoft.com/en-us/azure/azure-resource-manager/powershell-azure-resource-manager

Lab 44: Scheduling Auto and Stop Azure VMs

There might be many scenarios, when you may wish to start and stop Azure VMs. If you are working as a solutions architect, you might be also running many testing, development, QA, and staging virtual machines for the different projects. Since, Dev/QA/STG VMs usually not required in off hours and weekends, you may wish to keep them powered off and save a lot of money. The auto shutdown action can be scheduled in the VM's properties option itself, but there is no option to set auto start schedule in VM's properties. And, manually daily starting your Azure VMs might be very painful. Here, we will explain how to schedule Auto Start and Stop Schedule for your Azure VMs.

Schedule Auto Start Azure VM

To schedule Auto Stop Azure VM, you need to perform the following steps:

1. In **Azure Portal**, select the desired VM such as **MyTestWeb1** that you want to auto shutdown.
2. On the **Auto Shutdown** blade, enable Auto Shutdown and specify the following settings:
   - **Enabled**: Select **On** to enable
   - **Scheduled shutdown**: Set the **time** when the VM will be powered off.
   - **Time Zone**: Select your **time zone**
   - **Send notification before auto shutdown**: **Yes** to receive notification (requires a SendGrid account). **No** to not receive notification.
3. For the demo purpose, let's set the settings as per the following figure and click **Save** to save the changes.

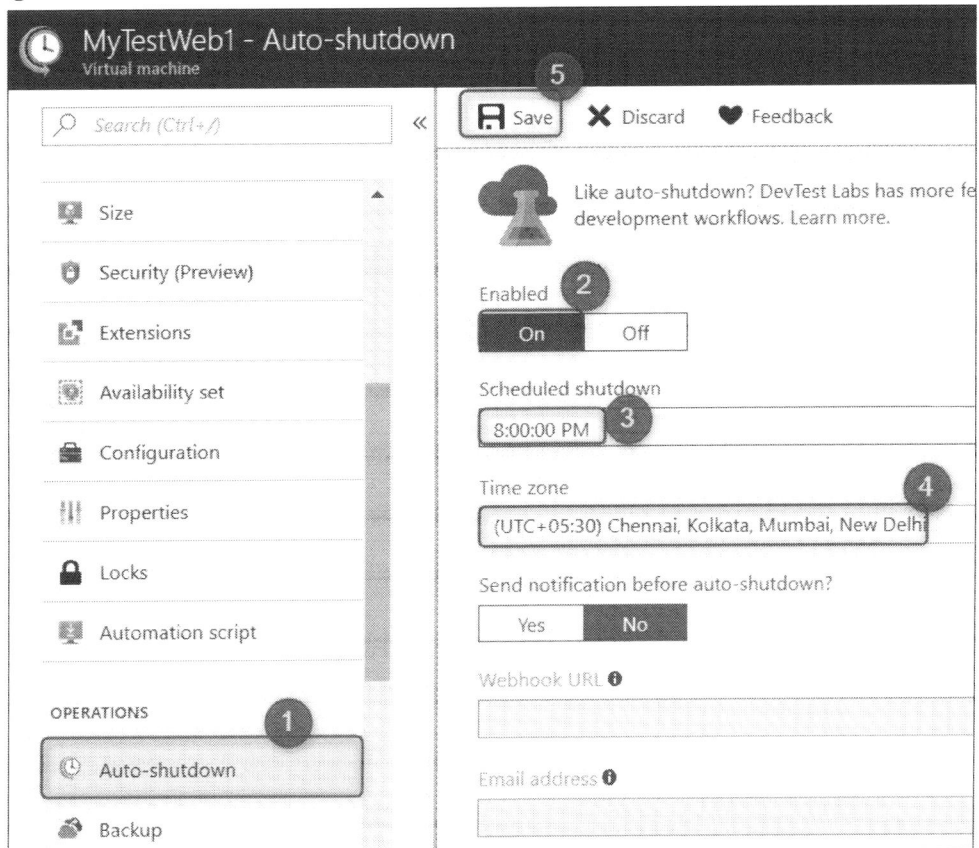

4. As per the above settings, this VM will be powered off daily at 8:00 PM IST. You can adjust your timing as per your requirements.

Schedule Auto Start Azure VM

Unlike Auto Shutdown Azure VM, auto start Azure VMs is not a straightforward method. It requires some additional configuration. To schedule auto start an Azure VM, first you need an automation account. And, the automation account must be in the same subscription where your Azure VMs are deployed.

To create an Automation Account, you need to perform the following steps:

1. In Azure Portal, navigate to **All Services** > **Automation Accounts** as shown in the following figure.

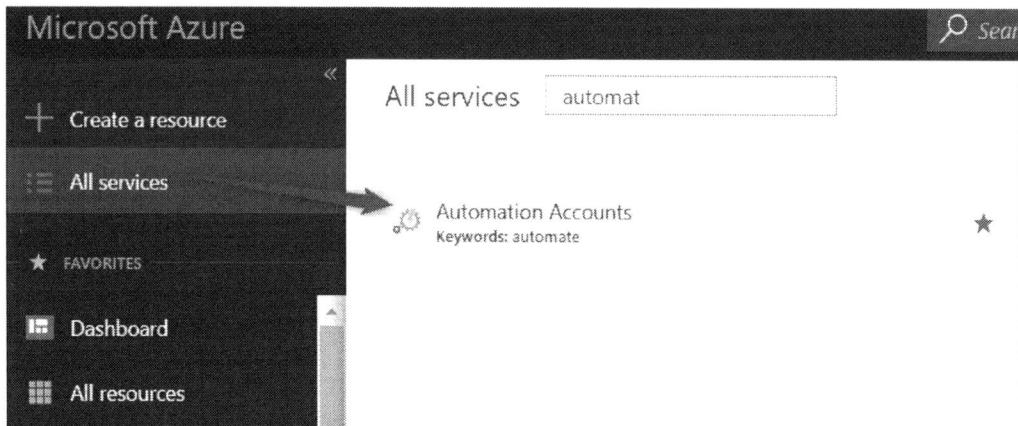

2. In the **Automation Accounts** blade, click **Add**, specify an account name, select resource group and location as per your choice as shown in the following figure.

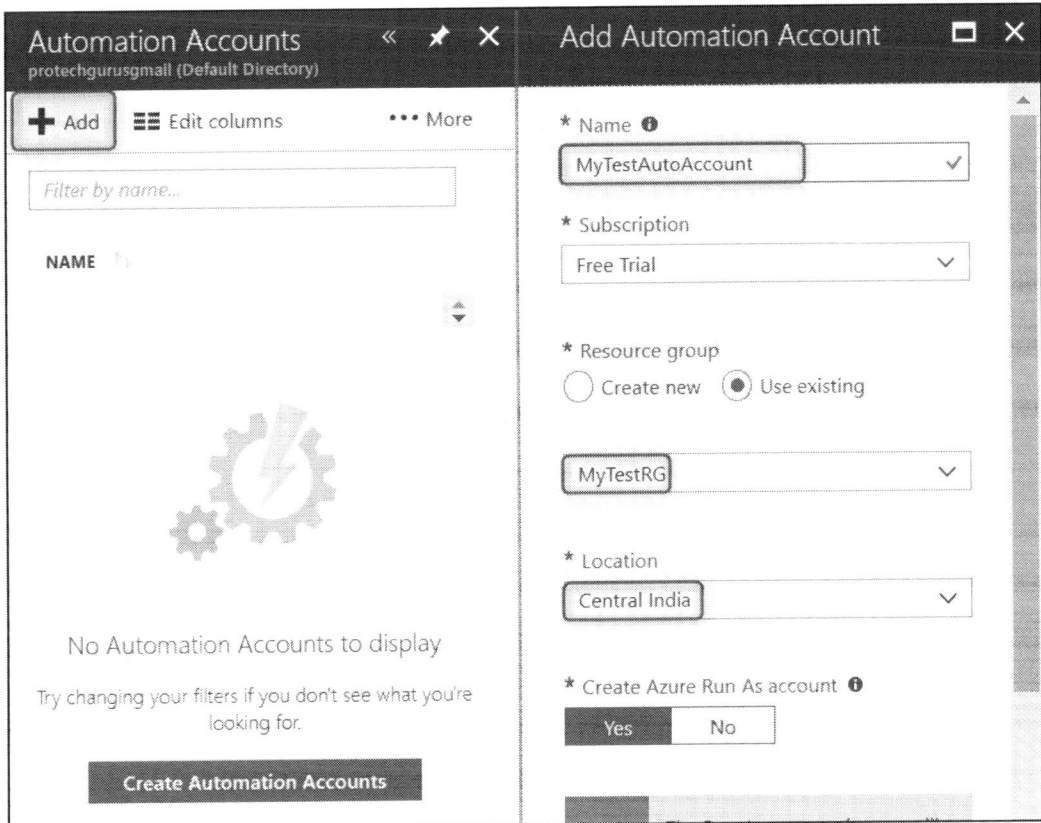

3. Click **Create** to create Automation Account.
4. Now, you need to configure Runbooks. For this, you need to perform the following steps:
5. Select your created automation account and scroll-down to **Runbooks** option.
6. Here, you will see a few pre-created runbooks. To add a new **Runbook**, click **Browse gallery** as shown in the following figure.

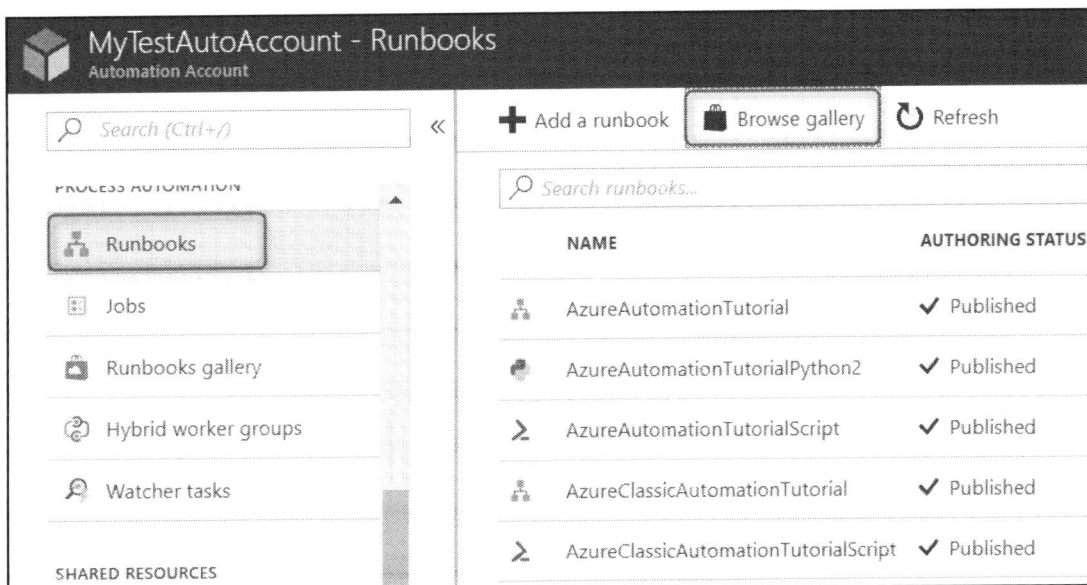

7. In the **Browse gallery** blade, you will see many pre-configured easy to use runbooks. Various runbooks provide the various types of capabilities, functions, and features.

8. For this lab exercise, let's select **Start Azure V2 VMs** runbook as shown in the following figure.

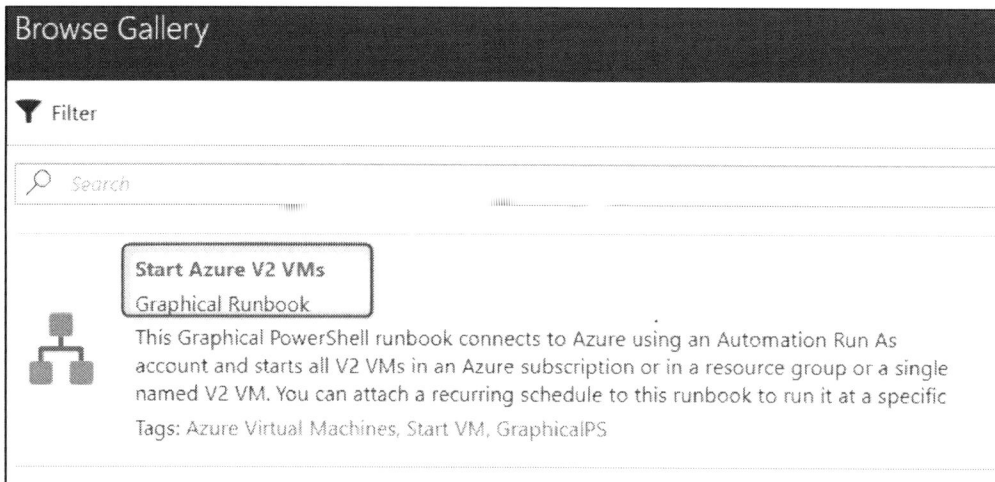

9. On the **Start Azure V2 VMs** blade, click **Import** to import the selected runbook as shown in the following figure.

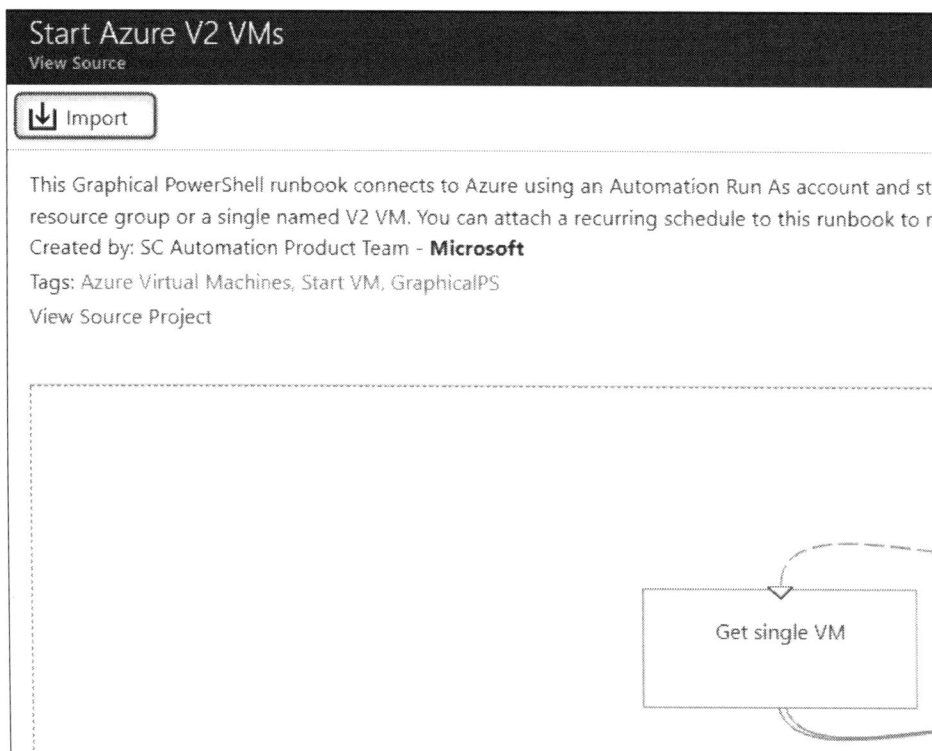

10. On the **Import** blade, specify the runbook name and description as shown in the following figure.

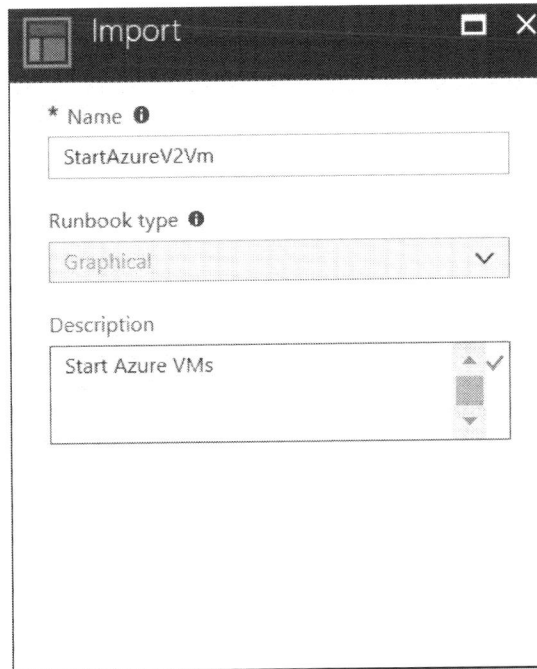

Import

* Name ⓘ

StartAzureV2Vm

Runbook type ⓘ

Graphical ⌄

Description

Start Azure VMs

11. Click **OK** to import the selected runbook.
12. Once the runbook imported, click **Edit** as shown in the following figure.

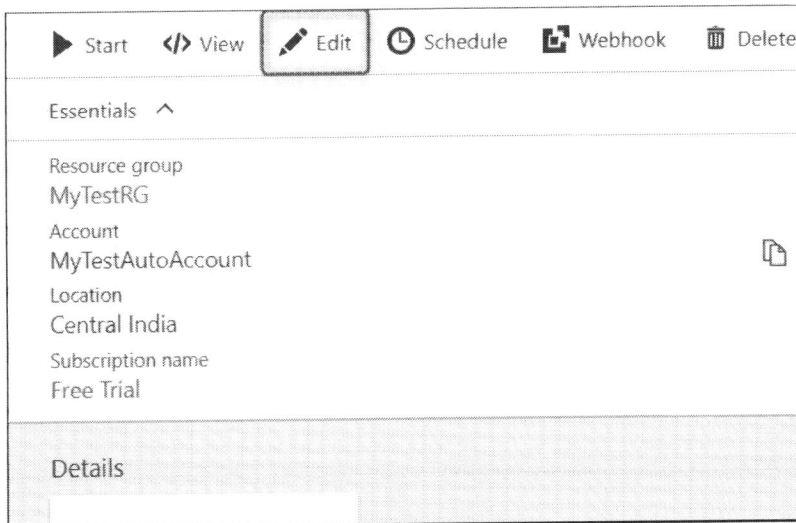

▶ Start   </> View   ✏ Edit   🕐 Schedule   📤 Webhook   🗑 Delete

Essentials ⌃

Resource group
MyTestRG

Account
MyTestAutoAccount

Location
Central India

Subscription name
Free Trial

Details

13. Here, you can modify the runbook. For the demo purpose, just accept the default settings as-is and click **Publish** to publish it as shown in the following figure.

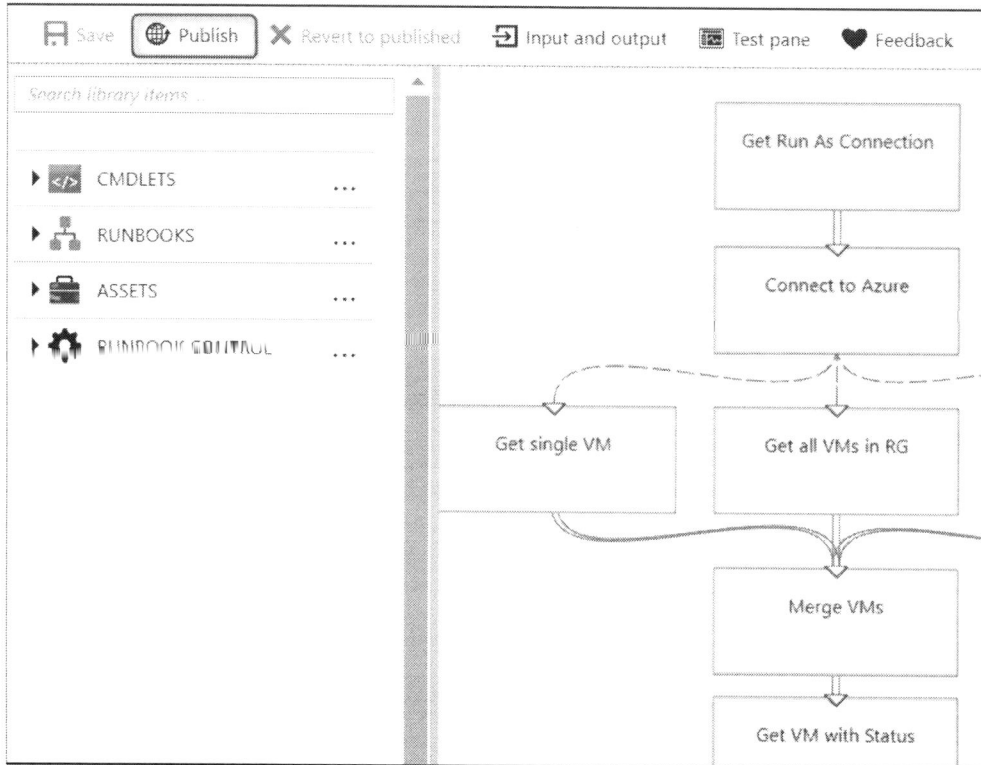

14. Now, click **Schedule** to set the scheduler to run this runbook as shown in the following figure.

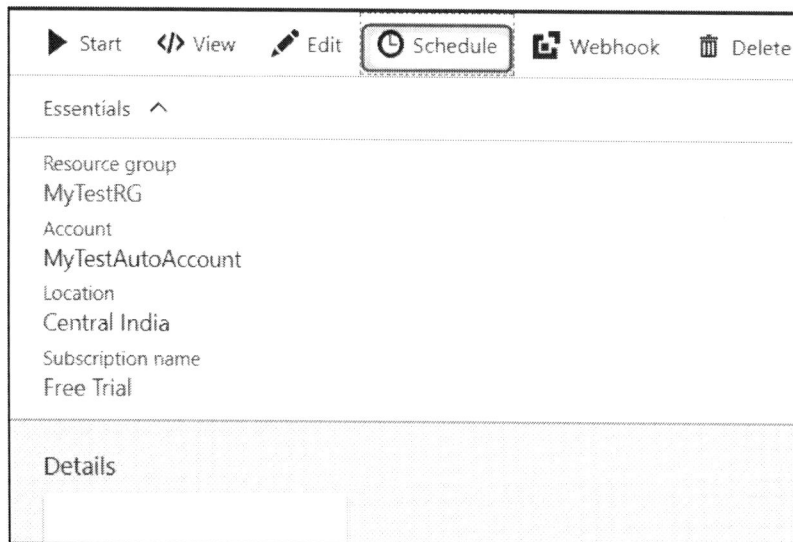

15. On the **Schedule Runbook** blade, click **Link a schedule to your runbook** and the click **Create a new schedule** as shown in the following figure.

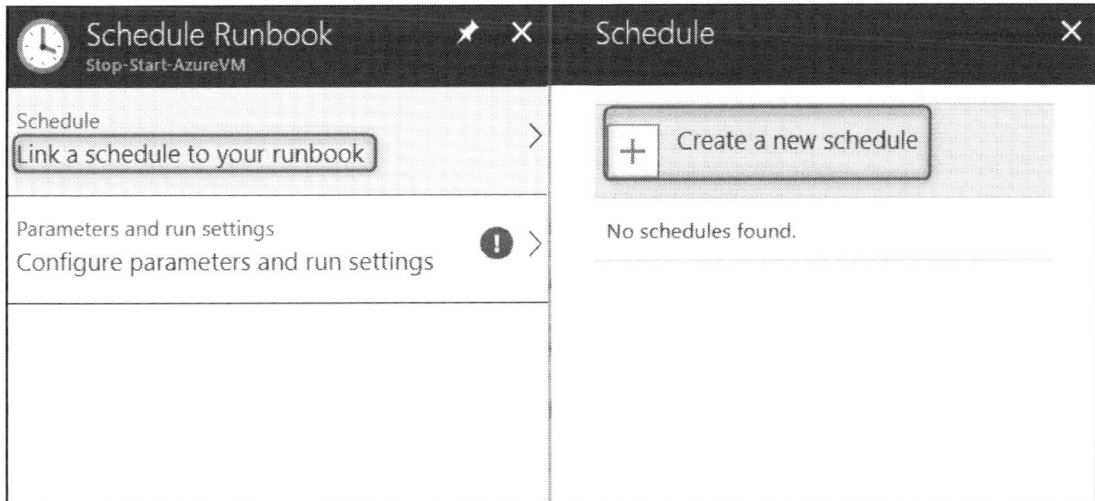

16. On the **New Schedule** blade, specify the desired **Name**, **Time Zone**, and **schedule** to run this runbook as shown in the following figure.

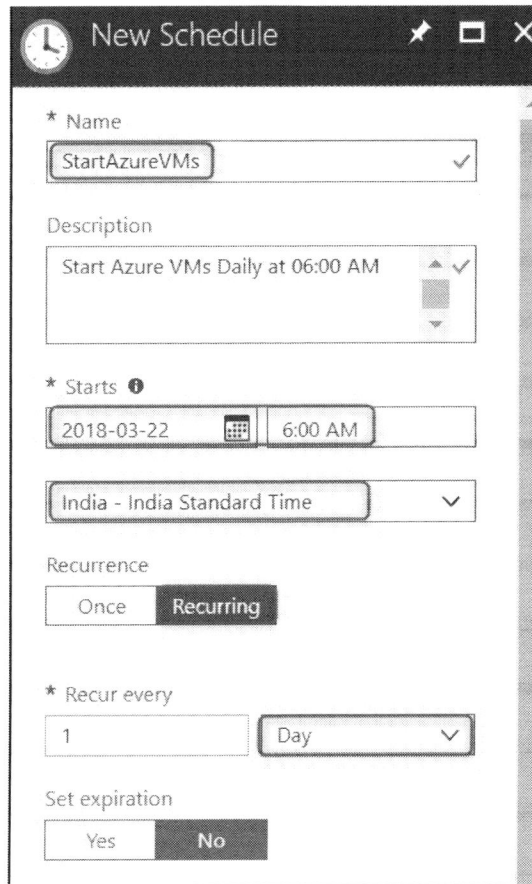

17. As per the above schedule, if all goes well, it will start Azure VMs automatically daily at 06:00 AM IST.

Other Helpful IT eBooks

You may also be interested in the following eBooks:

1. AWS Solutions Architect Associate - Exam Practice Questions
2. Step By Step Windows Server 2016 Lab Manual/Practical Guide
3. Step By Step AWS Cloud Lab Manual/Practical Guide for Ultimate Beginners
4. Step By Step CCNA Lab Manual/Practical Guide for Ultimate Beginners
5. Step By Step Windows Server 2012 R2 Lab Manual/Practical Guide
6. Step By Step VMware Workstation Player Lab Manual/Practical Guide

For more step by step tutorials, please visit our blog tutorials (https://protechgurus.com).

Printed in Poland
by Amazon Fulfillment
Poland Sp. z o.o., Wrocław